HOW TO READ
A BOOK

The Art of Getting
a Liberal Education

BY

MORTIMER J. ADLER

SIMON AND SCHUSTER
NEW YORK

TO
MARK and ARTHUR

Preface

I HAVE *tried to write a light book about heavy reading.*

Those who take no pleasure in knowing and understanding should not bother to read it. Those who believe that all their leisure time should be devoted to the effortless pleasures of the movies, the radio, and light romances should not bother to read it.

I am talking to the rest of us.

Reading—as explained (and defended) in this book—is a basic tool in the living of a good life. I need not defend the goodness of living humanly or reasonably, though it looks as if we might have to defend our right to do so.

Reading, I repeat, is a basic tool. Those who can use it to learn from books, as well as be amused by them, have access to the stores of knowledge. They can furnish their minds so that the prospect of hours spent alone is less bleak. Nor, in the hours they spend with others, need they fear that hollow sound of empty conversation.

Most of us find conversation dull. We seem to have little to say after the first few familiar topics are exhausted by the repetition of the same old remarks. The press and the radio provide the topics. They are the same for the most part, and so are the commonplaces we utter in comment. That is why we turn to gossip and scandal, or give up conversation entirely for bridge or movies. And if we cannot talk to one another interestingly, what dull company we must be when we are left to ourselves.

*One—though not the only—justification of liberal edu-
cation (and this is a book about liberal education) is that
it enriches us. It makes men of us. It makes us able to lead
the distinctively human life of reason. Vocational training
at its best can only help us earn the living which supports
our leisure. Everyone knows, I hope, that education is
only begun, not completed, in school and college. Even if
our colleges were doing a much better job than they are,
it would still be necessary for all of us to continue our
education thereafter. As it is, most of us have the problem
of getting the education which schools and colleges failed
to give us. Education is still open to all of us—whether we
have had a schooling or in spite of it. But only if we know
how to read.*

*With this in mind, I have written a book about reading.
Those who write about sex, or money-making, often give
the impression that it is the whole of life. I do not want
to give a similar impression about reading, but I do want
to persuade you that it is a substantial part of the life of
reason.*

*In the first part of this book, I have discussed the role
of reading in relation to learning and thinking, both in
school and out. In the second part, I have tried to outline
the steps one must take in learning how to read. As you
will see, there is not only the problem of how to read,
but also of what to read. The title indicates that I am concerned mainly with the reading of* books, *but the art of
reading which I describe applies to* any *kind of communication. In the life of unreason that is now upon us,
you can use such skill to see through the propaganda of
conflicting White Papers and around neutrality proclama-*

tions, and even to read between the lines of the too-brief war communiqués.

There is a third part. It is the most important. In a democracy, we must discharge the responsibilities of free men. Liberal education is here an indispensable means to this end. It not only makes men of us by cultivating our minds, but it frees our minds by disciplining them. Without free minds, we cannot act like free men. I shall try to show you that the art of reading well is intimately related to the art of thinking well—clearly, critically, freely. Hence, the third part of this book is devoted to the rest of the reader's life.

This is, in short, a book about reading in relation to life, liberty, and the pursuit of happiness. I said it was a "light book." I meant that it was much easier than the great and good books you must learn to read. I hope you find it so, and more, that as you learn to read, the heavier reading you once put aside will cease to be burdensome. You will enjoy learning. All books will become light in proportion as you find light in them.

MORTIMER J. ADLER

Chicago
September, 1939

Table of Contents

PART I

THE ACTIVITY
OF READING

CHAPTER ONE

To the Average Reader

THIS is a book for readers who cannot read. That may sound rude, though I do not mean to be. It may sound like a contradiction, but it is not. The appearance of rudeness and contradiction arises only from the variety of senses in which the word "reading" can be used.

The reader who has read thus far surely can read, in some sense of the word. You can guess, therefore, what I must mean. It is that this book is intended for those who can read in some sense of "reading" but not in others. There are many kinds of reading and degrees of ability to read. It is not contradictory to say that this book is for readers who want to read better or want to read in some other way than they now can.

For whom is this book not intended, then? I can answer that question simply by naming the two extreme cases. There are those who cannot read at all or in any way: infants, imbeciles, and other innocents. And there *may be* those who are masters of the art of reading—who can do every sort of reading and do it as well as is humanly possible. Most authors would like nothing better than such persons to write for. But a book, such as this, which is concerned with the art of reading itself and which aims to help its readers read better, cannot solicit the attention of the already expert.

Between these two extremes we find the average reader,

and that means most of us who have learned our ABC's. We have been started on the road to literacy. But most of us also know that we are not expert readers. We know this in many ways, but most obviously when we find some things too difficult to read, or have great trouble in reading them; or when someone else has read the same thing we have and shown us how much we missed or misunderstood.

If you have not had experiences of this sort, if you have never felt the effort of reading or known the frustration when all the effort you could summon was not equal to the task, I do not know how to interest you in the problem. Most of us, however, have experienced difficulties in reading, but we do not know why we have trouble or what to do about it.

I think this is because most of us do not regard reading as a complicated activity, involving many different steps in each of which we can acquire more and more skill through practice, as in the case of any other art. We may not even think there is an *art* of reading. We tend to think of reading almost as if it were something as simple and natural to do as looking or walking. There is no art of looking or walking.

Last summer, while I was writing this book, a young man visited me. He had heard what I was doing, and he came to ask a favor. Would I tell him how to improve his reading? He obviously expected me to answer the question in a few sentences. More than that, he appeared to think that once he had learned the simple prescription, success would be just around the corner.

I tried to explain that it was not so simple. It took many pages of this book, I said, to discuss the various rules of reading and to show how they should be followed. I told him that this book was like a book on how to play tennis.

As written about in books, the art of tennis consists of rules for making each of the various strokes, a discussion of how and when to use them, and a description of how to organize these parts into the general strategy of a successful game. The art of reading has to be written about in the same way. There are rules for each of the different steps you must take to complete the reading of a whole book.

He seemed a little dubious. Although he suspected that he did not know how to read, he also seemed to feel that there could not be so much to learn. The young man was a musician. I asked him whether most people, who can hear the sounds, know how to listen to a symphony. His reply was, of course not. I confessed I was one of them, and asked whether he could tell me how to listen to music as a musician expected it to be heard. Of course he could, but not in a few words. Listening to a symphony was a complicated affair. You not only had to keep awake, but there were so many different things to attend to, so many parts of it to distinguish and relate. He could not tell me briefly all that I would have to know. Furthermore, I would have to spend a lot of time listening to music to become a skilled auditor.

Well, I said, the case of reading was similar. If I could learn to hear music, he could learn to read a book, but only on the same conditions. Knowing how to read well was like any other art or skill. There were rules to learn and to follow. Through practice good habits must be formed. There were no insurmountable difficulties about it. Only willingness to learn and patience in the process were required.

I do not know whether my answer fully satisfied him. If it didn't, there was one difficulty in the way of his learning to read. He did not yet appreciate what reading involved. Because he still regarded reading as something almost anyone can do, something learned in the primary grades, he may have doubted still that learning to read was just like learning to hear music, to play tennis, or to become expert in any other complex use of one's senses and one's mind.

This difficulty is, I fear, one that most of us share. That is why I am going to devote the first part of this book to explaining the kind of activity reading is. For unless you appreciate what is involved, you will not be prepared (as this young man was not when he came to see me) for the kind of instruction that is necessary.

I shall assume, of course, that you want to learn. My help can go no further than you will help yourself. No one can make you learn more of an art than you want to learn or think you need. People often say that they would try to read if they only knew how. As a matter of fact, they might learn how if they would only try. And try they would, if they wanted to learn.

- 2 -

I did not discover I could not read until after I had left college. I found it out only after I tried to teach others how to read. Most parents have probably made a similar discovery by trying to teach their youngsters. Paradoxically, as a result, the parents usually learn more about reading than their children. The reason is simple. They have to be more active about the business. Anyone who teaches anything has to.

To get back to my story. So far as the registrar's records were concerned, I was one of the satisfactory students in my day at Columbia. We passed courses with creditable marks. The game was easy enough, once you caught on to the tricks. If anyone had told us then that we did not know much or could not read very well, we would have been shocked. We were sure we could listen to lectures and read the books assigned in such a way that we could answer examination questions neatly. That was the proof of our ability.

Some of us took one course which increased our self-satisfaction enormously. It had just been started by John Erskine. It ran for two years, was called General Honors, and was open to a select group of juniors and seniors. It consisted of nothing but "reading" the great books, from the Greek classics through the Latin and medieval masterpieces right down to the best books of yesterday, William James, Einstein, and Freud. The books were in all fields: they were histories and books of science or philosophy, dramatic poetry and novels. We read a book a week, some sixty in two years, and we discussed them with our teachers one night a week in informal, seminar fashion.

That course had two effects on me. For one thing, it made me think I had struck educational gold for the first time. Here was real stuff, handled in a real way, compared to the textbook and lecture courses that merely made demands on one's memory. But the trouble was I not only thought I had struck gold; I also thought that I owned the mine. Here were the great books. I knew how to read. The world was my oyster.

If, after graduation, I had gone into business or medicine or law, I would probably still be harboring the conceit that I knew how to read and was well read beyond the ordinary. Fortunately, something woke me from this dream. For every illusion that the classroom can nourish, there is a school of hard knocks to destroy it. A few years of practice awaken the lawyer and the doctor. Business or newspaper work disillusions the boy who thought he was a trader or a reporter when he finished the school of commerce or journalism. Well, I thought I was liberally educated, that I knew how to read, and had read a lot. The cure for that was teaching, and the punishment that precisely fitted my crime was having to teach, the year after I graduated, in this very Honors course which had so inflated me.

As a student I had read all the books I was now going to teach but, being very young and conscientious, I decided to read them again—you know, just to brush up each week for class. To my growing amazement, week after week, I discovered that the books were almost brand new to me. I seemed to be reading them for the first time, these books which I thought I had "mastered" thoroughly.

As time went on, I found out not only that I did not know very much about any of these books, but also that I did not know how to read them very well. To make up for my ignorance and incompetence I did what any young teacher might do who was afraid of both his students and his job. I used secondary sources, encyclopedias, commentaries, all sorts of books about books about these books. In that way, I thought, I would appear to know more than the students. They wouldn't be able to tell that my questions or points did not come from my better reading of the book they too were working on.

Fortunately for me I was found out, or else I might have been satisfied with getting by as a teacher just as I had got by as a student. If I had succeeded in fooling others, I might soon have deceived myself as well. My first good fortune was in having as a colleague in this teaching Mark Van Doren, the poet. He led off in the discussion of poetry, as I was supposed to do in the case of history, science, and philosophy. He was several years my senior, probably more honest than I, certainly a better reader. Forced to compare my performance with his, I simply could not fool myself. I had not found out what the books contained by reading them, but by reading *about* them.

My questions about a book were of the sort anyone could ask or answer without having read the book—anyone who had had recourse to the discussions which a hundred secondary sources provide for those who cannot or do not want to read. In contrast, his questions seemed to arise from the pages of the book itself. He actually seemed to have some intimacy with the author. Each book was a large world, infinitely rich for exploration, and woe to the student who answered questions as if, instead of traveling therein, he had been listening to a travelogue. The contrast was too plain, and too much for me. I was not allowed to forget that *I did not know how to read.*

My second good fortune lay in the particular group of students who formed that first class. They were not long in catching on to me. They knew how to use the encyclopedia, or a commentary, or the editor's introduction which usually graces the publication of a classic, just as well as I did. One of them, who has since achieved fame as a critic, was particularly obstreperous. He took what seemed to me endless delight in discussing the various theories about the book, which could be obtained from secondary sources, always to show me and the rest of the class that the book itself still remained to be discussed. I do not mean that he or the other students could really read the book better than I, or had done so. Clearly none of us, with the exception of Mr. Van Doren, was doing the job of reading.

After that first year of teaching, I had few illusions left

about my literacy. Since then, I have been teaching students how to read books, six years at Columbia with Mark Van Doren and for the last ten years at the University of Chicago with President Robert M. Hutchins. In the course of years, I think I have gradually learned to read a little better. There is no longer any danger of self-deception, of supposing that I have become expert. Why? Because reading the same books year after year, I discover each time what I found out the first year I began to teach: the book I am rereading is almost new to me. For a while, each time I reread it I thought, naturally enough, that I had mastered it, that I had really read it well at last, only to have the next reading show up my inadequacies and misinterpretations. After this happens several times, even the dullest of us is likely to learn that perfect reading lies at the end of the rainbow. Although practice makes perfect, in this art of reading as in any other, the long run needed to prove the maxim is longer than the allotted span.

- 3 -

I am torn between two impulses. I certainly want to encourage you to undertake this business of learning to read, but I do not want to fool you by saying that it is quite easy or that it can be done in a short time. I am sure you do not want to be fooled. As in the case of every other skill, learning to read well presents difficulties to be overcome by effort and time. Anyone who undertakes anything is prepared for that, I think, and knows that the achievement seldom exceeds the effort. After all, it takes time and trouble to grow up from the cradle, to make a fortune, raise a family, or gain the wisdom that some old men have. Why should it not take time and trouble to learn to read and to read what is worth reading?

Of course, it would not take so long if we got started when we were in school. Unfortunately, almost the opposite happens: *one gets stopped.* I shall discuss the failure of the schools more fully later. Here I wish only to record this fact about our schools, a fact which concerns us all, because in large part they have made us what we are today—people who cannot read well enough to enjoy reading for profit or to profit by reading for enjoyment.

But education does not stop with schooling, nor does the responsibility for the ultimate educational fate of each of us rest entirely on the school system. Everyone can and must decide for himself whether he is satisfied with the education he got, or is now getting if he is still in school. If he is not satisfied, it is up to him to do something about it. With schools as they are, more schooling is hardly the remedy. One way out—perhaps the only one available to most people—is to learn to read better, and then, by reading better, to learn more of what can be learned through reading.

That way out and how to take it is what this book tries to show. It is for adults who have gradually become aware of how little they got from all their schooling, as well as for those who, lacking such opportunities, have been puzzled to know how to overcome a deprivation they need not regret too much. It is for students in school and college who may occasionally wonder how to help themselves to education. It is even for teachers who may sometimes realize that they are not giving all the help they should, and that maybe they do not know how.

When I think of this large potential audience as the average reader, I am not neglecting all the differences in training and ability, in schooling or experience, and certainly not the different degrees of interest or sorts of motivation which can be brought to this common task. But what is of primary importance is that all of us share a recognition of the task and its worth.

We may be engaged in occupations which do not require us to read for a living, but we may still feel that that living would be graced, in its moments of leisure, by some learning—the sort we can do by ourselves through reading. We may be professionally occupied with matters that demand a kind of technical reading in the course of our work: the physician has to keep up with the medical literature; the lawyer never stops reading cases; the businessman has to read financial statements, insurance policies, contracts, and so forth. No matter whether the reading is to learn or to earn, it can be done poorly or well.

We may be college students—perhaps candidates for a higher degree—and yet realize that what is happening to us is stuffing, not education. There are many college students who know, certainly by the time they get their bachelor's degree, that they spent four years taking courses and finishing with them by passing examinations. The mastery attained in that process is not of subject matter, but of the teacher's personality. If the student remembers enough of what was told him in lectures and textbooks, and if he has a line on the teacher's pet prejudices, he can pass the course easily enough. But he is also passing up an education.

We may be teachers in some school, college, or university. I hope that most of us teachers know we are not expert readers. I hope we know, not merely that our students cannot read well, but also that we cannot do much better. Every profession has a certain amount of humbug about it necessary for impressing the laymen or the clients to be served. The humbug we teachers have to practice is the front we put on of knowledge and expertness. It is not entirely humbug, because we usually know a little more and can do a little better than our best students. But we must not let the humbug fool ourselves. If we do not know that our students cannot read very well, we are worse than humbugs: we do not know our business at all. And if we do not know that we cannot read very much better than they, we have allowed our professional imposture to deceive ourselves.

Just as the best doctors are those who can somehow retain the patient's confidence not by hiding but by confessing their limitations, so the best teachers are those who make the fewest pretensions. If the students are on all fours with a difficult problem, the teacher who shows that he is only crawling also, helps them much more than the pedagogue who appears to fly in magnificent circles far above their heads. Perhaps, if we teachers were more honest about our own reading disabilities, less loath to reveal how hard it is for us to read and how often we fumble, we might get the students interested in the game of learning instead of the game of passing.

- 4 -

I trust I have said enough to indicate to readers who cannot read that I am one who cannot read much better than they. My chief advantage is the clarity with which I know *that I cannot,* and perhaps *why I cannot.* That is the best fruit of years of experience in trying to teach others. Of course, if I am just a little better than someone else, I can help him somewhat. Although none of us can read well

enough to satisfy ourselves, we may be able to read better
than someone else. Although few of us read well for the
most part, each of us may do a good job of reading in some
particular connection, when the stakes are high enough to
compel the rare exertion.

The student who is generally superficial may, for a special reason, read some one thing well. Scholars who are as
superficial as the rest of us in most of their reading often do
a careful job when the text is in their own narrow field, especially if their reputations hang on what they say. On cases
relevant to his practice, a lawyer is likely to read analytically. A physician may similarly read clinical reports which
describe symptoms he is currently concerned with. But both
these learned men may make no similar effort in other fields
or at other times. Even business assumes the air of a learned
profession when its devotees are called upon to examine
financial statements or contracts, though I have heard it
said that many businessmen cannot read these documents
intelligently even when their fortunes are at stake.

If we consider men and women generally, and apart from
their professions or occupations, there is only one situation
I can think of in which they almost pull themselves up by
their bootstraps, making an effort to read better than they
usually do. When they are in love and are reading a love
letter, they read for all they are worth. They read every word
three ways; they read between the lines and in the margins;
they read the whole in terms of the parts, and each part in
terms of the whole; they grow sensitive to context and ambiguity, to insinuation and implication; they perceive the
color of words, the odor of phrases, and the weight of sentences. They may even take the punctuation into account.
Then, if never before or after, they read.

These examples, especially the last, are enough to suggest a first approximation of what I mean by "reading." That is not enough, however. What this is all about can be more accurately understood only if the different *kinds* and *grades* of reading are more definitely distinguished. To read this book intelligently—which is what this book aims to help its readers do with all books—such distinctions must be grasped. That belongs to the next chapter. Here suffice it if it is understood that this book is not about reading in every sense but only about that kind of reading which its readers do not do well enough, or at all, except when they are in love.

••••••

CHAPTER TWO

The Reading of "Reading"

- I -

ONE of the primary rules for reading anything is to spot the most important words the author uses. Spotting them is not enough, however. You have to know how they are being used. Finding an important word merely begins the more difficult search for the meanings, one or more, common or special, which the word is used to convey as it appears here and there in the text.

You already know that "reading" is one of the most important words in this book. But, as I have already suggested, it is a word of many meanings. If you take for granted that you know what I mean by the word, we are likely to get into difficulties before we proceed much further.

This business of using language to talk about language— especially if one is campaigning against its abuse—is risky. Recently Mr. Stuart Chase wrote a book which he should have called *Words About Words*. He might then have avoided the barb of the critics who so quickly pointed out that Mr. Chase himself was subject to the tyranny of words. Mr. Chase recognized the peril when he said, "I shall frequently be caught in my own trap by using bad language in a plea for better."

Can I avoid such pitfalls? I am writing about reading, and so it would appear that I do not have to obey the rules of reading but of writing. My escape may be more apparent than real, if it turns out that a writer should keep in mind the rules which govern reading. You, however, are reading about reading. You cannot escape. If the rules of reading I am going to suggest are sound, you must follow them in reading this book.

But, you will say, how can we follow the rules until we learn and understand them? To do that we shall have to read some part of this book without knowing what the rules are. The only way I know to help you out of this dilemma is by making you reading-conscious readers as we proceed. Let us start at once by applying the rule about *finding and interpreting the important words*.

- 2 -

When you set out to investigate the various senses of a word, it is usually wise to begin with a dictionary and your own knowledge of common usage. If you looked up "read" in the large Oxford Dictionary, you would find, first, that the same four letters constituted an obsolete noun referring to the fourth stomach of a ruminant, and the commonly used verb which refers to a mental activity involving words or symbols of some sort. You would know at once that we need not bother with the obsolete noun except, perhaps, to note that reading has something to do with rumination. You would discover next that the verb has twenty-one more or less closely related meanings, more or less common.

One uncommon meaning of "to read" is to think or suppose. This meaning passes into the more usual one of conjecturing or predicting, as when we speak of reading the stars, one's palm, or one's future. That leads eventually to the meaning of the word in which it refers to perusing books or other written documents. There are many other meanings, such as verbal utterance (when an actress reads her lines for the director); such as detecting what is not perceptible from what is (when we say we can read a person's character in his face); such as instruction, academic or personal (when we have someone read us a lecture).

The slight variations in usage seem endless: a singer reads music; a scientist reads nature; an engineer reads his instruments; a printer reads proof; we read between the lines; we read something into a situation, or someone out of the party.

We can simplify matters by noting what is common to many of these senses; namely, that mental activity is involved and that, in one way or another, symbols are being interpreted. That imposes a first limitation on our use of the word. We are not concerned with a part of the intestinal tract, nor are we concerned with enunciation, with speaking something out loud. A second limitation is needed, because we shall not consider—except for some points of comparison—the interpretation, clairvoyant or otherwise, of natural signs such as stars, hands, or faces. We shall limit ourselves to one kind of readable symbol, the kind which men invent for the purposes of communication—the words of human language. This eliminates the reading of other artificial signs such as the pointers on dials of physical apparatus, thermometers, gauges, speedometers, and so forth.

Henceforth, then, you must read the word "reading," as it occurs in this text, to refer to the process of interpreting or understanding what presents itself to the senses in the form of words or other sensible marks. This is not arbitrary legislation about what the word "reading" *really* means. It is simply a matter of defining our problem, which is reading in the sense of receiving communication.

Unfortunately, that is not simple to do, as you would realize at once if someone asked: "What about listening? Isn't that receiving communication, too?" I shall subsequently discuss the relation of reading and listening, for the rules of good reading are for the most part the rules of good listening, though perhaps harder to apply in the latter case. Suffice it for the present to distinguish reading from listening by restricting the communication being received to what is written or printed rather than spoken.

I shall try to use the word "reading" in the limited and special sense noted. But I know that I will not succeed without exception. It will be impossible to avoid using the word in some of its other senses. Sometimes I shall be thoughtful enough to mention explicitly that I am shifting the meaning. Other times I may suppose that the context is sufficient warning to you. Infrequently (I hope) I may shift the meaning without being aware of it myself.

Be stout, gentle reader, for you are just beginning. What has gone before is just preliminary to finding out the even *narrower* sense in which the word "reading" will be used. We must now face the problem which the first chapter indicated. We must distinguish between the sense in which you can read this book, for instance, and are now doing so, and the sense in which you may learn from it to read better or differently than you now can.

Notice that I said "better" *or* "differently." The one word points to a difference in *degrees* of ability, the other to a distinction in *kinds*. I suspect we shall find that the better reader can also do a different *kind* of reading. The poorer can probably do only one kind—the simplest kind. Let us first examine the range of ability in reading to determine what we mean by "better" and "poorer."

- 3 -

One obvious fact shows the existence of a wide range of degrees in ability to read. It is that reading begins in the primary grades and runs through every level of the educational system. Reading is the first of the three R's. It is first because we have to learn to read in order to learn by reading. Since what we have to learn, as we ascend in our education, becomes more difficult or complex, we must improve our ability to read proportionately.

Literacy is everywhere the primary mark of education, but it has many degrees, from a grammar-school diploma, or even less, up to a bachelor's degree or a Ph.D. But, in his recent commentary on American democracy, called *Of Human Freedom,* Jacques Barzun cautions us not to be misled by the boast that we have the most literate population in the world. "Literacy in this sense is not education; it is not even 'knowing how to read' in the sense of taking in quickly and correctly the message of the printed page, to say nothing of exercising a critical judgment upon it."

Supposedly, *gradations* in reading go along with *graduations* from one educational level to another. In the light of what we know about American education today, that supposition is not well founded. In France it is still true that the candidate for the doctor's degree must show an ability to read sufficient to admit him to that higher circle of literacy. What the French call *explication de texte* is an art which must be practiced at every educational level and in which improvement must be made before one moves up the scale. But in this country there is often little discernible difference between the *explication* which a high-school student would give and one by a college senior or even a doctoral candidate. When the task is to read a book, the high-school students and college freshmen are often better, if only because they are less thoroughly spoiled by bad habits.

The fact that there is something wrong with American education, so far as reading is concerned, means only that the gradations have become obscure for us, not that they do not exist. Our task is to remove that obscurity. To make the distinction in grades of reading sharper, we must define the criteria of better and worse.

What are the criteria? I think I have already suggested what they are, in the previous chapter. Thus, we say that one man is a better reader than another if he can read more difficult material. Anyone would agree, if Jones is able to read only such things as newspapers and magazines, whereas Brown can read the best current nonfiction books, such as Einstein and Infeld's *Evolution of Physics* or Hogben's *Mathematics for the Millions,* that Brown has more ability than Jones. Among readers at the Jones level, further discrimination may be made between those who cannot rise above the tabloids and those who can master *The New York Times.* Between the Jones group and the Brown group, there are still others measured by the better and worse magazines, better and worse current fiction, or by nonfiction books of a more popular nature than Einstein or Hogben, such as Gunther's *Inside Europe* or Heiser's *An American Doctor's Odyssey.* And better than Brown is the man who can read Euclid and Descartes as well as Hogben, or Galileo and Newton as well as Einstein and Infeld's discussion of them.

The first criterion is an obvious one. In many fields we measure a man's skill by the difficulty of the task he can perform. The accuracy of such measurement depends, of course, on the independent precision with which we can grade the tasks in difficulty. We would be moving in circles if we said, for instance, that the more difficult book is one which only the better reader can master. That is true, but not helpful. In order to understand what makes some books more difficult to read than others, we would have to know what demands they make on the skill of the reader. If we knew that, we would know what distinguishes better and worse readers. In other words, the difficulty of the reading matter is a convenient, objective sign of degrees of reading ability, but it does not tell us what the difference is in the reader, so far as his skill is concerned.

The first criterion has some use, nevertheless, to whatever extent it is true that the more difficult a book is the fewer readers it will have at any given time. There is some truth in this, because it is generally the case that, as one mounts the scale of excellence in any skill, the number of practitioners diminishes: the higher, the fewer. Counting noses, therefore, gives us some independent indication of whether one thing is more difficult to read than another. We can construct a crude scale and measure men accordingly. In a sense, that is the way all the scales, which employ reading tests made by the educational psychologists, are constructed.

The second criterion takes us further, but is harder to state. I have already suggested the distinction between active and passive reading. Strictly, all reading is active. What we call passive is simply less active. Reading is better or worse according as it is more or less active. And one reader is better than another in proportion as he is capable of a greater range of activity in reading. In order to explain this point, I must first be sure that you understand why I say that, strictly speaking, there is no absolutely passive reading. It only seems that way in contrast to more active reading.

No one doubts that writing and speaking are active undertakings, in which the writer or speaker is clearly doing something. Many people seem to think, however, that reading and listening are entirely passive. No work need be done. They think of reading and listening as *receiving* communication from someone who is actively *giving* it. So far they are right, but then they make the error of supposing that receiving communication is like receiving a blow, or a legacy, or a judgment from the court.

Let me use the example of baseball. Catching the ball is just as much an activity as pitching or hitting it. The pitcher or batter is the *giver* here in the sense that his activity initiates the motion of the ball. The catcher or fielder is the *receiver* in the sense that his activity terminates it. Both are equally active, though the activities are distinctly different. If anything is passive here, it is the ball: it is pitched and caught. It is the inert thing which is put in motion or stopped, whereas the living men are active, moving to pitch, hit, or catch. The analogy with writing and reading is almost perfect. The thing which is written and read, like the ball, is the passive object in some way common to the two activities which begin and terminate the process.

We can go a step farther with this analogy. A good catcher is one who stops the ball which has been hit or pitched. The art of catching is the skill of knowing how to do this as well as possible in every situation. So the art of reading is the skill of catching every sort of communication as well as possible. But the reader as "catcher" is more like the fielder than the man behind the plate. The catcher signals for a particular pitch. He knows what to expect. In a sense, the pitcher and catcher are like two men with but a single thought before the ball is thrown. Not so, however, in the case of the batter and fielder. Fielders may wish that batters would obey signals from them, but that isn't the way the game is played. So readers may sometimes wish that writers would submit completely to their desires for reading matter, but the facts are usually otherwise. The reader has to go after what comes out into the field.

The analogy breaks down at two points, both of which are instructive. In the first place, the batter and the fielder, being on opposite sides, do not have the same end in view. Each thinks of himself as successful only if he frustrates the other. In contrast, pitcher and catcher are successful only to the extent that they co-operate. Here the relation of writer and reader is more like that between the men on the battery. The writer certainly isn't trying *not to be caught,* although the reader may often think so. Successful communication occurs in any case where what the writer wanted to have received finds its way into the reader's possession. The writer's and the reader's skill converge upon a common end.

In the second place, the ball is a simple unit. It is either *completely* caught or not. A piece of writing, however, is a complex object. It can be received more or less completely, all the way from very little of what the writer intended to the whole thing. The amount the reader gets will usually depend on the amount of activity he puts into the process, as well as upon the skill with which he executes the different mental acts that are involved.

Now we can define the second criterion for judging reading ability. Given the same thing to read, one man reads it better than another, first, by reading it more actively, and second, by performing each of the acts involved more successfully. These two things are related. Reading is a complex activity, just as writing is. It consists of a large number of separate acts, all of which must be performed in a good reading. Hence, the man who can perform more of these various acts is better able to read.

- 4 -

I have not really told you what good and bad reading are. I have talked about the differences only in a vague and general way. Nothing else is possible here. Until you know the rules which a good reader must follow, you will not be able to understand what is involved.

I know of no short cut by which you can be shown *now*, clearly and in detail, what I hope you will see before you have finished. You may not see it even then. Reading a book on how to play tennis may not be sufficient to make you perceive *from the side lines* the various shades of skill in playing. If you stay on the side lines, you will never know how it feels to play better or worse. Similarly, you have to put the rules of reading into practice before you are really able to understand them and competent to judge your own accomplishment or that of others.

But I can do one thing more here which may help you get the feel of what reading is. I can distinguish different types of reading for you.

I discovered this way of talking about reading under the dire necessity which a lecture platform sometimes imposes. I was lecturing about education to three thousand schoolteachers. I had reached the point where I was bemoaning

the fact that college students couldn't read and that nothing
was being done about it. I could see from their faces that
they didn't know what I was talking about. Weren't they
teaching the children how to read? In fact, that was being
done in the very lowest grades. Why should I be asking that
four years of college be spent primarily in learning to read
and in reading great books?

Under the provocation of their general incredulity, and
their growing impatience with my nonsense, I went further.
I said that most people could not read, that many university
professors I knew could not, that probably my audience
could not read either. The exaggeration only made matters
worse. They knew they could read. They did it every day.
What in the world was this idiot on the platform raving
about? Then it was that I figured out how to explain. In
doing so, I distinguished two *kinds* of reading.

The explanation went something like this. Here is a
book, I said, and here is your mind. The book consists of
language written by someone for the sake of communicating something to you. Your success in reading is determined
by the extent to which you get all that the writer intended
to communicate.

Now, as you go through the pages, either you understand
perfectly everything the author has to say or you do not.
If you do, you may have gained information, but you could
not have increased your understanding. If, upon effortless
inspection, a book is completely intelligible to you, then
the author and you are as two minds in the same mold. The
symbols on the page merely express the common understanding you had before you met.

Let us take the second alternative. You do not understand the book *perfectly at once*. Let us even assume—what

unhappily is not always true—that you understand enough to know that you do not understand it all. You know there is more in the book than you understand and, hence, that the book contains something which can increase your understanding.

What do you do then? You can do a number of things. You can take the book to someone else who, you think, can read better than you, and have him explain the parts that troubled you. Or you can get him to recommend a textbook or commentary which will make it all plain by telling you what the author meant. Or you may decide, as many students do, that what's over your head isn't worth bothering about, that you understand enough, and the rest doesn't matter. If you do any of these things, you are not doing the job of reading which the book requires.

That is done in one way only. Without external help, you take the book into your study and work on it. With nothing but the power of your own mind, you operate on the symbols before you in such a way that you gradually lift yourself from a state of understanding less to one of understanding more. Such elevation, accomplished by the mind working on a book, is reading, the kind of reading that a book which challenges your understanding deserves.

Thus I roughly defined what I meant by reading: the process whereby a mind, with nothing to operate on but the symbols of the readable matter, and with no help from outside, elevates itself by the power of its own operations. The mind passes from understanding less to understanding more. The operations which cause this to happen are the various acts which constitute the art of reading. "How many of these acts do you know?" I asked the three thousand teachers. "What things would you do by yourself if your life depended on understanding something readable which at first perusal left you somewhat in the dark?"

Now their faces frankly told a different story. They plainly confessed that they wouldn't know what to do. They signified, moreover, that they would be willing to admit there was such an art and that some people must possess it.

Clearly not all reading is of the sort I have just described. We do a great deal of reading by which we are in no way *elevated,* though we may be informed, amused, or irritated. There would appear to be several types of reading: for information, for entertainment, for understanding. This sounds at first as if it were only a difference in the purpose with which we read. That is only partly so. In part, also, it depends on a difference in the thing to be read and the way of reading it. You cannot gain much information from the funny sheet or much intellectual elevation from an almanac. As the things to be read have different values, we must use them accordingly. We must satisfy each of our different purposes by going to the right sort of material for each. More than that, we must know how to satisfy our purposes by being able to read each sort of material appropriately.

Omitting, for the present, reading for amusement, I wish to examine here the other two main types: reading for information and reading to understand more. I think you will see the relation between these two types of reading and the degrees of reading ability. The poorer reader is usually able to do only the first sort of reading: for information. The better reader can do that, of course, and more. He can increase his understanding as well as his store of facts.

To pass from understanding less to understanding more, by your own intellectual effort in reading, is something like pulling yourself up by your bootstraps. It certainly feels that way. It is a major exertion. Obviously, it would be a more active kind of reading, entailing not only more varied activity but more skill in the performance of the various acts required. Obviously, too, the things which are usually regarded as more difficult to read, and hence only for the better reader, are those which are most likely to deserve and demand this type of reading.

Things you can comprehend without effort, such as magazines and newspapers, require a minimum of reading. You need very little art. You can read in a relatively passive way. For everyone who can read at all, there is some material of this sort, though it may be different for different individuals. What for one man requires no or little effort may demand genuine exertion from another. How far any man may get by expending every effort will depend on how much skill he has or is able to acquire, and that is somehow relative to his native intelligence.

The point, however, is not to distinguish good and bad readers according to the favors or deprivations of birth. The point is that for each individual there exist two sorts of readable matter: on the one hand, something which he can read effortlessly to be informed, because it communicates nothing which he cannot immediately comprehend; on the other, something which is above him, in the sense of challenging him to make the effort to understand. It may, of course, be too far above him, forever beyond his grasp. But this he cannot tell until he tries, and he cannot try until he develops the art of reading—the skill to make the effort.

- 5 -

Most of us do not know what the limits of our comprehension are. We have never tried our powers to the full. It is my honest belief that *almost all of the great books in every field are within the grasp of all normally intelligent men,* on the condition, of course, that they acquire the skill necessary for reading them and make the effort. Of course, those more favored by birth will reach the goal more readily, but the race is not always to the swift.

There are several minor points here which you must observe. It is possible to be mistaken in your judgment of something you are reading. You may think you understand it, and be content with what you get from an effortless reading, whereas in fact much may have escaped you. The first maxim of sound practice is an old one: the beginning of wisdom is a just appraisal of one's ignorance. So the beginning of reading as a conscious effort to understand is an accurate perception of the line between what is intelligible and what is not.

I have seen many students read a difficult book just as if they were reading the sports page. Sometimes I would ask at the beginning of a class if they had any questions about the text, if there was anything they did not understand. Their silence answered in the negative. At the end of two hours, during which they could not answer the simplest questions leading to an interpretation of the book, they would admit their deficiency in a puzzled way. They were puzzled because they were quite honest in their belief that they had read the text. They had, indeed, but not in the right way.

If they had allowed themselves to be puzzled *while* reading, instead of after the class was over; if they had encouraged themselves to note the things they did not understand, instead of putting such matters immediately out of mind, almost in shame and embarrassment, they might have discovered that the book in front of them was different from their usual diet.

Let me summarize now the distinction between these two types of reading. We shall have to consider both because the line between what is readable in one way and what must be read in the other is often hazy. To whatever extent we can keep the two kinds of reading distinct, we can use the word "reading" in two distinct senses.

The first sense is the one in which we speak of ourselves as reading newspapers, magazines, or anything else which, according to our skill and talents, is at once thoroughly intelligible to us. Such things may increase the store of information we remember, but they cannot improve our understanding, for our understanding was equal to them before we started. Otherwise, we would have felt the shock of puzzlement and perplexity which comes from getting in over our depth—that is, if we were both alert and honest.

The second sense is the one in which I would say a man has to read something that at first he does not completely understand. Here the thing to be read is initially better than the reader. The writer is communicating something which can increase the reader's understanding. Such communication between unequals must be possible, or else one man could never learn from another, either through speech or writing. Here by "learning" I mean understanding more, not remembering more information which has the same degree of intelligibility as other information you already possess.

There is clearly no difficulty about getting new information in the course of reading if, as I say, the novel facts are of the same sort as those you already know, so far as their intelligibility goes. Thus, a man who knows some of the facts of American history and understands them in a certain light can readily acquire by reading, in the first sense, more such facts and understand them in the same light. But suppose he is reading a history which seeks not merely to give him some more facts but to throw a new and, perhaps, more profound light on all the facts he knows. Suppose there is greater understanding here than he possesses before he starts to read. If he can manage to acquire that greater understanding, he is reading in the second sense. He has literally elevated himself by his own activity, though indirectly, of course, this was made possible by the writer who had something to teach him.

What are the conditions under which this kind of reading takes place? There are two. In the first place, there is initial inequality in understanding. The writer must be superior to the reader, and his book must convey in readable form the insights he possesses and his potential readers lack. In the second place, the reader must be able to overcome this inequality in some degree, seldom perhaps fully, but always approaching equality with the writer. To the extent that equality is approached, the communication is perfectly consummated.

In short, we can learn only from our betters. We must know who they are and how to learn from them. The man who has this sort of knowledge possesses the art of reading in the sense with which I am especially concerned. Everyone probably has some ability to read in this way. But all of us, without exception, can learn to read better and gradually gain more by our efforts through applying them to more rewarding materials.

CHAPTER THREE

Reading Is Learning

- I -

ONE rule of reading, as you have seen, is to pick out and interpret the important words in a book. There is another and closely related rule: to discover the important sentences and to understand what they mean.

The words "reading is learning" make a sentence. That sentence is obviously important for this discussion. In fact, I would say that it is the most important sentence so far. Its importance is indicated by the weightiness of the words which compose it. They are not only important words but also ambiguous ones, as we have seen in the case of "reading."

Now, if the word "reading" has many meanings, and similarly the word "learning," and if that little word "is" takes the prize for ambiguity, you are in no position to affirm or deny the sentence. It means a number of things, some of which may be true and some false. When you have found out the meaning of each of the three words, *as I have used them*, you will have discovered the proposition I am trying to convey. Then, and only then, can you decide whether you agree with me.

Since you know that we are not going to consider reading for amusement, you might charge me with inaccuracy for not having said: "*Some* reading is learning." My defense is one which you as a reader will soon come to anticipate. The *context* made it unnecessary for me to say "some." It was

understood that we were going to ignore reading for amusement.

To interpret the sentence, we must first ask: What is
learning? Obviously, we cannot discuss learning adequately
here. The only brief way out is to make a rough approximation in terms of what everybody knows: that learning is
acquiring knowledge. Don't run away. I am not going to
define "knowledge." If I tried to do that, we would be
swamped by the number of other words which would suddenly become important and demand explication. For our
purposes your present understanding of "knowledge" is
sufficient. You have knowledge. You know that you know
and what you know. You know the difference between
knowing and not knowing something.

If you were called upon to give a philosophical account
of the nature of knowledge, you might be stumped; but so
have many philosophers been. Let us leave them to their
worries, and proceed to use the word "knowledge" on the
assumption that we understand each other. But, you may
object, even if we assume that we have a sufficient grasp of
what we mean by "knowledge," there are other difficulties
in saying that learning is acquiring knowledge. One learns
how to play tennis or cook. Playing tennis and cooking are
not knowledge. They are ways of doing something which
require skill.

The objection has point. Although knowledge is involved in every skill, having a skill is having something
more than knowledge. The person who has a skill not only
knows something but can *do* something which the person
lacking it cannot do at all or as well. There is a familiar
distinction here, which all of us make when we speak of
knowing *how* (to do something) as opposed to knowing *that*

(something is the case). One can learn *how* as well as *that*. You have already acknowledged this distinction in recognizing that one has to learn how to read in order to learn from reading.

An initial restriction is thus imposed on the word "learning" as we are using it. Reading is learning only in the sense of gaining knowledge and not skill. You cannot learn how to read just by reading this book. All you can learn is the nature of reading and the rules of the art. That may help you learn how to read, but it is not sufficient. In addition, you must follow the rules and practice the art. Only in that way can the skill be acquired, which is something over and above the knowledge that a mere book can communicate.

- 2 -

So far, so good. But now we must return to the distinction between reading for information and reading for understanding. In the preceding chapter, I suggested how much more active the latter sort of reading must be, and how it feels to do it. Now we must consider the difference in what you get out of these two kinds of reading. Both information and understanding are knowledge in some sense. Getting more information is learning, and so is coming to understand what you did not understand before. What is the difference?

To be informed is to know simply that something is the case. To be enlightened is to know, in addition, what it is all about: why it is the case, what its connections are with other facts, in what respects it is the same and different, and so forth.

Most of us are acquainted with this distinction in terms

of the difference between being able to remember something and being able to explain it. If you remember what an author says, you have learned something from reading him. If what he says is true, you have even learned something about the world. But whether it is a fact about the book or the world, you have gained nothing but information if you have exercised only your memory. You have not been enlightened. That happens only when, in addition to knowing what an author says, you know what he means and why he says it.

A single example may help us here. What I am going to report happened in a class in which we were reading Thomas Aquinas's treatise on the passions, but the same thing has happened in countless other classes with many different sorts of material. I asked a student what St. Thomas had to say about the order of the passions. He quite correctly told me that love, according to St. Thomas, is the first of all the passions and that the other emotions, which he named accurately, follow in a certain order. Then I asked him what it meant to say this. He looked startled. Had he not answered my question correctly? I told him he had, but repeated my request for an explanation. He had told me what St. Thomas *said*. Now I wanted to know what St. Thomas *meant*. The student tried, but all he could do was to repeat, in slightly altered order, the same words he had used to answer my original question. It soon became obvious that he did not know what he was talking about, even though he would have made a good score on any examination which went no further than my original question or questions of a similar sort.

I tried to help him. I asked him whether love was first in the sense of being a cause of other emotions. I asked him how hate and anger, hope and fear, depended on love. I asked him about the relation of joy and grief to love. And what is love? Is love hunger for food and thirst for drink, or is it only that wonderful feeling which is supposed to make the world go round? Is the desire for money or fame, knowledge or happiness, love? In so far as he could answer these questions by repeating more or less accurately the words of St. Thomas, he did. When he made errors in reporting, other members of the class could be called upon to correct them. But neither he nor they could make any headway with explaining what it was all about.

I tried still another tack. I asked them, begging their pardon, about their own emotional experiences. They were all old enough to have had a few passions. Did they ever hate anybody, and did it have anything to do with loving that person or somebody else? Had they ever experienced a sequence of emotions, one of which somehow led into another? They were very vague, not because they were embarrassed or because they had never been emotionally upset but because they were totally unaccustomed to thinking about their experiences in this way. Clearly they had not made any connection between the words they had read in a book about the passions and their own experiences. These things were as in worlds apart.

It was becoming apparent why they did not have the faintest understanding of what they had read. It was just words they had memorized to be able to repeat somehow when I shot a question at them. That was what they did in other courses. I was asking too much of them.

I still persisted. Perhaps, if they could not understand Aquinas in the light of their own experience, they might be able to use the vicarious experience they got from reading novels. They had read some fiction. Here and there some of them had even read a great novel. Did passions occur in these stories? Were there different passions and how were they related? They did as badly here as before. They answered by telling me the story in a superficial summary of the plot. They understood the novels they had read about as little as they understood St. Thomas.

Finally, I asked whether they had ever taken any other courses in which passions or emotions had been discussed. Most of them had had an elementary course in psychology, and one or two of them had even heard of Freud, and perhaps read a little of him. When I discovered that they had made no connection whatsoever between the physiology of emotion, in which they had probably passed creditable examinations, and the passions as St. Thomas discussed them; when I found out they could not even see that St. Thomas was making the same basic point as Freud, I realized what I was up against.

These students were college juniors and seniors. They could read in one sense but not in another. All their years in school they had been reading for information only, the sort of information you have to get from something assigned in order to answer quizzes and pass examinations. They never connected one book with another, one course with another, or anything that was said in books or lectures with what happened to them in their own lives.

Not knowing that there was something more to do with a book than commit its more obvious statements to memory, they were totally innocent of their dismal failure when they came to class. According to their lights, they had conscientiously prepared the day's lesson. It had never occurred to them that they might be called upon to show that they understood what they had read. Even when a number of such class sessions began to make them aware of this novel requirement, they were helpless. At best they became a little more aware that they did not understand what they were reading, but they could do little about it. Here, near the end of their schooling, they were totally unskilled in the art of reading to understand.

- 3 -

When we read for information, we acquire facts. When we read to understand, we learn not only facts but their significance. Each kind of reading has its virtue, but it must be used in the right place. If a writer does not understand more than we do, or if in a particular passage he makes no effort to explain, we can only be informed by him, not enlightened. But if an author has insights we do not possess and if, in addition, he has tried to convey them in what he has written, we are neglecting his gift to us if we do not read him differently from the way in which we read newspapers or magazines.

The books we acknowledge to be great or good are usually those which deserve the better sort of reading. It is true, of course, that anything can be read for information as well as understanding. One should be able to remember what the author said as well as know what he meant. In a sense, being informed is prerequisite to being enlightened. The point, however, is not to stop at being informed. It is as wasteful to read a great book solely for information as to use a fountain pen for digging worms.

Montaigne speaks of "an abecedarian ignorance that precedes knowledge, and a doctoral ignorance that comes

after it." The one is the ignorance of those who, not knowing their ABC's, cannot read at all. The other is the ignorance of those who have misread many books. They are, as
Pope rightly calls them, bookful blockheads, ignorantly
read. There have always been literate ignoramuses who have
read too widely and not well. The Greeks had a name for
such mixture of learning and folly, which might be applied
to the bookish but poorly read of all ages. They are all
sophomores.

Being well read too often means the quantity, too seldom
the quality, of reading. It was not only the pessimistic and
misanthropic Schopenhauer who inveighed against too
much reading, because he found that, for the most part,
men read passively and glutted themselves with toxic over-
doses of unassimilated information. Bacon and Hobbes
made the same point. Hobbes said: "If I read as many books
as most men"—he meant "misread"—"I should be as dull-
witted as they." Bacon distinguished between "books to be
tasted, others to be swallowed, and some few to be chewed
and digested." The point that remains the same throughout rests on the distinction between different kinds of reading appropriate to different kinds of literature.

- 4 -

We have made some progress in interpreting the sentence
"reading is learning." We know that some, but not all, reading is learning. We know that some, but not all, learning
can be achieved through reading: the acquisition of knowledge but not of skill. If we concluded, however, that the
kind of reading which results in increased information or
understanding is *identical* with the kind of learning which

results in more knowledge, we would be making a serious error. We would be saying that no one can acquire knowledge except through reading, which is clearly false.

To avoid this error, we must now consider one further distinction in types of learning. This distinction has a significant bearing on the whole business of reading, and its relation to education generally. (If the point I am now going to make is unfamiliar to you, and perhaps somewhat difficult, I suggest that you take the following pages as a challenge to your skill in reading. This is a good place to begin *active* reading—marking the important words, noting the distinctions, seeing how the meaning of the sentence with which we started expands.)

In the history of education, men have always distinguished between instruction and discovery as sources of knowledge. Instruction occurs when one man teaches another through speech or writing. We can, however, gain knowledge without being taught. If this were not the case, and every teacher had to be taught what he in turn teaches others, there would be no beginning in the acquisition of knowledge. Hence, there must be discovery—the process of learning something by research, by investigation, or by reflection, without being taught.

Discovery stands to instruction as learning without a teacher to learning through the help of one. In both cases, the activity of learning goes on in the one who learns. It would be a great mistake to suppose that discovery is active learning and instruction passive. There is no passive learning, as there is no completely passive reading.

The difference between the two activities of learning is with respect to the materials on which the learner works. When he is being taught or instructed, the learner acts on something communicated to him. He performs operations on discourse, written or oral. He learns by acts of reading or listening. Note here the close relation between reading and listening. If we ignore the minor differences between these two ways of receiving communication, we can say that reading and listening are the same art—the art of being taught. When, however, the learner proceeds without the help of any sort of teacher, the operations of learning are performed on nature rather than discourse. The rules of such learning constitute the art of discovery. If we use the word "reading" loosely, we can say that discovery is the art of reading nature, as instruction (being taught) is the art of reading books or, to include listening, of learning from discourse.

What about thinking? If by "thinking" we mean the use of our minds to gain knowledge, and if instruction and discovery exhaust the ways of gaining knowledge, then clearly all our thinking must take place during one or the other of these two activities. We must think during the course of reading and listening, just as we must think in the course of research. Naturally, the kinds of thinking are different—as different as the two ways of learning are.

The reason why many people regard thinking as more closely associated with research and discovery than with being taught is that they suppose reading and listening to be passive affairs. It is probably true that one does less thinking when one reads for information than when one is undertaking to discover something. That is the less active sort of reading. But it is not true of the more active reading —the effort to understand. No one who has done this sort of reading would say it can be done thoughtlessly.

Thinking is only one part of the activity of learning. One

must also use one's senses and imagination. One must observe, and remember, and construct imaginatively what cannot be observed. There is, again, a tendency to stress the role of these activities in the process of research or discovery and to forget or minimize their place in the process of being taught through reading or listening. A moment's reflection will show that the sensitive as well as the rational powers must be employed in reading and listening. The art of reading, in short, includes all the same skills that are involved in the art of discovery: keenness of observation, readily available memory, range of imagination, and, of course, a reason trained in analysis and reflection. Though in general the skills are the same, they may be differently employed in the two major types of learning.

– 5 –

I would like to stress again the two errors which are so frequently made. One is made by those who write or talk about an art of thinking as if there were any such thing in and by itself. Since we never think apart from the work of being taught or the process of research, there is no art of thinking apart from the art of reading and listening, on the one hand, and the art of discovery, on the other. To whatever extent it is true that reading is learning, it is also true that reading is thinking. A complete account of the art of thinking can be given only in the context of a complete analysis of reading and research.

The other error is made by those who write about the art of thinking as if it were identical with the art of discovery. The outstanding example of this error, and one which has tremendously influenced American education, is John

Dewey's *How We Think*. This book has been the bible for thousands of teachers who have been trained in our schools of education. Professor Dewey limits his discussion of thinking to its occurrence in learning by discovery. But that is only one of the two main ways we think. It is equally important to know how we think when we read a book or listen to a lecture. Perhaps, it is even more important for teachers who are engaged in instruction, since the art of teaching must be related to the art of being taught, as the art of writing is related to the art of reading. I doubt whether anyone who does not know how to read well can write well. I similarly doubt whether anyone who does not have the art of being taught is skilled in teaching.

The cause of these errors is probably complex. Partly, they may be due to the false supposition that teaching and research are activities, whereas reading and being taught are merely passive. In part also, these errors are due to an exaggeration of the scientific method, which stresses investigation or research as if it were the only occasion for thought. There probably was a time when the opposite error was made: when men overemphasized the reading of books and paid too little attention to the reading of nature. That does not excuse us, however. Either extreme is equally bad. A balanced education must place a just emphasis on both types of learning, and on the arts they require.

Whatever their causes, the effect of these errors on American education is only too obvious. They may account for the almost total neglect of intelligent reading throughout the school system. Much more time is spent in training students how to discover things for themselves than in training them how to learn from others. There is no particular virtue, it seems to me, in wasting time to find out for yourself what has already been discovered. One should save one's skill in research for what has not yet been discovered, and exercise one's skill in being taught for learning what others already know and therefore can teach.

A tremendous amount of time is wasted in laboratory courses in this way. The usual apology for the excess of laboratory ritual is that it trains the student how to think. True enough, it does, but only in one type of thinking. A roundly educated man, even a research scientist, should also be able to think while reading. Each generation of men should not have to learn everything for themselves, as if nothing had ever been learned before. In fact, they cannot.

Unless the art of reading is cultivated, as it is not in American education today, the use of books must steadily diminish. We may continue to gain some knowledge by speaking to nature, for it will always answer, but there is no point in our ancestors speaking to us unless we know how to listen.

You may say there is little difference between reading books and reading nature. But remember that the things of nature are not symbols communicating something from another human mind, whereas the words we read and listen to are. And remember also that when we seek to learn from nature directly, our ultimate aim is to understand the world in which we live. *We neither agree nor disagree with nature,* as we often do in the case of books.

Our ultimate aim is the same when we seek to learn from books. But, in this second case, we must first be sure we understand what the book is saying. Only then can we decide whether we agree or disagree with its author. The

process of understanding nature *directly* is different from
that of coming to understand it through interpreting a
book. The critical faculty need be employed only in the
latter case.

- 6 -

I have been proceeding as if reading and listening could
both be treated as learning from teachers. To some extent
that is true. Both are ways of being instructed, and for both
one must be skilled in the art of being taught. Listening to
a course of lectures is in many respects like reading a book.
Many of the rules I shall formulate for the reading of books
apply to taking lecture courses. Yet there is good reason for
limiting our discussion to the art of reading, or at least
placing our primary emphasis on reading, and letting the
other applications become a secondary concern. The reason
is that listening is learning from a living teacher, while
reading is learning from a dead one, or at least one who is
not present to us except through his writing.

If you ask a living teacher a question, he may really
answer you. If you are puzzled by what he says, you may
save yourself the trouble of thinking by asking him what
he means. If, however, you ask a book a question, you must
answer it yourself. In this respect a book is like nature.
When you speak to it, it answers you only to the extent
that you do the work of thinking and analysis yourself.

I do not mean, of course, that if the teacher answers your
question, you have no further work. That is so only if the
question is simply one of fact. But if you are seeking an
explanation, you have to understand it or nothing has been
explained to you. Nevertheless, with the living teacher
available to you, you are given a lift in the direction of

understanding him, as you are not when the teacher's words in a book are all you have to go by.

But books can also be read under the guidance and with the help of teachers. So we must consider the relation between books and teachers—between being taught by books with and without the aid of teachers. That is a matter for the next chapter. Obviously, it is a matter which concerns those of us who are still in school. But it also concerns those of us who are not, for we may have to depend on books alone as the means for continuing our education, and we ought to know how to make books teach us well. Perhaps we are better off for lacking living teachers, perhaps worse.

CHAPTER FOUR

Teachers, Dead or Alive

- I -

WE CAN be instructed by listening to a lecture as well as through reading a book. That is what brings us to the consideration now of books and teachers, to complete our understanding of reading as learning.

Teaching, as we have seen, is the process whereby one man learns from another through communication. *Instruction* is thus distinguished from *discovery*, which is the process whereby a man learns something by himself, through observing and thinking about the world, and not by receiving communication from other men. It is true, of course, that these two kinds of learning are intimately and intricately fused in the actual education of any man. Each may help the other. But the point remains that we can always tell, if we take the pains to do so, whether we learned something we know from someone else or whether we found it out for ourselves.

We may even be able to tell whether we have learned it from a book or from a teacher. But, by the meaning of the word "teaching," the book which taught us something can be called a "teacher." We must distinguish, therefore, between writing teachers and speaking teachers, teachers we learn from by reading and teachers we learn from by listening.

For convenience of reference, I shall call the speaking

48

teacher a "live teacher." He is a human being with whom we have some personal contact. And I shall call books "dead teachers." Please note that I do not mean to say that the author of the book is dead. In fact, he may be the very alive teacher who not only lectures at us but makes us read a textbook he has written.

Whether or not the author is dead, the book is a dead thing. It cannot talk back to us, or answer questions. It does not grow and change its mind. It is a communication, but we cannot converse with it, in the sense in which we may succeed, once in a while, in communicating something to our living teachers. The rare cases in which we have been able to converse profitably with the author of a book we have read may make us realize our deprivation when the author is dead or at least unavailable for conversation.

- 2 -

What is the role of the live teacher in our education? A live teacher may help us to acquire certain skills: may teach us *how* to cut pin wheels in kindergarten, how to form and recognize letters in the early grades, or how to spell and pronounce, how to do sums and long division, how to cook, sew, and do carpentry. A live teacher may assist us to develop any art, even the arts of learning itself, such as the art of experimental research or the art of reading.

In giving such aid, more than communication is usually involved. The live teacher not only tells us what to do, but is particularly useful in *showing* us how and, even more directly, in helping us to go through the motions. On these latter counts, there is no question that a live teacher can be more helpful than a dead one. The most successful how-

to-do book cannot take you by the hand or say at the right
moment, "Stop doing it that way. Do it this way."

Now, one thing is immediately clear. With respect to all
the knowledge we gain by discovery, a live teacher can perform only one function. He obviously cannot teach us that
knowledge, for then we would not gain it by discovery. He
can only teach us the art of discovery, that is, tell us how to
do research, how to observe and think in the process of
finding things out. He may, in addition, help us to become
expert in the motions. In general this is the province of a
book like Dewey's *How We Think* and of those who have
tried to help students practice according to its rules.

Since we are primarily concerned with reading—and with
the other kind of learning, through instruction—we can
limit our discussion to the role of the teacher as one who
communicates knowledge or helps us to learn from communication. And, for the time being, let us even limit ourselves to considering the live teacher as a source of knowledge, and not as a preceptor who helps us learn how to do
something.

Considered as a source of knowledge, the live teacher
either competes with or co-operates with dead teachers,
that is, with books. By *competition* I mean the way in which
many live teachers tell their students by lectures what the
students could learn by reading the books the lecturer
himself digested. Long before the magazine existed, live
teachers earned their living by being "readers' digests." By
co-operation I mean the way in which the live teacher somehow divides the function of teaching between himself and
available books: some things he tells the student, usually
boiling down what he himself has read, and some things
he expects the student to learn by reading.

If these were the only functions a live teacher performed with respect to the communication of knowledge, it would follow that anything which can be learned in school can be learned outside of school and without live teachers. It might take a little more trouble to read for yourself than to have books digested for you. You might have to read more books, if books were your only teachers. But to whatever extent it is true that the live teacher has no knowledge to communicate except what he himself learned by reading, you can learn it directly from books yourself. You can learn it as well if you can read as well.

I suspect, moreover, that if what you seek is understanding rather than information, reading will take you further. Most of us are guilty of the vice of passive reading, of course; but most people are even more likely to be passive in listening to a lecture. A lecture has been well described as the process whereby the notes of the teacher become the notes of the student without passing through the mind of either.

Note taking is usually not an active assimilation of what is to be understood, but an almost automatic record of what was said. The habit of doing it becomes a more pervasive substitute for learning and thinking as one spends more years in educational institutions. It is worst in the professional schools, such as law and medicine, and the graduate school. Someone said you can tell the difference between graduate and undergraduate students in this way. If you walk into a classroom and say "Good morning," and the students reply, they are undergraduates. If they write it down, they are graduate students.

There are two other functions a live teacher performs, by which he is related to books. One is *repetition*. We have all taken courses in school in which the teacher said in class the very same things we were assigned to read in a textbook written by him or one of his colleagues. I have been guilty of teaching that way myself. I remember the first course I ever taught. It was elementary psychology. A textbook was assigned. The examination which the department set for all the sections of this course indicated that the student need only learn what the textbook said. My only function as a living teacher was to help the textbook do its work. In part, I asked questions of the sort that might be asked on an examination. In part, I lectured, repeating the book chapter by chapter, in words not very different from those the author used.

Occasionally I may have tried to explain a point, but if the student had done a job of reading for understanding, he could have understood the point by himself. If he could not read that way, he probably could not listen to my explanation in an understanding way either.

Most of the students were taking the course for credit, not merit. Since the examination did not measure understanding but information, they probably regarded my explanations as a waste of their time—sheer exhibitionism on my part. Why they continued to come to class, I do not know. If they had spent as much time reading the textbook as the sports page, and with the same diligence for details of information, they could have passed the examination without being bored by me.

- 3 -

The function which remains to be discussed is difficult to name. Perhaps I can call it "original communication." I am thinking of the living instructor who knows something which cannot be found in books anywhere. It must be something which he has himself discovered and has not yet made available for readers. This happens rarely. It happens today most frequently in the fields of scholarship or scientific research. Every now and then the graduate school is graced by a course of lectures which constitute an original communication. If you are not fortunate enough to hear the lectures, you usually console yourself by saying that they will probably appear in book form shortly.

The printing of books has now become such a routine and common affair that it is not likely any more that original communications must be heard or lost. Before Caxton, however, the living teacher probably performed this function more frequently. That was why students traveled all over medieval Europe to hear a famous lecturer. If one goes back far enough in the history of European learning, one comes to the early time before knowledge had been funded, before there was a tradition of learning which one generation received from its predecessor and passed on to the next. Then, of course, the teacher was primarily a man of knowledge and a communicator secondarily. I mean he had first to get knowledge by *discovering it himself*, before he could teach it to anyone else.

The present situation is at the other extreme. The living teacher today is primarily a man of learning, rather than a discoverer. He is one who has learned most of what he knows from other teachers, alive or dead. Let us consider the average teacher today as one who has no original communication to make. In relation to dead teachers, therefore, he must be either a repeater or a digester. In either case, his students could learn everything he knows by reading the books he has read.

With respect to the communication of knowledge, the only justification for the living teacher, then, is a practical one. The flesh being weak, it takes the easier course. The paraphernalia of lectures, assignments, and examinations may be a surer and more efficient way of getting a certain amount of information, and even a little understanding, into the rising generation's heads. Even if we had trained them how to read well, we might not be able to trust them to keep at the hard work of reading in order to learn.

The self-educated man is as rare as the self-made man. Most men do not become genuinely learned or amass large fortunes through their own efforts. The existence of such men, however, shows it can be done. Their rarity indicates the exceptional qualities of character—the stamina and self-discipline, the patience and perseverance—which are required. In knowledge as in wealth, most of us have to be spoon-fed to the little we possess.

These facts, and their practical consequences for institutional education, do not alter the main point, however. What is true of the average teacher is equally true of all textbooks, manuals, and syllabi. These, too, are nothing but repetitions, compilations, and condensations of what can be found in other books, often other books of the same sort.

There is one exception, however, and that makes the point. Let us call those living teachers who perform the function of original communication the primary teachers. There are a few in every generation, though most are secondary teachers in the sense described. Just as there are primary and secondary teachers who are alive now, so among dead teachers we can make the same distinction. There are primary and secondary books.

The primary books are those which contain original communications. They need not be original in entirety, of course. On the contrary, complete originality is both impossible and misleading. It is impossible except at the hypothetical beginning of our cultural tradition. It is misleading because no one should try to discover for himself what he can be taught by others. The best sort of originality is obviously that which adds something to the fund of knowledge made available by the tradition of learning. Ignorance or neglect of the tradition is likely to result in a false or shallow originality.

The great books in all fields of learning are, in some good sense of the word, "original" communications. These are the books which are usually called "classics," but that word has for most people a wrong and forbidding connotation—wrong in the sense of referring to antiquity, and forbidding in the sense of sounding unreadable. Great books are being written today and were written yesterday as well as long ago. And I am going to try to show that, far from being unreadable, the great books are the most readable and those which most deserve to be read.

- 4 -

What I have said so far may not help you to pick out the great books from all others on the shelves. In fact, I shall postpone stating the criteria which betoken a great book—criteria which also help you tell good books from bad—until much later (in Chapter Sixteen, to be precise). It might seem logical to tell a person what to read before telling him how, but I think it is wiser pedagogy to explain the requirements of reading first. Unless one is able to read carefully and critically, the criteria for judging books, however sound they may be in themselves, are likely to become in use just arbitrary rules of thumb. Only after you have read some great books competently will you have an intimate grasp of the standards by which other books can be judged as great or good. If you are impatient to know the titles of the books which most competent readers have agreed upon as great, you can turn now to the Appendix in which they are listed; but I would advise waiting until you have read the discussion of their characteristics and contents in Chapter Sixteen.

There is, however, one thing I can say about the great books here. This may explain why they are generally readable, even if it does not explain why they should be generally read. They are like popularizations in that most of them are written for ordinary men and not for pedants or scholars. They are like textbooks in that they are intended for beginners and not for specialists or advanced students. You can see why that must be so. To the extent that they are original, they have to address themselves to an audience which starts from scratch. There is no prerequisite for reading a great book except another great book in the tradition of learning, by which the later teacher may have himself been taught.

Unlike textbooks and popularizations, the great books assume an audience of readers who are thoroughly competent to read. That is one of their major distinctions, and probably why they are so little read today. They are not only original communications, rather than digests or repetitions, but unlike the latter they do not go in for spoon-feeding. They say: "Here is knowledge worth having. Come and get it."

The proliferation of textbooks and lecture courses in our

educational system today is the surest sign of our declining literacy. Truer than the quip that those who can't teach, teach teachers, is the insight that teachers who cannot help their students read the great books write textbooks for them, or at least use those their colleagues have written. A textbook or manual might almost be defined as a pedagogical invention for getting "something" into the heads of those who cannot read well enough to learn more actively. An ordinary classroom lecture is a similar device. When teachers no longer know how to perform the function of reading books *with* their students, they are forced to lecture *at* them instead.

Textbooks and popularizations of all sorts are written for people who do not know how to read or can read only for information. As dead teachers, they are like the live secondary teachers who wrote them. Alive or dead, the secondary teacher tries to impart knowledge without requiring too much or too skillful activity on the part of the learner. Theirs is an art of teaching which demands the least art of being taught in the student. They stuff the mind rather than enlighten it. The measure of their success is how much the sponge will absorb.

Our ultimate goal is understanding rather than information, though information is a necessary steppingstone. Hence we must go to the primary teachers, for they have understanding to give. Can there be any question that the primary teachers are better sources of learning than the secondary ones? Is there any doubt that the effort they demand of us leads to the vital cultivation of our minds? We can avoid effort in learning, but we cannot avoid the results of effortless learning—the assorted vagaries we collect by letting secondary teachers indoctrinate us.

If, in the same college, two men were lecturing, one a man who had discovered some truth, the other a man who was repeating secondhand what he had heard reported of the first man's work, which would you rather go to hear? Yes, even supposing that the repeater promised to make it a little simpler by talking down to your level, would you not suspect that the secondhand stuff lacked something in quality or quantity? If you paid the greater price in effort, you would be rewarded by better goods.

It happens to be the case, of course, that most of the primary teachers are dead—the men are dead, and the books they have left us are dead teachers—whereas most of the living teachers are secondary. But suppose that we could resuscitate the primary teachers of all times. Suppose there were a college or university in which the faculty was thus composed. Herodotus and Thucydides taught the history of Greece, and Gibbon lectured on the fall of Rome. Plato and St. Thomas gave a course in metaphysics together; Francis Bacon and John Stuart Mill discussed the logic of science; Aristotle, Spinoza, and Immanuel Kant shared the platform on moral problems; Machiavelli, Thomas Hobbes, and John Locke talked about politics.

You could take a series of courses in mathematics from Euclid, Descartes, Riemann, and Cantor, with Bertrand Russell and A. N. Whitehead added at the end. You could listen to St. Augustine and William James talk about the nature of man and the human mind, with perhaps Jacques Maritain to comment on the lectures. Harvey discussed the circulation of the blood, and Galen, Claude Bernard, and Haldane taught general physiology.

Lectures on physics enlisted the talent of Galileo and Newton, Faraday and Maxwell, Planck and Einstein.

Boyle, Dalton, Lavoisier, and Pasteur taught chemistry.
Darwin and Mendel gave the main lectures on evolution
and genetics, with supporting talks by Bateson and T. H.
Morgan.

Aristotle, Sir Philip Sidney, Wordsworth, and Shelley
discussed the nature of poetry and the principles of literary
criticism, with T. S. Eliot thrown in to boot. In economics,
the lectures were by Adam Smith, Ricardo, Karl Marx, and
Marshall. Boas discussed the human race and its races,
Thorstein Veblen and John Dewey, the economic and political problems of American democracy, and Lenin lectured on communism.

Etienne Gilson analyzed the history of philosophy, and
Poincaré and Duhem, the history of science. There might
even be lectures on art by Leonardo da Vinci, and a lecture
on Leonardo by Freud. Hobbes and Locke might discuss
the use and abuse of words, with passing references to
Ogden and Richards, Korzybski and Stuart Chase. A much
larger faculty than this is imaginable, but this will suffice.

Would anyone want to go to any other university, if he
could get into this one? There need be no limitation of
numbers. The price of admission—the only entrance requirement—is the ability and willingness to read. This
school exists for everybody who is willing and able to learn
from first-rate teachers, though they be dead in the sense of
not jolting us out of our lethargy by their living presence.
They are not dead in any other sense. If contemporary
America dismisses them as dead, then, as a well-known
writer recently said, we are repeating the folly of the ancient
Athenians who supposed that Socrates died when he drank
the hemlock.

The great books can be read in or out of school. If they

are read in school, in classes under the supervision of live teachers, the latter must properly subordinate themselves to the dead ones. We can learn only from our intellectual betters. The great books are better than most living teachers as well as their students.

The secondary teacher is simply a better student, and he should regard himself as learning from the masters along with his younger charges. He should not act as if he were the primary teacher, using a great book as if it were just another textbook of the sort one of his colleagues might write. He should not masquerade as one who knows and can teach by virtue of his original discoveries, if he is only one who has learned through being taught. The primary sources of his own knowledge should be the primary sources of learning for his students, and such a teacher functions honestly only if he does not aggrandize himself by coming between the great books and their young readers. He should not "come between" as a nonconductor, but he should come between as a mediator—as one who helps the less competent make more effective contacts with the best minds.

- 5 -

All this is not news, or, at least, it should not be. For many centuries, education was regarded as the elevation of a mind by its betters. If we are honest, most of us living teachers should be willing to admit that, apart from the advantages which age bestows, we are not much better than our students in intellectual caliber or attainment. If elevation is to take place, better minds than ours will have to do the teaching. That is why, for many centuries, education was thought to be produced by contact with the great minds of past and present.

There is only one fly in the ointment. We, the teachers, must know how to read for understanding. Our students must know how. Anyone, in school or out, must know how, if the formula is to work.

But, you may say, it isn't as simple as all that. These great books are too difficult for most of us, in school or out. That is why we are forced to get our education from secondary teachers, from classroom lectures, textbooks, popularizations, which repeat and digest for us what would otherwise forever remain a closed book. Even though our aim be understanding, not information, we must be satisfied with a less rich diet. We suffer incurable limitations. The masters are too far above us. It is certainly better to gather a few crumbs which have dropped from the table than to starve in futile adoration of the feast we cannot reach.

This I deny. For one thing, the less rich diet is likely not to be genuinely nourishing at all, if it is predigested food which can be passively acquired and only temporarily retained rather than actively assimilated. For another, as Professor Morris Cohen once told a class of his, the pearls which are dropped before real swine are likely to be imitation.

I am not denying that the great books are likely to require more arduous and diligent effort than the digests. I am only saying that the latter cannot be substituted for the former, because you cannot get the same thing out of them. They may be all right if all you want is some kind of information, but not if it is enlightenment you seek. There is no royal road. The path of true learning is strewn with rocks, not roses. Anyone who insists upon taking the easier way ends up in a fool's paradise—a bookful blockhead, ignorantly read, a sophomore all his life.

At the same time, I am saying that the great books can be read by every man. The help he needs from secondary teachers does not consist of the get-learning-quick substitutes. It consists of help in learning how to read, and, more than that when possible, help actually in the course of reading the great books.

Let me argue a bit further the point that the great books are the most readable. In one sense, of course, they are difficult to read. They require the greatest ability to read. Their art of teaching demands a corresponding and proportionate art of being taught. But, at the same time, the great books are the most competent to instruct us about the subject matters with which they deal. If we had the skill necessary to read them well, we would find them the easiest, because the most facile and adequate, way to master the subject matters in question.

There is something of a paradox here. It is due to the fact that two different kinds of mastery are involved. There is, on the one hand, the author's mastery of his subject matter; on the other, there is our need to master the book he has written. These books are recognized as great because of their mastery, and we rate ourselves as readers according to the degree of our ability to master these books.

If our aim in reading is to gain knowledge and insight, then the great books are the most readable, both for the less and for the more competent, because they are the most instructive. Obviously I do not mean *"most* readable" in the sense of "with the *least* effort"—even for the expert reader. I mean that these books reward every degree of effort and ability to the maximum. It may be harder to dig for gold than for potatoes, but each unit of successful effort is more amply repaid.

The relation between the great books and their subject matters, which makes them what they are, cannot be changed. That is an objective and unalterable fact. But the relation between the original competence of the beginning reader and the books which most deserve to be read can be altered. The reader can be made more competent, through guidance and practice. To the extent that this happens, he is not only more able to read the great books, but, as a consequence, comes nearer and nearer to understanding the subject matter as the masters have understood it. Such mastery is the ideal of education. It is the obligation of secondary teachers to facilitate the approach to this ideal.

- 6 -

In writing this book I am a secondary teacher. My aim is to help and mediate. I am not going to read any books for you to save you the trouble of reading them yourself. This book has only two functions to perform: to interest you in the profit of reading and to assist you in cultivating the art.

If you are no longer in school, you may be forced to use the services of a dead teacher of the art, such as this book. And no how-to-do book can ever be as helpful, in as many ways, as a good living guide. It may be just a little harder to develop skill when you have to practice according to the rules you find in a book, without being stopped, corrected, and shown how. But it certainly can be done. Too many men have done it to leave the possibility in doubt. It is never too late to begin, but we all have reason to be vexed with a school system which failed to give us a good start early in life.

The failure of the schools, and their responsibility, belong to the next chapter. Let me end this one by calling your attention to two things. The first is that you have learned something about the rules of reading. In earlier chapters you saw the importance of picking out important words and sentences and interpreting them. In the course of this chapter you have followed an argument about the readability of the great books and their role in education. Discovering and following an author's arguments is another step in reading. I shall discuss the rule for doing so more fully later.

The second point is that we have now pretty well defined the purpose of this book. It has taken many pages to do that, but I think you can see why it would have been unintelligible if I had stated it in the first paragraph. I could have said: "This book is intended to help you develop the art of reading for understanding, not information; therefore, it aims to encourage and assist you in reading the great books." But I do not think you would have known what I meant.

Now you do, even though you may still have some reservations about the profit or significance of the enterprise. You may think there are many books, other than the great ones, which are worth reading. I agree, of course. But you must admit in turn that the better the book, the more it is worth reading. Furthermore, if you learn how to read the great books, you will have no difficulty in reading other books, or for that matter anything else. You can use your skill to go after easier game. May I remind you, however, that the sportsman doesn't hunt lame ducks?

CHAPTER FIVE

"The Defeat of the Schools"

- I -

IN THE course of the preceding chapters, I have said some things about the school system which are libelous unless they are true. But if true they constitute a grave indictment of the educators who have violated a public trust. Though this chapter may seem like a long digression from the business of teaching you how to read, it is needed to explain the situation in which most of us find ourselves or our children —"educated" but illiterate. If the schools were doing their job, this book would not be necessary.

So far I have spoken largely from my own experience as a teacher in high school, college, and university. But you need not take my uncorroborated word for the deplorable failures of American education. There are many other witnesses who can be called to the stand. Better than ordinary witnesses, who may also speak from their own experience, there is something like scientific evidence on the point. We can listen to the experts report the results of tests and measurements.

As far back as I can remember, there have been complaints about the schools for not teaching the young to write and speak well. The complaints have focused mainly on the products of high school and college. An elementary-school diploma never was expected to certify great competence in these matters. But after four or eight more years in school, it seemed reasonable to hope for a disciplined ability to perform these basic acts. English courses were, and for the most part still are, a staple ingredient in the high-school curriculum. Until recently, freshman English was a required course in every college. These courses were supposed to develop skill in writing the mother tongue. Though less emphasized than writing, the ability to speak clearly, if not with eloquence, was also supposed to be one of the ends in view.

The complaints came from all sources. Businessmen, who certainly did not expect too much, protested the incompetence of the youngsters who came their way after school. Newspaper editorials by the score echoed their protests and added a voice of their own, expressing the misery of the editor who had to blue-pencil the stuff college graduates passed across his desk.

Teachers of freshman English in college have had to do over again what should have been completed in high school. Teachers of other college courses have complained about the impossibly sloppy and incoherent English which students hand in on term papers or examinations.

And anyone who has taught in the graduate school or in a law school knows that a B.A. from our best colleges means very little with reference to a student's skill in writing or speaking. Many a candidate for the Ph.D. has to be coached in the writing of his dissertation, not from the point of view of scholarship or scientific merit but with respect to the minimum requirements of simple, clear, straightforward English. My colleagues in the law school frequently cannot tell whether a student does or does not know the law because of his inability to express himself coherently on a point in issue.

I have mentioned only writing and speaking, not reading.

schooling should lack rudimentary information, how much more so is it that they should be disbarred from using the only means that can remedy the situation. If they could read—not to mention write and speak—they might be able to inform themselves throughout their adult life.

Notice that the defect which the tests discover is in the easier type of reading—reading for information. For the most part, the tests do not even measure ability to read for understanding. If they did, the results would cause a riot.

Last year Professor James Mursell, of Columbia's Teachers College, wrote an article in *The Atlantic Monthly*, entitled "The Defeat of the Schools." He based his allegation on "thousands of investigations" which comprise the "consistent testimony of thirty years of enormously varied research in education." A large mass of evidence comes from a recent survey of the schools of Pennsylvania carried on by the Carnegie Foundation. Let me quote his own words:

> What about English? Here, too, there is a record of failure and defeat. Do pupils in school learn to read their mother tongue effectively? Yes and no. Up to the fifth and sixth grade, reading, on the whole, is effectively taught and well learned. To that level we find a steady and general improvement, but beyond it the curves flatten out to a dead level. This is not because a person arrives at his natural limit of efficiency when he reaches the sixth grade, for it has been shown again and again that with special tuition much older children, and also adults, can make enormous improvement. Nor does it mean that most sixth-graders read well enough for all practical purposes. A great many pupils do poorly in high school because of sheer ineptitude in getting meaning from the printed page. They can improve; they need to improve; but they don't.
>
> The average high-school graduate has done a great deal of

reading, and if he goes on to college he will do a great deal more; but he is likely to be a poor and incompetent reader. (Note that this holds true of the *average* student, not the person who is a subject for special remedial treatment.) He can follow a simple piece of fiction and enjoy it. But put him up against a closely written exposition, a carefully and economically stated argument, or a passage requiring critical consideration, and he is at a loss. It has been shown, for instance, that the average high-school student is amazingly inept at indicating the central thought of a passage, or the levels of emphasis and subordination in an argument or exposition. To all intents and purposes he remains a sixth-grade reader till well along in college.

Even after he has finished college, I must add, he is not much better. I think it is true that no one can get through college who cannot read for information with reasonable efficiency. It may even be that he could not get into college were he thus deficient. But if we keep in mind the distinction between the types of reading, and remember that the tests measure primarily the ability to do the simpler sort, we cannot take much consolation from the fact that college students read better than sixth-graders. Evidence from the graduate and professional schools tends to show that, so far as reading for understanding is concerned, they are still sixth-graders.

Professor Mursell writes even more dismally of the range of reading in which the schools succeed in engaging the interest of students:

> Pupils in school, and also high-school and college graduates, read but little. Medium-grade magazines and fair-to-medium fiction are the chief standbys. Reading choices are made on hearsay, casual recommendations, and display advertising. Education is clearly not producing a discriminating or venturesome reading public. As one investigator con-

cludes, there is no indication "that the schools are developing permanent interest in reading as a leisure-time activity."

It is somewhat sanguine to talk about students and graduates reading the great books, when it appears that they do not read even the good nonfiction books which come out every year.

I pass rapidly over Mursell's further report of the facts about writing: that the average student cannot express himself "clearly, exactly, and correctly in his native tongue"; that "a great many high-school pupils are not able to discriminate between what is a sentence and what is not"; that the average student has an impoverished vocabulary. "As one goes from senior year in high school to senior year in college, the vocabulary content of written English hardly seems to increase at all. After twelve years in school a great many students still use English in many respects childish and undeveloped; and four years more bring slight improvement." These facts have a bearing on reading. The student who cannot "express fine and precise shades of meaning" certainly cannot detect them in the expression of anyone else who is trying to communicate above the level of subtlety which a sixth-grader can grasp.

There is more evidence to cite. Recently the Board of Regents of New York State solicited an inquiry into the achievement of its schools. This was carried out by a commission under the supervision of Professor Luther Gulick of Columbia. One of the volumes of the report treats of the high schools, and in this a section is devoted to the "command of the tools of learning." Let me quote again:

> Large numbers even of the high school graduates are seriously deficient in the basic tools of learning. The tests given to leaving pupils by the Inquiry included a test of

ability to read and understand straightforward English. . . .
The passages presented to the pupils consisted of paragraphs
taken from simple scientific articles, historical accounts, discussions of economic problems, and the like. The test was
originally constructed for eighth grade pupils.

They discovered that the average high-school senior
could pass a test designed to measure an achievement proper
in the eighth grade. This is certainly not a remarkable vic-
tory for the high schools. But they also discovered that "a
disturbingly large proportion of New York State boys and
girls leave the secondary schools,—even go on to higher
schools,—without having attained a desirable minimum."
One must agree with their sentiment when they say that
"in skills which everyone must use"—such as reading and
writing—"everyone should have at least a minimum of
competence." It is clear that Professor Mursell is not using
language too strong when he speaks of "the defeat of the
schools."

The Regents' Inquiry investigated the kind of learning
which high-school students do by themselves, apart from
school and courses. This, they rightly thought, could be
determined by their out-of-school reading. And they tell us,
from their results, "that once out of school, most boys and
girls read solely for recreation, chiefly in magazines of mediocre or inferior fiction and in daily newspapers." The range
of their reading, in school and out, is woefully slight and
of the simplest and poorest sort. Nonfiction is out of the
question. They are not even acquainted with the best novels
published during their years in school. They know the
names only of the most obvious best sellers. Worse than
that, "once out of school, they tend to let books alone.
Fewer than 40 per cent. of the boys and girls interviewed

had read any book or any part of a book in the two weeks preceding the interviews. Only one in ten had read non-fiction books." For the most part, they read magazines, if anything. And even here the level of their reading is low: "fewer than two young people in a hundred read magazines of the type of *Harper's, Scribner's,* or *The Atlantic Monthly.*"

What is the cause of this shocking illiteracy? The Regents' Inquiry report points its finger at the heart of the trouble when it says that "the reading habits of these boys and girls are no doubt directly affected by the fact that many of them have never learned to read understandingly." Some of them "apparently felt that they were completely educated, and that reading was therefore unnecessary." But, for the most part, they do not know how to read, and therefore do not enjoy reading. *The possession of skill is an indispensable condition of its use and of enjoyment in its exercise.* In the light of what we know about their general inability to read—for understanding and even, in some cases, for information—it is not surprising to discover the limited range of reading among high-school graduates, and the poor quality of what they do read.

The serious consequences are obvious. "The inferior quality of reading done by large numbers of these boys and girls," this section of the Regents' report concludes, "offers no great hope that their independent reading will add very much to their educational stature." Nor, from what we know of the achievement in college, is the hope for the college graduate much greater. He is only a little more likely to do much serious reading after he graduates, because he is only a little more skilled in reading after four more years spent in educational institutions.

I want to repeat, because I want you to remember, that however distressing these findings may seem, they are not half as bad as they would be if the tests were themselves more severe. The tests measure a relatively simple grasp of relatively simple passages. The questions the students be-ing measured must answer after they have read a short para-graph call for very little more than a precise knowledge of what the writer said. They do not demand much in the way of interpretation, and almost nothing of critical judgment.

I say that the tests are not severe enough, but the standard I would set is certainly not too stringent. Is it too much to ask that a student be able to read a whole book, not merely a paragraph, and report not only what was said therein but show an increased understanding of the subject matter be-ing discussed? Is it too much to expect from the schools that they train their students not only to interpret but to criti-cize; that is, to discriminate what is sound from error and falsehood, to suspend judgment if they are not convinced, or to judge with reason if they agree or disagree? I hardly think that such demands would be exorbitant to make of high school or college, yet if such requirements were incor-porated into tests, and a satisfactory performance were the condition of graduation, not one in a hundred students now getting their diplomas each June would wear the cap and gown.

- 3 -

You may think that the evidence I have so far presented is local, being restricted to New York and Pennsylvania, or that it places too much weight on the average or poorer high-school student. That is not the case. The evidence represents what is going on in the country generally. The schools of New York and Pennsylvania are better than average. And the evidence includes the best high-school seniors, not merely the poorer ones.

Let me support this last statement by one other citation. In June, 1939, the University of Chicago held a four-day conference on reading for teachers attending the summer session. At one of the meetings, Professor Diederich, of the department of education, reported the results of a test given at Chicago to top-notch high-school seniors who came there from all parts of the country to compete for scholarships. Among other things, these candidates were examined in reading. The results, Professor Diederich told the thousand teachers assembled, showed that most of these very "able" students simply could not understand what they read.

Moreover, he went on to say, "our pupils are not getting very much direct help in understanding what they read or hear, or in knowing what they mean by what they say or write." Nor is the situation limited to high schools. It applies equally to colleges in this country, and even in England, as indicated by the recent researches of Mr. I. A. Richards concerning the linguistic skill of undergraduates in Cambridge University.

Why are the students not getting any help? It cannot be because the professional educators are unaware of the situation. That conference at Chicago ran for four days—with many papers presented at morning, afternoon, and evening sessions—all on the problem of reading. It must be because the educators simply do not know what to do about it; in addition, perhaps, because they do not realize how much time and effort must be expended to teach students how to read, write, and speak well. Too many other things, of much less importance, have come to clutter up the curriculum.

Some years ago I had an experience which is illuminating in this connection. Mr. Hutchins and I had undertaken to read the great books with a group of high-school juniors and seniors in the experimental school which the university runs. This was thought to be a novel "experiment" or worse, a wild idea. Many of these books were not being read by college juniors and seniors. They were reserved for the delectation of graduate students. And we were going to read them with high-school boys and girls!

At the end of the first year, I went to the principal of the high school to report on our progress. I said that these younger students were clearly interested in reading the books. The questions they asked showed that. The acuteness and vitality of their discussion of matters raised in class showed that they had enough intelligence to do the work. In many respects, they were better than older students who had been dulled by years of listening to lectures, taking notes, and passing examinations. They had much more edge than college seniors or graduate students. But, I said, it was perfectly obvious that they did not know how to read a book. Mr. Hutchins and I, in the few hours a week we had with them, could not discuss the books and also teach them how to read. It was a shame that their native talents were not being trained to perform a function that was plainly of the highest educational importance.

"What was the high school doing about teaching students how to read?" I asked. It developed that the principal had been thinking about this matter for some time. He suspected that the students couldn't read very well, but there wasn't time in the program for training them. He enumerated all the more important things they were doing. I refrained from saying that, if the students knew how to read, they could dispense with most of these courses and learn the same thing by reading the books. "Anyway," he went on, "even if we had the time, we couldn't do much about reading until the school of education has finished its researches on the subject."

I was puzzled. In terms of what I knew about the art of reading, I could not imagine what kind of experimental research was being done that might help the students learn to read or their teachers to train them in doing so. I knew the experimental literature on the subject pretty well. There have been thousands of investigations and countless reports to constitute the "psychology of reading." They deal with eye movements in relation to different kinds of type, page layout, illumination, and so forth. They treat of other aspects of optical mechanics and sensory acuity or disability. They consist of all sorts of tests and measurements leading to the standardization of achievement at different educational levels. And there have been both laboratory and clinical studies which bear on the emotional aspects of reading. The psychiatrists have found out that some children get into emotional tantrums about reading, as others do about mathematics. Sometimes emotional difficulties seem to cause reading disability; sometimes they result from it.

All of this work has, at best, two practical applications. The tests and measurements facilitate school administration, the classification and gradation of students, the determination of the efficiency of one or another procedure. The work on the emotions and the senses, especially the eye, in its movements and as an organ of vision, has led to the

therapeutic program which is part of "remedial reading."
But none of this work even begins to touch on the problem
of how to teach the young the art of reading well, for enlightenment as well as information. I do not mean that the
work is useless or unimportant, or that remedial reading
may not save a lot of children from the most serious disabilities. I mean only that it has the same relation to making
good readers as the development of proper muscular co-
ordination has to the development of a novelist who must
use his hand and eye in penmanship or typewriting.

One example may make this point clear. Suppose you
want to learn how to play tennis. You go to a tennis coach
for lessons in the art. He looks you over, watches you on
the court for a while, and then, being an unusually discriminating fellow, he tells you that he cannot teach you.
You have a corn on your big toe, and papilloma on the ball
of one foot. Your posture is generally bad, and you are
muscle-bound in your shoulder movements. You need
glasses. And, finally, you seem to have the jitters whenever
the ball comes at you, and a tantrum whenever you miss it.

Go to a chiropodist and an osteopath. Have a masseur
get you relaxed. Get your eyes attended to, and your emotions straightened out somehow, with or without the aid of
psychoanalysts. Do all these things, he says, and then come
back and I'll try to teach you how to play tennis.

The coach who said this would not only be discriminating but sound in his judgment. There would be no point
in trying to instruct you in the art of tennis while you were
suffering from all these disabilities. The educational psychologists have made this sort of contribution. They have
diagnosed the disabilities which prevent or hinder a person
from learning how to read. Better than the coach, they have

devised all sorts of therapy which contribute to remedial reading. But when all this work is done, when the maximum in therapy is accomplished, you still have to learn how to read or play tennis.

The doctors who fix your feet, prescribe your glasses, correct your posture, and relieve your emotional tensions cannot make you into a tennis player, though they transform you from a person who cannot learn how to one who can. Similarly, the psychologists who diagnose your reading disabilities and prescribe their cure do not know how to make you a good reader. They only make you able to be trained by one who knows the art. That art is not theirs, any more than the art of tennis belongs to the chiropodist or optician.

Most of this educational research is merely preliminary to the main business of learning to read. It spots and removes obstacles. It helps cure *disability*, but it does not remove *inability*. At best it makes those who are abnormal in one way or another more like the normal person whose native gifts make him freely susceptible to training.

But the normal individual has to be trained. He is gifted with the power to learn to read, but he is not born with the art. That must be cultivated. The cure of abnormality may overcome the inequalities of birth or the accidents of early development. Even if it succeeded in making all men approximately equal in their initial capacity to learn, it could go no further. At that point, the development of skill would have to begin. Genuine instruction in the art of reading begins, in short, where the educational psychologists leave off.

It *should* begin. Unfortunately, it does not, as all the evidence shows. And, as I have already suggested, there are two reasons why it does not. *First,* the curriculum and the educational program in general, from grammar school through college, is too crowded with other time-consuming things to permit enough attention to be given the basic skills. *Second,* most educators do not seem to know how to teach the art of reading. The three R's exist in the curriculum today only in their most rudimentary form. They are regarded as belonging to the primary grades, instead of extending all the way up to the bachelor's degree. As a result, the bachelor of arts is not much more competent in reading and writing than a sixth-grader.

- 4 -

I would like to discuss these two reasons in a little more detail. With respect to the first, the issue is not whether the three R's belong in education, but to what extent they belong and how far they must be developed. Everyone, even the most extreme progressive educator, admits that children must be given the basic skills, must be taught to read and write. But there isn't general agreement about how much skill is the absolute minimum for an educated man to possess, and how much educational time it would take to give the minimum to the average student.

Last year I was invited to participate in a national broadcast on the Town Meeting hour. The subject was education in a democracy. The other two participants were Professor Gulick of Columbia and Mr. John Studebaker, national commissioner of education. If you heard the broadcast, or read the pamphlet containing the speeches, you observed that there appeared to be agreement among all of us about the three R's as indispensable training for democratic citizenship.

The agreement was only apparent and superficial, however. For one thing, I meant by the three R's, the arts of reading, writing, and reckoning as these should be possessed by a bachelor of those arts; whereas my colleagues meant only the most rudimentary sort of grammar-school training. For another thing, they mentioned such things as reading and writing as only a few of the many ends which education, especially in a democracy, must serve. I did not deny that reading and writing are only a part and not the whole, but I did disagree about the order of importance of the several ends. If one could enumerate all the essentials which a sound educational program must consider, I would say that the techniques of communication, which make for literacy, are our first obligation, and more so in a democracy than in any other kind of society, because it depends on a literate electorate.

This is the issue in a nutshell. First things should come first. Only after we are assured that we have adequately accomplished them is there any time or energy for less important considerations. That, however, is not the way things are done in the schools and colleges today. Matters of unequal importance are given equal attention. The relatively trivial is often made the whole of an educational program, as in certain colleges which are little better than finishing schools. What used to be regarded as extracurricular activity has seized the center of the stage, and the basic curricular elements are piled up somewhere in the wings, marked for cold storage or the junkman. In this process, begun by the elective system and completed by the excesses of progressive education, the basic intellectual disciplines got pushed into a corner or off the stage entirely.

In their false liberalism, the progressive educators confused discipline with regimentation, and forgot that true freedom is impossible without a mind made free by discipline. I never tire of quoting John Dewey at them. He said long ago: "The discipline that is identical with trained power is also identical with freedom. . . . Genuine freedom, in short, is intellectual; it rests in the trained power of thought." A disciplined mind, trained in the power of thought, is one which can read and write critically, as well as do efficient work in discovery. The art of thinking, as we have seen, is the art of learning through being taught or through unaided research.

I am not saying, let me repeat, that knowing how to read and learning through books are the whole of education. One should also be able to carry out investigation intelligently. Beyond that one should be well informed in all the areas of fact which are a necessary groundwork for thinking. There is no reason why all these things cannot be accomplished in the educational time at our disposal. But if one had to make a choice among them, one should certainly place the primary emphasis on the fundamental skills and let information of any sort take second place. Those who make the opposite choice must regard an education as a burden of fact one acquires in school and tries to carry around for the rest of life, though the baggage becomes heavier as it progressively proves less useful.

The sounder view of education, it seems to me, is one which emphasizes discipline. In this view, what one gets in school is not so much learning as the technique of learning. the arts of educating oneself through all the media the environment affords. Institutions educate only if they enable one to continue learning forever after. The art of reading and the technique of research are the primary instruments of learning, of being taught things and of finding them out. That is why they must be the primary objectives of a sound educational system.

Although I do not agree with Carlyle that "*all* that a university or final highest school can do for us is still what the first school began,—teach us to read," I do agree with Professor Tenney of Cornell that if the school does teach students to read, it has placed in their hands "the primary instrument of all higher education. Thereafter, the student, if he so wills, can educate himself." If the schools taught their *pupils* to read well, they would make *students* of them, and students they would be out of school and after it as well.

Let me call your attention, in passing, to a fault of reading which many persons commit, especially professors. A writer says he thinks something is of primary importance, or more important than something else. The bad reader interprets him as saying that nothing else but the thing he stresses is important. I have read many reviews of President Hutchins' *Higher Learning in America* which have stupidly or even viciously mistaken his insistence upon literacy as indispensable to liberal or general education for an exclusion of everything else. To affirm, as he does clearly, that nothing else comes first is not to deny that other things come second, third, and so forth.

What I have been saying will probably be similarly misinterpreted by the professors or the professionals in education. They will probably go further, and charge me with neglecting "the whole man" because I have not discussed the discipline of emotion in education and the formation of moral character. Everything that is not discussed is not necessarily denied, however. If that were the implication of omissions, writing about any one subject would involve infinite possibilities of error. This book is about reading, not about everything. The context should therefore indicate that we are primarily concerned with intellectual education, and not the whole of education.

If I were asked, as I was from the floor on the night of the Town Meeting broadcast, "Which do you consider the most important to a student, the three R's or a good moral character?" I would answer now, as I did then:

> The choice between the intellectual and the moral virtues is a hard one to make; but if I had to make the choice, I would choose the moral virtues always, because the intellectual virtues without the moral virtues can be viciously misused, as they are misused by anyone who has knowledge and skill, but doesn't know the ends of life.

Knowledge and skill of mind are not the most important items in this life. Loving the right things is more important. Education as a whole must consider more than man's intellect. I am saying only that, in so far as it concerns the intellect, there is nothing more important than the skills by which it must be disciplined to function well.

- 5 -

I turn now to tne second reason why the schools have failed in the matter of reading and writing. The first reason was that they underestimated the importance and extent of the task, and hence misconceived the relatively greater time and effort which must be devoted to it than to anything else. The second is that the arts have been almost lost.

The arts I am referring to now are the liberal arts which once were called grammar, logic, and rhetoric. These are the arts which a B.A. is supposed to be a bachelor of, and an M.A. a master. These are the arts of reading and writing, speaking and listening. Anyone who knows anything about the rules of grammar, logic, and rhetoric knows that they govern the operations we perform with language in the process of communication.

The various rules of reading, to which I have already more or less explicitly referred, involve points of grammar or logic or rhetoric. The rule about words and terms, or the one about sentences and propositions, has a grammatical and a logical aspect. The rule about proof and other types of argument is obviously logical. The rule about interpreting the emphasis a writer places on one thing rather than another entails rhetorical considerations.

I shall discuss these different aspects of the rules of reading later. Here the only point is that the loss of these arts is in large part responsible for our inability to read and to teach students how to read. It is highly significant that when Mr. I. A. Richards writes a book about *Interpretation in Teaching*, which is really a book on some aspects of reading, he finds it necessary to resuscitate the arts, and to divide his treatment into three main parts: grammar, rhetoric, and logic.

When I say that the arts are lost, I do not mean that the sciences of grammar and logic, for instance, are gone. There are still grammarians and logicians in the universities. The scientific study of grammar and logic is still pursued, and in some quarters and under certain auspices with renewed vigor. You have probably heard about the "new" discipline which has been advertised lately under the name

"semantics." It is not new, of course. It is as old as Plato
and Aristotle. It is nothing but a new name for the scientific
study of the principles of linguistic usage, combining grammatical and logical considerations.

The ancient and medieval grammarians, and an eighteenth-century writer such as John Locke, could teach the
contemporary "semanticists" a lot of principles they do not
know, principles they need not try to discover if they would
and could read a few books. It is interesting that, just about
the time when grammar has almost dropped out of the
grammar school, and when logic is a course taken by few
college students, these studies should be revived in the
graduate school with a great fanfare of original discovery.

The revival of the study of grammar and logic by the
semanticists does not alter my point, however, about the
loss of the arts. There is all the difference in the world
between studying the science of something and practicing
the art of it. We would not like to be served by a cook whose
only merit was an ability to recite the cookbook. It is an
old saw that some logicians are the least logical of men.
When I say that the linguistic arts have reached a new low
in contemporary education and culture, I am referring to
the practice of grammar and logic, not to acquaintance
with these sciences. The evidence for my statement is simply that we cannot write and read as well as men of other
ages could, and that we cannot teach the next generation
how to do so, either.

It is a well-known fact that those periods of European
culture in which men were least skillful in reading and
writing were periods in which the greatest hullabaloo was
raised about the unintelligibility of everything that had
been written before. This is what happened in the decadent

Hellenistic period and in the fifteenth century, and it is happening again today. When men are incompetent in reading and writing, their inadequacy seems to express itself in their being hypercritical about everybody else's writing. A psychoanalyst would understand this as a pathological projection of one's own inadequacies on to others. The less well we are able to use words intelligently, the more likely we are to blame others for their unintelligible speech. We may even make a fetish of our nightmares about language, and then we become semanticists for fair.

The poor semanticists! They do not know what they are confessing about themselves when they report all the books they are unable to understand. Nor does semantics seem to have helped them when, after practicing its rituals, they still find so many passages unintelligible. It has not helped them to become better readers than they were before they supposed that "semantics" had the magic of "sesame." If they only had the grace to assume that the trouble was not with the great writers of the past and present, but with them as readers, they might give semantics up or, at least, use it to try to learn how to read. If they could read a little better, they would find that the world contained a much larger number of intelligible books than they now suppose. As matters now stand for them, there are almost none.

- 6 -

The fact that the liberal arts are no longer generally practiced, in school or out, is plain from its consequence: namely, that students do not learn to read and write, and teachers do not know how to help them. But the cause of this fact is complicated and obscure. To explain how we got the way we are today, educationally and culturally, would probably require an elaborate history of modern times from the fourteenth century on. I shall be content to offer two incomplete and superficial explanations of what has happened.

The *first* is that science is the major achievement of modern times. Not only do we worship it for all the comforts and utilities, all the command over nature, which it bestows, but we are captivated by its method as the elixir of knowledge. I am not going to argue (though I think it true) that the experimental method is not the magic key to every mansion of knowledge. The only point I wish to make is that, under such cultural auspices, it is natural for education to emphasize the kind of thinking and learning the scientist does, either to the neglect or to the total exclusion of all others.

We have come to disdain the kind of learning which consists in being taught by others, in favor of the kind which is discovering things for ourselves. As a result, the arts appropriate to the first kind of learning, such as the art of reading, are neglected, while the arts of independent inquiry flourish.

The *second* explanation is related to the first. In the age of science, which is progressively discovering new things and adding to our knowledge every day, we tend to think that the past can teach us nothing. The great books on the shelves of every library are of antiquarian interest only. Let those who wish to write the history of our culture dabble in them, but we who are concerned to know about ourselves, the aims of life and society, and the world of nature in which we live, must either be scientists or read the newspaper reports of the most recent scientific meeting.

We need not bother to read the great works of scientists now dead. They can teach us nothing. The same attitude soon extends to philosophy, to moral, political, and economic problems, to the great histories that were written before the latest researches were completed, and even to the field of literary criticism. The paradox here is that we thus come to disparage the past even in fields which do not employ the experimental method and cannot be affected by the changing content of experimental findings.

Since, in any generation, only a few great books get written, most of the great ones necessarily belong to the past. After we have stopped reading the great ones of the past, we soon do not even read the few great ones of the present, and content ourselves with second- and third-hand accounts of them. There is a vicious circle in all this. Because of our preoccupation with the present moment and the latest discovery, we do not read the great books of the past. Because we do not do this sort of reading, and do not think it is important, we do not bother about trying to learn to read difficult books. As a result, we do not learn to read well at all. We cannot even read the great books of the present, though we may admire them from the distance and through the seven veils of popularization. Lack of exercise breeds flabbiness. We end up by not being able to read even the good popularizations well.

The vicious circle is worth looking at more closely. Just as you cannot improve your tennis game by playing only against opponents you can readily beat, so you cannot improve your skill in reading unless you work on something that taxes your effort and demands new resources. It follows, therefore, that in proportion as the great books have fallen from their traditional place as major sources of learning, it has become less and less possible to teach students how to read. You cannot cultivate their skill above the low level of their daily practice. You cannot teach them how to read well if, for the most part, they are not called upon to use the skill in its highest forms.

So much for the vicious circle as it moves in one direction. Now, coming around the other way, we find there is not much point in trying to read the great books with students who have no preparation at all in the art of reading from their prior schooling and are not getting any in the rest of their education. That was the trouble with the Honors course at Columbia in my day, and I suspect it still is the case with similar reading courses now given there.

In one course, which takes a small part of the student's time, you cannot discuss the books with him and also teach him how to read them. This is especially true if he comes from an elementary and secondary schooling which has paid little attention even to the rudiments of reading skill, and if the other courses in college which he is taking concurrently make no demands on his ability to read for enlightenment.

That has been our experience here in Chicago, too. Mr. Hutchins and I have been reading the great books with students these last ten years. For the most part, we have failed if our aim was to give these students a liberal education. By a liberally educated student, one who deserves the degree of bachelor of liberal arts, I mean one who is able to read well enough to read the great books and who has in fact read them well. If that is the standard, we have seldom succeeded. The fault may be ours, of course, but I am more inclined to think that we could not, in one course out of many, overcome the inertia and lack of preparation due to the rest of the antecedent and concurrent schooling.

The reform of education must start far below the college level and it must take place radically at the college level itself, if the art of reading is to become well developed and the range of reading is to be adequate by the time the bachelor's degree is awarded. Unless that does happen, the bachelor's degree must remain a travesty on the liberal arts from which it takes its name. We will continue to graduate, not liberal artists but chaotically informed and totally undisciplined minds.

There is only one college that I know of in this country which is trying to turn out liberal artists in the true sense. That is St. John's College in Annapolis, Maryland. There they recognize that four years must be spent in training students how to read, write, and reckon, and how to observe in a laboratory, at the same time that they are reading the great books in all fields. There they realize that there is no point in trying to read the books without developing all the arts needed to read them, and likewise that it is impossible to cultivate these basic intellectual skills without at the same time giving the students the right matter to exercise them on.

They have many handicaps to overcome at St. John's, but not lack of interest in the students or unwillingness to do the work which is required of no other college students today. The students do not feel that their sacred liberties are being trampled on because they do not have the freedom of elective choices. What is good for them educationally is prescribed. The students are interested and are doing the work. But one of the major handicaps is that the students come to St. John's from high schools which turn them out totally unprepared. Another is the inability of the American public, the parents as well as the educators, to appreciate what St. John's is trying to do for American education.

This is the deplorable state of American education today, despite the pronouncements and programs of some of its leaders.

President Butler has written eloquently, in his annual reports and elsewhere, of the primary importance of such intellectual disciplines as manifest themselves in good writing and reading. He has summarized the truth about the tradition of learning in a single paragraph:

> Only the scholar can realize how little that is being said and thought in the modern world is in any sense new. It was the colossal triumph of the Greeks and Romans and of the great thinkers of the middle ages to sound the depths of almost every problem which human nature has to offer, and to interpret human thought and human aspiration with astounding profundity and insight. Unhappily, these deep-lying facts which should be controlling in the life of a civilized people, are known only to a few, while the many grasp, now at an ancient and well-demonstrated falsehood and now at an old and well-proved truth, as if each had all the attractions of novelty.

The many need not be thus unfortunate, if schools and colleges trained them to read and made them read the books which constitute their cultural heritage. But it is not being done, certainly not to any great extent, at Columbia or Harvard, at Princeton, Yale, or California. It is not being done at Chicago, where President Hutchins has been even more outspoken than Dr. Butler, and has been unquestionably explicit in his plan for the reform of the college curriculum so that the ends of liberal education may be served.

Why? There are many causes, not the least of which are such familiar ones as the inertia of vested interests; the devotion of most college teachers to competence in some field of specialized research rather than in general or liberal education; and undue magnification of the scientific method and its latest findings. But one other cause, certainly, is a general apathy about this whole business of reading, an apathy which comes, I think, from an equally general lack of understanding of what is involved. I have often wondered if the situation could be changed until the faculties themselves had learned to read the great books and had read them—not the few which belong to their own academic niche, but all of them.

- 7 -

The situation I have described exists not only in school but outside as well. The public is paying for the education; it must be satisfied with what it is getting. The only way that one can account for the failure of the public to rise up in arms is that it doesn't care or that it really doesn't understand what's wrong. I cannot believe the first. It must be the second. An educational system and the culture in which it exists tend to perpetuate each other.

There is a vicious circle here, too. Perhaps it can be broken by adult education, by making the adult population aware of what is wrong with the schools they went through and to which they are now sending their children. One of the first things to do is to make them appreciate what a liberal education could be in terms of skill in reading and writing, and the profit in books to be read. I would rather try to overcome their apathy than to address myself to some of my colleagues in the educational business.

That the general public is also apathetic about reading cannot be questioned. You know it, and do not have to be told. The publishers know it also. It might interest you to eavesdrop on the publishers talking about you, the general public, their trade. Here is one addressing his fellow publishers in their weekly trade journal.

He begins by saying that "college graduates who do not know how to read constitute a major indictment of American educational methods, and a constant challenge to the country's publishers and booksellers. Large numbers of college graduates do know how to read, but there are far too many whose acute reading apathy might be described as an occupational disease."

He knows what the trouble is: "Students are taught by teachers who are themselves victims of the same educational process, and who openly or sub-consciously have a positive distaste for disinterested reading. . . . Instead of stepping forth as an eager candidate for continuing education, who should look forward to a lifetime of learning and reading *after* commencement, we get an unripe bachelor of arts, who is scarcely an adult and who shuns education like the plague."

He calls upon the publishers and booksellers to do their share in winning the nation back to books, and concludes thus:

> If the five million college graduates of this country increased their book-reading time by even as little as ten per cent., the results would be tremendous. If people generally changed their intellectual fuel or re-charged their mental batteries with the same regularity they devoted to changing

motor oil every thousand miles, or replacing frayed playing cards, there might be something like a rebirth of learning in our republic. . . . As it is, we are distinctly not a book-reading country. We wallow in magazines, and drug ourselves with movies. . . .

People sometimes marvel at spectacular best-sellers like *The Outline of History, The Story of Philosophy, The Art of Thinking,* or *Van Loon's Geography*—books which sell in hundreds of thousands, and sometimes reach a million readers. My comment is "Not enough!" I look at the census figures, and behold the intellectual apathy of most college men, and exclaim "Wait till the graduates begin reading!" I applaud Walter B. Pitkin's commencement day advice. "Don't sell your books and keep your diplomas. Sell your diplomas, if you can get anyone to buy them, and keep your books."

To sum it all up, too many men and women use their college degrees as an official license to "settle down" in an intellectual rut, as a social sanction exempting them from thinking their own thoughts, and buying their own books.

Another publisher says, "millions of people who can read and do read newspapers and magazines never read books." He figures out that they might be induced to read books if they were only made a little more like magazine articles— shorter, simpler, and designed in general for those who like to run while reading. This enterprise, called The People's Library, and described as "a scientific effort to increase the reading of serious books," seems to me to defeat its own avowed purpose. You cannot elevate people by going down to their level. If they succeed in getting you there, there they will keep you, for it is easier to get you to stay down than for them to move up.

Not by making books less like books, but by making people more like readers, must the change be effected. The plan behind The People's Library is as blind to the causes of the situation its sponsors are trying to cure as the people are at Harvard who complain about the rampant tutoring schools, without realizing that the way to remedy that evil is to lift the Harvard education above the level where the tutoring schools can prepare students more efficiently for examinations than the faculty can.

The publishers are not concerned so much about the reading of the great books as about the good new books they would like to publish if they could only find readers for them. But they know—or if they don't, they should—that these two things are connected. The ability to read for enlightenment, and consequent upon that the desire to do so, is the *sine qua non* of any serious reading. It may be that the causal sequence works either way. Starting with good current books, a reader may be led to the great books, or vice versa. I am sure that the reader who does one will eventually do the other. I would guess that the probability of his doing either is higher if he has ever once read a great book through and with sufficient skill to enjoy his mastery of the subject matter.

- 8 -

This has been a long jeremiad. There has been much weeping and gnashing of teeth about the state of the nation. Because you just dislike the words, you may despair of "a new deal," or maybe you are the hopeless type who says, " 'Twas ever thus." On the latter point, I must disagree. There have been times in European history when the level of reading was higher than it is now.

In the late Middle Ages, for instance, there were men who could read better than the best readers today. Of course, it is true that there were fewer men who could read, that they had fewer books to read, and that they depended upon read- ing more than we do as a source of learning. The point remains, however, that they mastered the books they val- ued, as we master nothing today. Maybe we do not respect any book as they valued the Bible, the Koran, or the Tal- mud; a text of Aristotle; a dialogue of Plato; or the *Insti- tutes* of Justinian. However that may be, they developed the art of reading to a higher point than it ever reached before or since.

We must get over all our funny prejudices about the Middle Ages and go to the men who wrote exegeses of Scrip- ture, glosses on Justinian, or commentaries on Aristotle for the most perfect models of reading. These glosses and com- mentaries were not condensations or digests. They were analytical and interpretative readings of a worthy text. In fact, I might as well confess here that I have learned much of what I know about reading from examining a medieval commentary. The rules I am going to prescribe are simply a formulation of the method I have observed in watching a medieval teacher read a book with his students.

Compared to the brilliance of the twelfth and thirteenth centuries, the present era is much more like the dark ages of the sixth and seventh centuries. Then the libraries had been burned or closed. There were few books available and fewer readers. Today, of course, we have more books and libraries than ever before in the history of man. In one sense, too, there are more men who can read. But it is the sense in which this is true that makes the point. So far as reading for understanding goes, the libraries might just as well be closed and the printing presses stopped.

But, you will say, we are living in a democratic era. It is

more important that many men should be able to read a
little than that a few men should be able to read well. There
is some truth in that, but not the whole truth. Genuine
participation in democratic processes of self-government
requires greater literacy than the many have yet been given.

Instead of comparing the present with the late middle
ages, let us make the comparison with the eighteenth century, for in its way that was a period of enlightenment
which sets a relevant standard for us. The democratization
of society had already then begun. The leaders of the movement, in this country and abroad, were liberally educated
men, as no college graduate is today. The men who wrote
and ratified the Constitution knew how to read and write.

While we have properly undertaken to make public education more widespread than it was in the eighteenth century, education need not become less liberal as it becomes
more universal. At every level and for all elements in the
population, the same kind of education—for freedom
through discipline—which enabled democracy to take root
in this country must be regained if its flowering is to be
protected today from the winds of violence abroad in the
world.

All you have to do is to read the writings of John Adams
and Thomas Jefferson, of Hamilton, Madison, and Jay, to
know that they could read and write better than we or our
leaders can today. If you look into the curriculum of the
colonial colleges, you may discover how this happened. You
will discover that a liberal education was once given in this
country. True, not everyone received this liberal education. Democracy had not yet matured to the point of widespread popular education.

Even today it may be true that some part of the population

must be vocationally trained, while another part is liberally educated. For even a democracy must have leaders, and its safety depends on their caliber, their liberalism. If we do not want leaders who boast of thinking with their blood, we had better educate and, more than that, cultivate a respect for those who can think with their minds, minds liberated by discipline.

One point more. There is a lot of talk today, among liberal educators who fear the rise of Fascism, about the dangers of regimentation and indoctrination. I have already pointed out that many of them confuse discipline with Prussian drill and the goose step. They confuse authority, which is nothing but the voice of reason, with autocracy or tyranny. But the error they make about indoctrination is the saddest. They, and most of us, do not know what docility is.

To be docile is to be teachable. To be teachable one must have the art of being taught and must practice it actively. The more active one is in learning from a teacher, dead or alive, and the more art one uses to master what he has to teach, the more docile one is. Docility, in short, is the precise opposite of passivity and gullibility. Those who lack docility—the students who fall asleep during a class—are the most likely to be indoctrinated. Lacking the art of being taught, whether that be skill in listening or in reading, they do not know how to be active in receiving what is communicated to them. Hence, they either receive nothing at all or what they receive they absorb uncritically.

Slighting the three R's in the beginning, and neglecting the liberal arts almost entirely at the end, our present education is essentially illiberal. It indoctrinates rather than disciplines and educates. Our students are indoctrinated with all sorts of local prejudices and predigested pap. They have been fattened and made flabby for the demagogues to prey upon. Their resistance to specious authority, which is nothing but the pressure of an opinion, has been lowered. They will even swallow the insidious propaganda in the headlines of some local newspapers.

Even when the doctrines they impose are sound democratic ones, the schools fail to cultivate free judgment because they have forsaken discipline. They leave their students open to opposite indoctrination by more powerful orators or, what is worse, to the sway of their own worst passions.

Ours is a demagogic rather than a democratic education. The student who has not learned to think critically, who has not come to respect reason as the only arbiter of truth in human generalizations, who has not been lifted out of the blind alleys of local jargons and shibboleths, will not be saved by the orator of the classroom from later succumbing to the orator of the platform and the press.

To be saved, we must follow the precept of the Book of Common Prayer: "Read, mark, learn, and inwardly digest."

CHAPTER SIX

——••••——

On Self-Help

• I •

ALL my cards are on the table now. Now you know that I have an ulterior motive in writing a book designed to help people learn how to read. For years I have watched the vicious circle which perpetuates things as they are and wondered how it could be broken. It has seemed hopeless. Today's teachers were taught by yesterday's, and they teach those of tomorrow. Today's public was educated in the schools of yesterday and today; it cannot be expected to demand that the schools change tomorrow. It cannot be expected to make demands if it does not know intimately, as a matter of its own experience, the difference between real education and all the current impostures. That "if" gave me the clue. Why couldn't it be made a matter of people's experience, instead of their having to rely on hearsay and all the crosscurrents of talk among disputing experts?

It could. If somehow out of school and after it, people generally could get some of the education they did not get in school, they might be motivated, as they are not now, to blow up the school system. And they could get the education they did not get, if they could read. Do you follow this reasoning? The vicious circle would be broken if the general public were better educated than the standard product of the schools and colleges. It would break at the point where they would really know themselves the kind of lit-

eracy they would like their children to get. All the regular
flimflam handed out by the educators could not talk them
out of it.

No one can be taught reading, or any other skill for that
matter, who will not help himself. The help I, or anyone
like me, may offer is insufficient. It is at best remote guidance. It consists of rules, examples, advice of all sorts. But
you have to be willing to *take* advice and to *follow* rules.
You can get no further than you take yourself. Hence, my
diabolical plan will not work without your co-operation in
its early stages. Once I got you started reading, I would let
nature take its course, and be fairly confident about the
ultimate outcome.

I have a deep conviction that anyone who has had even
a memorable taste of the kind of education Mr. Hutchins
is fighting for, and St. John's is trying to give, would want
it for others. Certainly, he would want it for his children.
It is not paradoxical that the most violent opposition to
the program comes from professional educators who seem
to have been least touched in their own lives by this type
of education.

More than educational reform is at stake. Democracy and
the liberal institutions we have cherished in this country
since its founding are in the balance, too. When Mr. Walter
Lippmann first discovered a book on the *Education of the
Founding Fathers of the Republic,* he was surprised that
"the men who had made the modern world should have
been educated in this old-fashioned way." The old-fashioned way is the way of the arts of reading and writing,
the way of reading the great books.

Mr. Lippmann, who passed through Harvard very credit-
ably, attributed his surprise to the fact that he had, natu-

rally enough, never challenged the standards of his generation. It must be said in his behalf, however, that since
leaving Harvard he has read a great many books. That has
some bearing on his insight:

> I began to think that perhaps it was very significant that
> men so educated had founded our liberties, and that we who
> are not so educated should be mismanaging our liberties and
> be in danger of losing them. Gradually I have come to believe
> that this fact is the main clue to the riddle of our epoch, and
> that men are ceasing to be free because they are no longer
> being educated in the arts of free men.

Do you see why I think there is dynamite in reading, not
only enough to blow up the school system but enough to
furnish the arsenal for the protection of our liberties?

- 2 -

I have hesitated some time before talking about self-help.
In fact, I have hesitated some time about writing this book,
because I have what is, perhaps, an irrational prejudice
against self-help books. They have always sounded like
patent-medicine advertisements to me. If only you will take
this or that in small, regular doses, you will be cured of all
your ills. The world will be saved. This means you. It all
depends on you. In my academic serenity, I was once above
and apart from such tawdry devices. When you write for
your scholarly peers, you do not make such appeals, probably because you would never think of expecting them to
help themselves.

Two things have brought me down from the tower. In

the first place, it may be serene up there, but after your eyes have been opened to the sham and the delusion which perpetuate the serenity, it seems more like the stillness that sometimes pervades a madhouse. In the second place, I have seen the fruits of adult education. It can be done. And anyone who has worked in adult education knows that he must appeal for self-help. There are no monitors to keep adults at the task. There are no examinations and grades, none of the machinery of external discipline. The person who learns something out of school is self-disciplined. He works for merit in his own eyes, not credit from the registrar.

There is only one caution I must add to keep the proceedings honest. Those self-help books which promise to do more than they can are bogus. No book, as I have said before, can direct you in the acquisition of a skill with as much efficiency as the tutor or coach who takes you by the hand and leads you through the motions.

Let me state now, simply and briefly, the conditions under which you can effectively help yourself. Any art or skill is possessed by those who have formed the habit of operating according to its rules. In fact, the artist or craftsman in any field differs thus from those who lack his skill. He has a habit they lack. You know what I mean by habit here. I do not mean drug addiction. Your skill in playing golf or tennis, your technique in driving a car or cooking soup, is a habit. You acquired it by performing the acts which constitute the whole operation.

There is no other way of forming a habit of operation than by operating. That is what it means to say one learns to do by doing. The difference between your activity before and after you have formed a habit is a difference in facility and readiness. You can do the same thing much better than when you started. That is what it means to say practice makes perfect. What you do very imperfectly at first you gradually come to do with the kind of almost automatic perfection that an instinctive performance has. You do something as if you were to the manner born, as if the activity were as natural to you as walking or eating. That is what it means to say that habit is second nature.

One thing is clear. Knowing the rules of an art is not the same as having the habit. When we speak of a man as skilled in any way, we do not mean that he knows the rules of doing something, but that he possesses the habit of doing it. Of course, it is true that knowing the rules, more or less explicitly, is a condition of getting the skill. You cannot follow rules you do not know. Nor can you acquire an artistic habit—any craft or skill—without following rules. The art as something which can be taught consists of rules to be followed in operation. The art as something which can be learned and possessed consists of the habit which results from operating according to the rules.

Everything I have said so far about the acquisition of skill applies to the art of reading. But there is one difference between reading and certain other skills. To acquire any art you must know the rules in order to follow them. But you need not in every case understand the rules, or at least not to the same degree. Thus, in learning to drive an automobile, you must know the rules but you do not have to know the principles of automotive mechanics which make them right. In other words, to *understand* the rules is to *know more than* the rules. It is to know the scientific principles which underlie them. If you wanted to be able to repair your car as well as drive it yourself, you would have to know its mechanical principles, and you would understand the rules of driving better than most drivers do. If understanding the rules were part of the test for a driver's license, the automobile industry would suffer a depression that would make the last one look like a boom.

The reason for this difference between reading and driving is that the one is more of an intellectual, the other more of a manual, art. All rules of art engage the mind in the activity they govern, of course; but the activity may not be principally an activity of the mind itself, as reading is. Reading and writing, scientific research and musical composition, are intellectual arts. That is why it is more necessary for their practitioners not only to know the rules but to find them intelligible.

It is more necessary, but it is not absolutely indispensable. It might be more accurate to say that it is a matter of degree. You must have *some* understanding of the rules of reading, if you are to form the habit of this intellectual operation intelligently. But you need not understand them perfectly. If complete understanding were essential, this book would be a hoax. To understand the rules of reading perfectly, you would have to know the sciences of grammar, rhetoric, and logic with consummate adequacy. Just as the science of automotive mechanics underlies the rules for driving and repairing cars, so the liberal sciences I have just named underlie the rules of liberal art which govern such things as reading and writing.

You may have observed that sometimes I speak of the arts of reading and writing as liberal arts, and sometimes I say the liberal arts are grammar, rhetoric, and logic. In the former case, I am referring to the operations which the rules direct us in performing well; in the latter, I am referring to the rules themselves which govern such operations. Furthermore, the fact that grammar and logic are sometimes regarded as sciences and sometimes as arts means that the rules of operation, which the arts prescribe, can be made intelligible by principles underlying the rules, which the sciences discuss.

It would take a book ten times as long as this one to expound the sciences which make the rules of reading and writing intelligible. If you started to study the sciences for the sake ultimately of understanding the rules and forming the habits, you might never get to the rules or form the habits. That is what happens to many logicians and grammarians who have spent their lives studying the sciences. They do not learn how to read and write. That is why courses in logic as a science, even if they were required of all college students, would not do the trick. I have met many students who have spent years of genuine devotion to the science of logic who could not read and write very well; in fact, did not even know the rules of the art, not to mention the habit of good performance according to the rules.

The solution of this riddle is indicated. We shall begin with the rules—the precepts which are most directly and intimately regulative of the acts you must perform to read well. I shall try to make the rules as intelligible as possible in a brief discussion, but I shall not go into the intricacies and subtleties of scientific grammar or logic. Suffice it if you realize that there is much more to know about the rules than you are learning from this book, and that the more you know of their underlying principles, the better you will understand them. Perhaps, if you learn to read by reading this book, you will be able later to read books about the sciences of grammar, rhetoric, and logic.

I am satisfied that this is a sound procedure. It might not

be generally so, but it must be so in the case of reading. If you do not know how to read very well to begin with, you cannot learn how by starting with scientific books about grammar and logic, because you cannot read them well enough either to understand them in themselves or to make practical applications of them by formulating rules of operation for yourself. Getting this aspect of our undertaking clear removes another possibility of dishonesty or pretension. I shall always try to tell you if my explanation of a rule is superficial or inadequate, as necessarily some of them will be.

I must caution you against one other thing. You will not learn to read just by reading this book, any more than you can learn to drive a car by perusing a driver's manual. You understand, I am sure, the point about the necessity of practice. But you may think that you can start right off in this business of reading, as soon as you know the rules. If you think so, you are going to be disappointed. I want to prevent that because such frustrations may lead you to abandon the whole enterprise in despair.

Do not take the list of rules in one hand, and a book to be read in the other, and try to perform at once as if you possessed the skill habitually. That would be as dangerous to your mental health as getting into an auto for the first time, with the wheel in one hand and a driving manual in the other, would be to your physical well-being. In both cases, an operation which is at first clumsy, disconnected, tedious, and painful becomes graceful and smooth, facile and pleasant, only through many hours of practice. If at first you do not succeed, the rewards of practice should induce you to try again.

Mr. Aaron Copland recently wrote a book on *What to Listen for in Music*. In its opening paragraph, he wrote:

> All books on understanding music are agreed about one point: You can't develop a better appreciation of the art merely by reading a book about it. If you want to understand music better, you can do nothing more important than listen to it. Nothing can possibly take the place of listening to music. Everything that I have to say in this book is said about an experience that you can only get outside this book. Therefore, you will probably be wasting your time in reading it unless you make a firm resolve to hear a great deal more music than you have in the past. All of us, professionals and nonprofessionals, are forever trying to deepen our understanding of the art. Reading a book may sometimes help us. But nothing can replace the prime consideration—listening to music itself.

Substitute the word "books" for "music," and "reading" for "listening," and you have the first and last word of advice about how to use the rules I am going to discuss. Learning the rules may help, but nothing can replace the prime consideration, which is reading books.

You may ask: How will I know whether I am really following the rules when I read? How can I tell whether I am really making the right amount of effort to get out of the rut of passive and sloppy reading? What are the signs which indicate that I am making progress toward reading more intelligently?

There are many ways of answering such questions. For one thing, you should be able to tell whether you are getting the lift which comes from managing to understand something which at first seemed unintelligible to you. For another, if you know the rules, you can always check your reading as one checks back on the sum of a column of figures. How many of the steps, which the rules prescribe, have you taken? You can measure your achievement in terms of the techniques you should have used to operate upon a book better than yourself, whereby to elevate yourself to its level.

The most direct sign that you have .done the work of reading is *fatigue*. Reading that is reading entails the most intense mental activity. If you are not tired out, you probably have not been doing the work. Far from being passive and relaxing, I have always found what little reading I have done the most arduous and active occupation. I often cannot read more than a few hours at a time, and I seldom read much in that time. I usually find it hard work and slow work. There may be people who can read quickly and well, but I am not one of them. The point about speed is irrelevant. I am sure that is a matter on which individuals differ. What is relevant is activity. To read books passively does not feed a mind. It makes blotting paper out of it.

- 3 -

By my own standards of good reading, I do not think I have read many books. I have, of course, obtained information from a large number. But I have not struggled for enlightenment with many. I have reread some of those quite often, but that is somewhat easier than the original reading. Perhaps you will get my point if I tell you that now I probably do not read to understand more than ten books a year—that is, books I have not read before. I haven't the time I once had. It always was and still is the hardest work I do. I seldom do it in the living room in an easy chair, largely for fear of being seduced into relaxation and eventually sleep. I do it sitting up at my desk, and almost always with a pencil in hand and a pad at the side.

That suggests another sign by which to tell whether you are doing the job of reading. Not only should it tire you, but there should be some discernible product of your mental activity. Thinking usually tends to express itself overtly in language. One tends to verbalize ideas, questions, difficulties, judgments that occur in the course of thinking. If you have been reading, you must have been thinking; you have something you can express in words. One of the reasons why I find reading a slow process is that I keep a record of the little thinking I do. I cannot go on reading the next page, if I do not make a memo of something which occurred to me in reading this one.

Some people are able to use their memory in such a way that they need not bother with notes. Again, this is a matter of individual differences. I find it more efficient not to burden my memory while reading and to use the margins of the book or a jot pad instead. The work of memory can be undertaken later and, of course, should be. But I find it easier not to let it interfere with the work of understanding which constitutes the main task of reading. If you are like me—rather than like those who can keep on reading and remembering at the same time—you will be able to tell whether you have been reading actively by your pencil and paper work.

Some people enjoy making notes on the back cover or the end papers of a book. They find, as I do, that this often saves them the trouble of an extra reading to rediscover the main points they had intended to remember. Marking a

book or writing on its end papers may make you more re-
luctant to lend your books. They have become documents
in your intellectual autobiography, and you may not wish
to trust such records to any except the best of friends. I
seldom feel like confessing so much about myself even to
friends. But the business of making notes while reading is
so important that you should not be deterred from writing
in a book by the possible social consequences.

If for the reason mentioned, or some other, you have
prejudices against marking up a book, use a pad. If you
read a borrowed book, you have to use a pad. Then there
is the problem of keeping your notes for future reference,
on the assumption, of course, that you have made a significant record of your reading. I find writing in the book
itself the most efficient and satisfying procedure during a
first reading, although it is often necessary later to make
more extensive notes on separate sheets of paper. The latter procedure is indispensable if you are organizing a fairly
elaborate summary of the book.

Whatever procedure you choose, you can measure yourself as a reader by examining what you have produced in
notes during the course of reading a book. Do not forget.
here as elsewhere, that there is something more important
than quantity. Just as there is reading and reading, so there
is note taking and note taking. I am not recommending
the kind of notes most students take during a lecture. There
is no record of thought in them. At best, they are a sedulous
transcript. They later become the occasion for what has
been well described as "legalized cribbing and schoolboy
plagiarism." When they are thrown away after examinations are over, nothing is lost. Intelligent note taking is
probably as hard as intelligent reading. In fact, the one

must be an aspect of the other, if the notes one makes while reading are a record of thought.

Every different operation in reading calls for a different step in thinking, and hence the notes one makes at various stages in the process should reflect the variety of intellectual acts one has performed. If one is trying to grasp the structure of a book, one may make several tentative outlines of its main parts in their order, before one is satisfied with one's apprehension of the whole. Schematic outlines and diagrams of all sorts are useful in disengaging the main points from supporting and tangential matters. If one can and will mark the book, it is helpful to underline the important words and sentences as they seem to occur. More than that, one should note the shifts in meanings by numbering the places at which important words are used successively in different senses. If the author appears to contradict himself, some notation should be made of the places at which the inconsistent statements occur, and the context should be marked for possible indications that the contradiction is only apparent.

There is no point in enumerating further the variety of notations or markings that can be made. There will obviously be as many as there are things to do in the course of reading. The point here is simply that you can discover whether you are doing what you should be doing by the note taking or markings which have accompanied your reading.

One illustration of note taking may be helpful here. If I were reading the first few chapters of this book, I might have constructed the following diagram to keep the meanings of "reading" and "learning" clear, and to see them in relation to one another and to other things:

Types of Reading:
>   I. For amusement
>   II. For knowledge
>   A. For information
>   B. For understanding

Types of Learning:
>   I. By discovery: without teachers
>   II. By instruction: through aid of teachers
>   A. By live teachers: lectures; listening
>   B. By dead teachers: books; reading

Hence *Reading II* (*A* and *B*) is *Learning II* (*B*)

But books are also of different sorts:

Types of Books:
>   I. Digests and repetitions of other books
>   II. Original communications

And it appears that:

> *Reading II (A)* is related more closely to *Books I*
> *Reading II (B)* is related more closely to *Books II*

A scheme of this sort would give me a first grasp of some of the more important distinctions the author was making. I would keep a diagram of this sort before me as I read, to discover how much more filling-in it could take as the author proceeded to multiply distinctions and to draw conclusions from premises he constructed in terms of these distinctions. Thus, for instance, the distinction between primary and secondary teachers might be added by correlating them with the two types of books.

- 4 -

We are now prepared to proceed to the next part of this book in which the rules of reading will be discussed. It

you carefully examined the Table of Contents before you
started, you know what lies ahead of you. If you are like
many readers I know, you paid no attention to the Table
of Contents or at best gave it a cursory glance. But Tables of
Contents are like maps. They are just as useful in the first
reading of a book as a road map is for touring in strange
territory.

Suppose you look at the Table of Contents again. What
do you find? That the first part of this book, which you
have now finished, is a general discussion of reading; that
the second part is entirely devoted to the rules; that the
third part considers the relation of reading to other aspects
of one's life. (You will find all this in the Preface also.)

You might even guess that in the next part each of the
chapters, except the first, would be devoted to the statement and explanation of one or more rules, with examples
of their practice. But you could not tell from the titles of
these chapters how the rules were grouped into subsets and
what was the relation of the various subordinate sets to
each other. That, as a matter of fact, will be the business
of the first chapter in the next part to make clear. But I can
say this much about it here. The different sets of rules relate to different ways in which a book can be approached:
in terms of its being a complicated structure of parts, having some unity of organization; in terms of its linguistic
elements; in terms of the relation between author and
reader as if they were engaged in conversation.

Finally, you might be interested to know that there are
other books about reading, and what their relation is to
this one. Mr. I. A. Richards has written a long book, to
which I have already referred, called *Interpretation in
Teaching*. It is primarily concerned with rules of the sec-

ond sort described above, and attempts to go much further than this book into the principles of grammar and logic. Professor Tenney of Cornell, who has also been mentioned, recently wrote a book called *Intelligent Reading* which also deals primarily with rules of the second sort, though some attention is paid also to the third. His book suggests various exercises in the performance of relatively simple grammatical tasks. Neither of these books considers rules of the first sort, which means that neither of them faces the problem of *how to read a whole book*. They are rather concerned with the interpretation of small excerpts and isolated passages.

Someone might suggest that recent books on semantics would also prove helpful. I have some doubts here, for reasons I have already indicated. I would almost say that most of them are useful only in showing how not to read a book. They approach the problem as if most books are not worth reading, especially the great books of the past, or even those in the present by authors who have not undergone semantic purification. That seems to me the wrong approach. The right maxim is like the one which regulates the trial of criminals. We should assume that the author is intelligible until shown otherwise, not that he is guilty of nonsense and must prove his innocence. And the only way you can determine an author's guilt is to make the very best effort you can to understand him. Not until you have made such an effort with every available turn of skill have you a right to sit in final judgment on him. If you were an author yourself, you would realize why this is the golden rule of communication among men.

PART II

THE RULES

CHAPTER SEVEN

From Many Rules to One Habit

- I -

WHILE you are in the stage of learning to read, you have to go over a book more than once. If it is worth reading at all, it is worth three readings at least.

Lest you become unduly alarmed at the demands that are going to be made of you, let me hasten to say that the expert reader can do these three readings at the same time. What I have called "three readings" need not be three in time. They are, strictly speaking, three in manner. They are three *ways* of reading a book. To be well read, each book should be read in these three ways each time it is read. The number of distinct times you can read something profitably depends partly on the book and partly on you as a reader, your resourcefulness and industry.

Only at the beginning, I repeat, the three ways of reading a book must be done separately. Before you become expert, you cannot coalesce a lot of different acts into one complex, harmonious performance. You cannot telescope the different parts of the job so that they run into one another and fuse intimately. Each deserves your full attention while you are doing it. After you have practiced the parts separately, you not only can do each with greater facility and less attention but you can also gradually put them together into a smoothly running whole.

I am saying nothing here which is not common knowledge about learning a complex skill. I merely want to be sure you realize that learning to read is at least as complex as learning to typewrite or learning to play tennis. If you can recall your patience in any other learning experience you have had, perhaps you will be more tolerant of a tutor who is shortly going to enumerate a long list of rules for reading.

The experimental psychologists have put the learning process under glass for anyone to look at. The learning curves they have plotted, during countless laboratory studies of every sort of manual skill, show graphically the rate of progress from one stage of practice to another. I want to call your attention to two of their findings.

The first is called the "learning plateau." During a series of days in which a performance, such as typewriting or receiving the Morse code telegraphically, is practiced, the curve shows improvement both in speed and in the reduction of errors. Then suddenly the curve flattens out. For some days, the learner cannot make any advances. His hard work seems to yield no substantial effects either in speed or accuracy. The rule that every bit of practice makes a little more perfect appears to break down. Then, just as suddenly, the learner gets off the plateau and starts to climb again. The curve which records his achievements again shows steady progress from day to day. And this continues, though perhaps with a slightly diminishing acceleration, until the learner hits another plateau.

Plateaus are not found in all learning curves, but only in those which record progress in gaining a complex skill. In fact, the more complex the performance to be learned, the more frequently such stationary periods appear. The psychologists have discovered, however, that learning is going on during these periods, though it is hidden in the sense of having no manifest practice effects at the time. The discovery that "higher units" of skill are then being formed is the second of the two findings I referred to before. While the learner is improving in typing single letters, he makes progress in speed and accuracy. But he has to form the habit of typing syllables and words as units, and then later phrases and sentences.

The stage during which the learner is passing from a lower to a higher unit of skill appears to be one of no advance in efficiency, because the learner must develop a certain number of "word units" before he can perform at that level. When he has enough of these units mastered, he makes a new spurt of progress until he has to pass to a higher unit of operation. What at first consisted of a large number of single acts—the typing of each individual letter —becomes finally one complex act—the typing of a whole sentence. The habit is perfectly formed only when the learner has reached the highest unit of operation. Where before there seemed to be many habits, which it was difficult to make work together, now there is one habit by virtue of the organization of all the separate acts into one smoothly flowing performance.

The laboratory findings merely confirm what I think most of us know already from our own experience, though we might not have recognized the plateau as a period in which hidden learning is going on. If you are learning to play tennis, you have to learn how to serve the ball, how to receive your opponent's service or return, how to play net, or at the mid-court and base line. Each of these is part of the total skill. At first, each must be mastered separately, because there is a technique for doing each. But none of these by itself is the game of tennis. You have to pass from these lower units to the higher unit in which all the separate skills are put together and become one complex skill. You have to be able to move from one act to another so rapidly and automatically that your attention is free for the strategy of play.

Similarly in the case of learning to drive a car. At first, you learn to steer, shift gears, apply the brake. Gradually these units of activity are mastered and lose their separateness in the process of driving. You have learned to drive when you have learned to do all these things together without thinking about them.

The man who has had one experience in acquiring a complex skill knows that he need not fear the array of rules which present themselves at the beginning of something new to be learned. He knows that he does not have to worry about how all the different acts, in which he must become separately proficient, are going to work together. Knowing that the plateaus in learning are periods of hidden progress may prevent discouragement. Higher units of activity are getting formed even if they do not increase one's efficiency all at once.

The multiplicity of the rules indicates the complexity of the one habit to be formed, not the plurality of distinct habits. The part acts coalesce and telescope as each reaches the stage of automatic execution. When all the subordinate acts can be done more or less automatically, you have formed the habit of the whole performance. Then you can think about beating your opponent in tennis, or driving your car to the country. This is an important point. At the beginning, the learner pays attention to himself and his skill in the separate acts. When the acts have lost their separate·

ness in the skill of the whole performance, the learner can at last pay attention to the goal which the technique he has acquired enables him to reach.

- 2 -

What is true of tennis or driving holds for reading, not simply the grammar-school rudiments, but the highest type of reading for understanding. Anyone who recognizes that such reading is a complex activity will acknowledge this. I have made all this explicit so that you will not think that the demands to be made here are any more exorbitant or exasperating than in other fields of learning.

Not only will you become proficient in following each of the rules, but you will gradually cease to concern yourself with the rules as distinct and the separate acts they regulate. You will be doing a larger job, confident that the parts will take care of themselves. You will no longer pay so much attention to yourself as a reader, and be able to put your mind wholly on the book you are reading.

But for the present we must pay attention to the separate rules. These rules fall into three main groups, each dealing with one of the three indispensable ways a book must be read. I shall now try to explain why there must be three readings.

In the first place, you must be able to grasp what is being offered as knowledge. In the second place, you must judge whether what is being offered is really acceptable to you as knowledge. In other words, there is first the task of *understanding* the book, and second the job of *criticizing* it. These two are quite separate, as you will see more and more.

The process of understanding can be further divided. To understand a book, you must approach it, *first,* as a whole, having a unity and a structure of parts; and, *second,* in terms of its elements, its units of language and thought.

Thus, there are three distinct readings, which can be variously named and described as follows:

I.   The first reading can be called *structural* or analytic. Here the reader proceeds from the whole to its parts.

II. The second reading can be called *interpretative* or synthetic. Here the reader proceeds from the parts to the whole.

III. The third reading can be called *critical* or evaluative. Here the reader judges the author, and decides whether he agrees or disagrees.

In each of these three main divisions, there are several steps to be taken, and hence several rules. You have already been introduced to three of the four rules for doing the second reading: (1) you must discover and interpret the most important *words* in the book; (2) you must do the same for the most important *sentences,* and (3) similarly for the *paragraphs* which express arguments. The fourth rule, which I have not yet mentioned, is that you must know which of his problems the author solved, and which he failed on.

To accomplish the first reading you must know (1) what kind of book it is; that is, the subject matter it is about. You must also know (2) what the book as a whole is trying to say; (3) into what parts that whole is divided, and (4) what the main problems are that the author is trying to solve. Here, too, there are four steps and four rules.

Notice that the parts which you come to by analyzing the whole in this first reading are not exactly the same as the parts you start with to construct the whole in the second reading. In the former case, the parts are the ultimate divisions of the author's treatment of his subject matter or problem. In the latter case, the parts are such things as terms, propositions, and syllogisms; that is, the author's ideas, assertions, and arguments.

The third reading also involves a number of steps. There are first several general rules about how you must undertake the task of criticism, and then there are a number of critical points you can make—four in all. The rules for the third reading tell you what points can be made and how to make them.

In this chapter, I am going to discuss all the rules in a general way. Later chapters take them up separately. If you wish to see a single, compact tabulation of all these rules, you will find it on pages 266-7, at the opening of Chapter Fourteen.

Though you will understand it better later, it is possible to show you here how these various readings will coalesce, especially the first two. That has already been somewhat indicated by the fact that both have to do with whole and parts in some sense. Knowing what the whole book is about and what its main divisions are will help you discover its leading terms and propositions. If you can discover what the chief contentions of the author are and how he supports these by argument and evidence, you will be aided in determining the general tenor of his treatment and its major divisions.

The last step in the first reading is to define the problem or problems the author is trying to solve. The last step in

the second reading is to decide whether the author has
solved these problems, or which he has and which he has
not. Thus you see how closely the first two readings are
related, converging as it were in their final steps.

As you become more expert, you will be able to do these
two readings together. The better you can do them together, the more they will help each other get done. But
the third reading will never become, in fact never can become, absolutely simultaneous with the other two. Even
the most expert reader must do the first two and the third
somewhat separately. Understanding an author must always
precede criticizing or judging him.

I have met many "readers" who do the third reading
first. Worse than that, they fail to do the first two readings
at all. They pick up a book and soon begin to tell you what
is wrong with it. They are full of opinions which the book
is merely a pretext for expressing. They can hardly be
called "readers" at all. They are more like people you know
who think a conversation is an occasion for talking but not
listening. Not only are such people not worth your effort
in talking, but they are usually not worth listening to either.

The reason why the first two readings can grow together
is that both are attempts to understand the book, whereas
the third remains distinct because it undertakes criticism
after understanding is reached. But even after the first two
readings are habitually fused, they can still be analytically
separated. This is important. If you had to check your reading of a book, you would have to divide the whole process
into its parts. You might have to re-examine separately each
step you took, though at the time you did not take it separately, so habitual had the process of reading become.

For this reason, it is important to remember that the

various rules remain distinct from one another as rules even though they tend to lose their distinctness for you through causing you to form a single, complicated habit. They could not help you check your reading unless you could consult them as so many different rules. The teacher of English composition, going over a paper with a student and explaining his marks, points to this or that rule the student violated. At that time, the student must be reminded of the different rules, but the teacher does not want him to write with a rule sheet before him. He wants him to write well habitually, as if the rules were part of his nature. The same is true of reading.

- 3 -

Now there is one further complication. Not only must you read a book three ways (and at the beginning that may mean three times), but you must also be able to read two or more books in relation to one another in order to read any one of them well. I do not mean that you must be able to read *any* collection of books together. I am thinking only of books which are related because they deal with the same subject matter or treat of the same group of problems. If you cannot read such books in relation to one another, you probably cannot read any one of them very well. If the authors are saying the same or different things, if they are agreeing or disagreeing, what assurance can you have that you understand one of them unless you recognize such overlappings and divergences, such agreements and disagreements?

This point calls for a distinction between *intrinsic* and *extrinsic* reading. I hope these two words are not misleading. I know of no other way to name the difference. By "intrinsic reading" I mean reading a book in itself, quite apart from all other books. By "extrinsic reading" I mean reading a book in the light of other books. The other books may, in some cases, be only reference books, such as dictionaries, encyclopedias, almanacs. They may be secondary books, which are useful commentaries or digests. They may be other great books. Another extrinsic aid to reading is relevant experience. The experiences to which one may have to refer in order to understand a book may be either of the sort that occur only in a laboratory, or of the sort which men possess in the course of their daily lives. Intrinsic and extrinsic reading tend to fuse in the actual process of understanding, or even criticizing, a book.

What I said before about being able to read related books in relation to one another applies especially to the great books. Frequently, in lecturing about education, I refer to the great books. Members of the audience usually write to me later to ask for a list of such books. I tell them to get either the list which the American Library Association has published under the title Classics of the Western World, or the list printed by St. John's College, in Annapolis, Maryland, as part of its announcement. Later I am informed by these people that they have great difficulties in reading the books. The enthusiasm which prompted them to send for the list and to start reading has given way to a hopeless feeling of inadequacy.

There are two reasons for this. One, of course, is that they do not know how to read. But that is not all. The other reason is that they think they should be able to understand the first book they pick out, without having read the others to which it is closely related. They may try to read *The Federalist Papers* without having read the Articles of Confederation and the Constitution. Or they may try all these without having read Montesquieu's *The Spirit of the Laws,* Rousseau's *The Social Contract,* and John Locke's essay *Of Civil Government.*

Not only are many of the great books related, but they have actually been written in a certain order which should not be ignored. A later writer has been influenced by an earlier one. If you read the earlier writer first, he may help you understand the later book. Reading related books in relation to one another and in an order which renders the later ones more intelligible is a basic rule of extrinsic reading.

I shall discuss the extrinsic aids to reading in Chapter Fourteen. Until then, we shall be concerned only with the rules of intrinsic reading. Again, I must remind you that we have to make such separations in the process of learning, even though the learning is completed only when the separations disappear. The expert reader has other books in mind, or relevant experiences, while he is reading a particular book to which these other things are related. But for the present, you must pay attention to the steps in reading a single book, as if that book were a whole world in itself. I do not mean, of course, that your own experience can ever be excluded from the process of understanding what a book is saying. That much of extrinsic reference beyond the book is absolutely indispensable, as we shall see. After all, you cannot enter the world of a single book without bringing your mind along and with it the whole of your past experience.

These rules of intrinsic reading apply not only to reading a book but to taking a **course** of lectures. I am sure that a person who could read a whole book well could get more out of a course of lectures than most people do, in or out of college. The two situations are largely the same, though following a series of lectures may call for a greater exercise of memory or note taking. There is one other difficulty about the lectures. You can read a book three *times* if you have to read it separately in each of three ways. That is not possible with lectures. Lectures may be all right for those who are expert in receiving communication, but they are hard on the untrained.

This suggests an educational principle: perhaps it would be a sound plan to be sure that people knew how to read a whole book before they were encouraged to attend a course of lectures. It does not happen that way in college now. It does not happen in adult education either. Many people think that taking a course of lectures is a short cut to getting what they are not able to read in books. But it is not a short cut to the same goal. In fact, they might as well be going in the opposite direction.

- 4 -

There is one limitation on the applicability of these rules, which should be already obvious. I have repeatedly stressed that they aim to help you read a *whole* book. At least that is their primary aim, and they would be misused if applied mainly to excerpts or small parts out of context. You cannot learn to read by doing it fifteen minutes a day in the manner prescribed by the guidebook which goes along with the Harvard Classics.

It is not merely that fifteen minutes a day is somewhat

insufficient but that you should not read a little piece here and a little part there, as the guidebook recommends. The Five-Foot Shelf contains many of the great books, although it also includes some that are not so great. In many cases, whole books are included; in others, substantially large excerpts. But you are not told to read a whole book or a large part of one. You are directed to taste a little nectar here and sniff a little honey there. That will make you a literary butterfly, not a competent reader.

For example, one day you are to read six pages from the *Autobiography* of Benjamin Franklin; on the next, eleven pages of Milton's early lyrics, and on the next, ten pages of Cicero on friendship. Another sequence of days finds you reading eight pages by Hamilton from *The Federalist Papers*, then remarks by Burke on taste running fifteen pages, and then twelve pages from Rousseau's *Discourse on Inequality*. The only thing which determines the order is the historic connection between the thing to be read and a certain day of the month. But the calendar is hardly a relevant consideration.

Not only are the excerpts far too short for a sustained effort of reading, but the order in which one thing follows another makes it impossible to grasp any real whole in itself or to understand one thing in relation to another. This plan for reading the Harvard Classics must make the great books about as unintelligible as a college course under the elective system. Perhaps the plan was devised to honor Dr. Eliot, the sponsor of both the elective system and the Five-Foot Shelf. In any case, it offers us a good object lesson of what not to do if we wish to avoid intellectual St. Vitus's dance.

- 5 -

There is one further limitation on the use of these rules. We are here concerned with only one of the major purposes in reading, and not the other—with reading to learn, and not with reading for enjoyment. The purpose is not only in the reader but in the writer as well. We are concerned with books which aim to teach, which seek to convey knowledge. In the early chapters I distinguished between reading for knowledge and for amusement, and restricted our discussion to the former. We must now go a step further and distinguish two large classes of books which differ according to the intention of the author as well as in the satisfaction they can afford readers. We must do this because our rules apply strictly to one type of book and one type of purpose in reading.

There are no recognized, conventional names for these two classes of books. I am tempted to call one sort poetry or fiction, and the other exposition or science. But the word "poetry" today usually means lyrics, instead of naming all imaginative literature, or what is sometimes called belles-lettres. Similarly, the word "science" tends to exclude history and philosophy, though both of these are expositions of knowledge. Names aside, the difference is grasped in terms of the author's intention: the poet, or any writer who is a *fine* artist, aims to please or delight, just as the musician and the sculptor do, by making beautiful things to be beheld. The scientist, or any man of knowledge who is a *liberal* artist, aims to instruct by speaking the truth.

The problem of learning how to read poetical works well is at least as difficult as the problem of learning to read for knowledge. It is also radically different. The rules which

I have briefly enumerated and will presently discuss in detail are directions for reading to learn, not for adequately enjoying a work of fine art. The rules for reading poetry would differ necessarily. They would take a book as long as this to expound and explain.

In their general ground plan, they might resemble the three divisions of the rules for reading scientific or expository works. There would be rules concerning the appreciation of the whole in terms of its being a unified structure of parts. There would be rules for discerning the linguistic and imaginative elements that constitute a poem or story. There would be rules for making critical judgments about the goodness or badness of the work, rules which helped develop good taste and discrimination. Beyond that, however, the parallelism would cease, because the structure of a story and a science are so different; the linguistic elements are differently used to evoke imagination and to convey thought; the criteria of criticism are not the same when it is beauty rather than truth that is to be judged.

The category of books which delight or amuse has as many levels of quality in it as the category of books which instruct. What is called "light fiction" requires as little ability to read, as little skill or activity, as books which are merely informative, and do not require us to make an effort to understand. We can read the stories in a mediocre magazine as passively as we read its articles.

Just as there are expository books which merely repeat or digest what is better learned from the primary sources of enlightenment, so there is secondhand poetry of all sorts. I do not mean simply the twice-told tale, for all good tales are many times told. I mean rather the narrative or lyric which does not alter our sentiments or mold our imagination. In both fields, the great books, the primary books, are alike in being original works and our betters. As in the one case the great book is able to elevate our understanding, so in the other the great book inspires us, deepens our sensitivity to all human values, increases our humanity.

In both fields of literature, only books which are better than we are require skill and activity in reading. We can read the other stuff passively and with little technical proficiency. The rules for reading imaginative literature, therefore, aim primarily to help people read the great works of belles-lettres—the great epic poems, the great dramas, novels, and lyrics—just as the rules for reading to learn aim primarily at the great works of history, science, and philosophy.

I regret that both sets of rules cannot be adequately treated in a single volume, not only because both kinds of reading are necessary for a decent literacy, but because the best reader is one who possesses both sorts of skill. The two arts of reading penetrate and support each other. We seldom do one sort of reading without having to do a little of the other at the same time. Books do not come as neat and pure packages of science or poetry.

The greatest books most frequently combine these two basic dimensions of literature. A Platonic dialogue such as *The Republic* must be read both as a drama and as an intellectual discourse. A poem such as Dante's *The Divine Comedy* is not only a magnificent story but a philosophical disquisition. Knowledge cannot be conveyed without the supporting texture of imagination and sentiment; and feeling and imagery are inveterately infected with thought.

It remains the case, however, that the two arts of reading are distinct. It would be thoroughly confusing to proceed as if the rules we were going to expound applied *equally* to poetry and science. Strictly, they apply only to science or books conveying knowledge. I can think of two ways to compensate for the deficiency of this limited treatment of reading. One is to devote a chapter later to the problem of reading imaginative literature. Perhaps, after you have become acquainted with the detailed rules for reading non-fiction books, it will be possible to indicate briefly the analogous rules for reading fiction and poetry. I shall try to do this in Chapter Fifteen. In fact, I shall go further and there make the effort to generalize the rules so that they apply to reading *anything*. The other remedy is to suggest books on the reading of poetry or fiction. I shall name some here, and more later in Chapter Fifteen.

Books which treat of the appreciation or criticism of poetry are themselves scientific books. They are expositions of a certain kind of knowledge, sometimes called "literary criticism"; viewed more generally, they are books like this one, trying to instruct in an art—in fact, a different aspect of the same art, the art of reading. Now if this book helps you learn how to read any kind of expository book, you can read these other books by yourself and be helped by them to read poetry or belles-lettres.

The great traditional book of this sort is Aristotle's *Poetics*. More recently, there are the essays of Mr. T. S. Eliot, and two books by Mr. I. A. Richards, *The Principles of Criticism* and *Practical Criticism*. The *Critical Essays* of Edgar Allan Poe are worth consulting, especially the one on "The Poetic Principle." In his analysis of *The Poetic Experience*, Fr. Thomas Gilby illuminates the object and the manner of poetic knowledge. William Empson has written about *Seven Types of Ambiguity* in a way that is par ticularly helpful for reading lyric poetry. And recently, Gordon Gerould has published a book on *How to Read Fiction*. If you look into these books, they will lead you to others.

In general, you will find the greatest help from those books which not only formulate the rules but exemplify them in practice by discussing literature appreciatively and critically. Here, more than in the case of science, you need to be guided by someone who actually shows you how to read by doing it for you. Mr. Mark Van Doren has just published a book called simply *Shakespeare*. It gives you *his* reading of the plays of Shakespeare. There are no rules of reading in it, but he provides you with a model to follow. You may even be able to detect the rules which governed him by seeing them in operation. There is one other book I would like to mention, because it bears on the analogy between reading imaginative and expository literature. *Poetry and Mathematics* by Scott Buchanan illuminates the parallel between the structure of science and the form of fiction.

– 6 –

You may object to all this. You may say that I have forced a distinction where none can be drawn. You may say that there is only one way of reading all books, or that any book must be read in every way, if there are many ways.

I have anticipated this objection by pointing out already that most books have several dimensions, certainly a poetic and a scientific one. I have even said that most books, and especially the great books, must be read in both ways. But that does not mean that the two kinds of reading must be confused, or that we must entirely ignore our primary purpose in reading a book or the author's chief intention in writing it. I think most authors know whether they are primarily poets or scientists. Certainly the great ones do. Any good reader should be aware of what he wants when he goes to a book: knowledge primarily, or delight.

The further point is simply that one should satisfy one's purpose by going to a book written with a similar intention. If one seeks knowledge, it seems wiser to read books which offer to instruct, if there be such, than books which tell stories. If one seeks knowledge of a certain subject matter, one had better go to books which treat of it rather than others. It seems misguided to read a history of Rome, if it is astronomy one wishes to learn.

This does not mean that one and the same book cannot be read in different ways and according to different purposes. The author may have more than one intention, although I think one is always likely to be primary and to dictate the obvious character of the book. Just as a book may have a primary and secondary character—as the dialogues of Plato are primarily philosophical and secondarily dramatic, and *The Divine Comedy* is primarily narrative and secondarily philosophical—so the reader may deal with the book accordingly. He may even, if he wishes, invert the order of the author's purposes, and read Plato's dialogues mainly as drama, and *The Divine Comedy* chiefly as philosophy. This is not without parallel in other fields. A piece of music intended to be enjoyed as a work of fine art can be used to put the baby to sleep. A chair intended to be sat upon can be placed behind ropes in a museum and admired as a thing of beauty.

Such duplicity of purpose and such inversions of primary

and secondary character leave the main point unchanged. Whatever you do in the way of reading, whichever purpose you put first or second, you must know what you are doing and obey the rules for doing that sort of thing. There is no error in reading a poem as if it were philosophy, or science as if it were poetry, so long as you know which you are doing at a given time and how to do it well. You will not suppose, then, that you are doing something else, or that it makes no difference how you do whatever you are doing.

There are, however, two errors which must be avoided. One of them I will call "purism." This is the error of supposing that a given book can be read in only one way. It is an error because books are not pure in character, and that in turn is due to the fact that the human mind, which writes or reads them, is rooted in the senses and imagination and moves or is moved by emotions and sentiment.

The second error I call "obscurantism." This is the error of supposing that *all* books can be read in only one way. Thus, there is the extreme of estheticism, which regards all books as if they were poetry, refusing to distinguish other types of literature and other modes of reading. The other extreme is that of intellectualism, which treats all books as if they were instructive, as if nothing could be found in a book except knowledge. Both errors are epitomized in a single line by Keats—"Beauty is truth, truth beauty"—which may contribute to the effect of his ode, but which is false as a principle of criticism or as a guide to reading books.

You have been sufficiently warned now what to expect, and what not, from the rules which the following chapters will discuss in detail You will not be able to misuse them very much, because you will find that they do not work

outside their proper and limited field of applicability. The
man who sells you a frying pan seldom tells you that you
will not find it useful as a refrigerator. He knows you can
be trusted to find that out for yourself.

- - - - - -

CHAPTER EIGHT

Catching on From the Title

- I -

Just by their titles, you might not be able to tell in the case of *Main Street* and *Middletown* which was social science and which was fiction. Even after you had read them both you might still hesitate. There is so much social science in some contemporary novels, and so much fiction in most of sociology, that it is hard to keep them apart. (It was recently announced, for instance, that *The Grapes of Wrath* had been made required reading in the social-science courses of several colleges.)

As I have already said, books can be read in several ways. One can understand why some literary critics review a novel by Dos Passos or Steinbeck as if they were considering a scientific research or a piece of political oratory; or why some are tempted to read Freud's latest book, on Moses, as a romance. In many cases, the fault is with the book and author.

Authors sometimes have mixed motives. Like other human beings, they are subject to the failing of wanting to do too many things at once. If they are confused in their intentions, the reader cannot be blamed for not knowing which pair of reading glasses to put on. The best rules of reading will not work on bad books—except, perhaps, to help you find out that they are bad.

Let us put aside that large group of contemporary books which confuse science and fiction, or fiction and oratory.

There are enough books—the great books of the past and many good contemporary books—which are perfectly clear in their intention and which, therefore, deserve a discriminating reading from us. The first rule of reading requires us to be discriminating. I should say the first rule of the first reading. It can be expressed as follows: you must know what kind of book you are reading, and you should know this as early in the process as possible, preferably before you begin to read.

You must know, for instance, whether you are reading fiction—a novel, a play, an epic, or a lyric—or whether it is an expository work of some sort—a book which conveys knowledge primarily. Picture the confusion of a person who plodded through a novel, all the while supposing it to be a philosophical discourse; or of one who meditated on a scientific treatise as if it were a lyric. You cannot, because I have asked you to imagine what is almost impossible. For the most part, people know the kind of book they are reading before they start. They picked it out to read because it was of that kind. This is certainly true of the main distinction in types of books. People know whether they want amusement or instruction, and seldom go to the wrong counter for what they want.

Unfortunately, there are other distinctions which are not so simple and so commonly recognized. Since we have temporarily excluded imaginative literature from consideration, our problem here has to do with subordinate distinctions within the field of expository books. It is not merely a question of knowing which books are primarily instructive, but which are instructive in a particular way. The kinds of information or enlightenment which a history and a philosophical book afford are not the same. The problems dealt with by a book on physics and one on morals are not the same, nor are the methods that the writers employ in solving such different problems.

You cannot read books that differ thus, in the same way. I do not mean that the rules of reading are as radically different here as in the case of the basic distinction between poetry and science. All these books have much in common. They deal in knowledge. But they are also different, and to read them well we must read them in a manner appropriate to their differences.

I must confess that at this point I feel like a salesman who, having just persuaded the customer that the price is not too high, cannot avoid mentioning the sales tax which is additional. The customer's ardor begins to wilt. The salesman overcomes this obstacle by some more smooth talk, and then is forced to say that he cannot make delivery for several weeks. If the buyer does not walk out on him at that point, he is lucky. Well, I have no sooner finished persuading you that certain distinctions are worth observing, than I have to add: "But there are still more." I hope you will not walk out on me. I promise you that there is an end to the making of distinctions in types of reading. The end is in this chapter.

Let me repeat the rule again: *you must know what kind of (expository) book you are reading, and you should know this as early in the process as possible, preferably before you begin to read.* Everything is clear here except the last clause. How, you may ask, can the reader be expected to know what sort of book he is reading before he begins to read?

May I remind you that a book always has a title and, more than that, it usually has a subtitle, a table of contents, a preface or introduction by the author? I shall neglect the publisher's blurb. After all, you may have to read a book which has lost its jacket.

What is conventionally called the "front matter" is usually sufficient for the purpose of classification, anyway. The front matter consists of the title, subtitle, table of contents, and preface. These are the signals the author flies in your face to let you know which way the wind is blowing. It is not his fault if you will not stop, look, and listen.

- 2 -

The number of readers who pay no attention to the signals is larger than you might suspect, unless you happen to be one of those who are honest enough to admit it. I have had this experience again and again with students. I have asked them what a book was about. I have asked them to tell me, in the most general terms, what sort of book it was. This, I have found, is a good way, almost an indispensable way, to begin a discussion.

Many students are unable to answer this first and simplest question about the book. Sometimes they apologize by saying that they haven't finished reading it yet, and therefore do not know. That's no excuse, I point out. Did you look at the title? Did you study the table of contents? Did you read the preface or introduction? No, they did not. The front matter of a book seems to be like the ticking of a clock— something you notice only when it is not there.

One reason why titles and prefaces are ignored by so many readers is that they do not think it important to classify the book they are reading. They do not follow this first rule. If they tried to follow it, they would be grateful to the author for helping them. Obviously, the author thinks

it is important for the reader to know the kind of book he
is being given. That is why he goes to the trouble of making
it plain in the preface, and usually tries to make his title
more or less descriptive. Thus, Einstein and Infeld, in their
preface to *The Evolution of Physics*, tell the reader that
they expect him to know "that a scientific book, even though
popular, must not be read in the same way as a novel." They
also construct, as many authors do, an analytical table of
contents to advise the reader in advance of the details of
their treatment. In any case, the chapter headings listed
in the front serve the purpose of amplifying the significance
of the main title.

The reader who ignores all these things has only himself
to blame if he is puzzled by the question: What kind of
book is this? He is going to get more perplexed. If he cannot
answer that question, and if he never asks it of himself, he
is going to be unable to ask or answer a lot of other questions about the book.

Recently Mr. Hutchins and I were reading two books
together with a class of students. One was by Machiavelli,
the other by Thomas Aquinas. In the opening discussion,
Mr. Hutchins asked whether the two books were of the
same kind. He happened to pick on a student who had not
finished his reading of them. The student used that as an
excuse to avoid answering. "But," said Mr. Hutchins, "how
about their titles?" The student had failed to observe that
Machiavelli had written about *The Prince*, and St. Thomas
about *The Governance of Princes*. When the word "prince"
was put on the board and underlined, the student was willing to guess that both books were about the same problem.

"But what sort of problem is it?" Mr. Hutchins persisted.

"What kind of books are these?" The student now thought he saw a lead, and reported that he had read the two prefaces. "How does that help?" Mr. Hutchins asked. "Well," said the student, "Machiavelli wrote his little guidebook on how to be a dictator and get away with it for Lorenzo de' Medici, and St. Thomas wrote his for the King of Cyprus."

We did not stop at that point to correct the error in this statement. St. Thomas was not trying to help tyrants get away with it. The student had used one word, however, which almost answered the question. When asked which word it was, he did not know. When told that it was "guidebook," he did not realize the significance of what he had said. I asked him if he knew in general what sort of book a guidebook was? Was a cookbook a guidebook? Was a moral treatise a guidebook? Was a book on the art of writing poetry a guidebook? He answered all these questions affirmatively.

We reminded him of a distinction that had been made in class before between theoretical and practical books. "Oh," he said, with a burst of light, "these are both practical books, books which tell you what *should* be done rather than what *is* the case." At the end of another half-hour, with other students drawn into the discussion, we finally managed to get the two books classified as *practical* works in *politics*. The rest of the period was spent in trying to find out whether the two authors understood politics in the same way, and whether their books were equally practical or practical in the same way.

I report this story not merely to corroborate my statement about the general neglect of titles, but to make a further point. The clearest titles in the world, the most explicit front matter, will not help you classify a book, even if you pay attention to these signs, unless you have the broad lines of classification already in mind.

You will not know the sense in which Euclid's *Elements of Geometry* and William James's *Principles of Psychology* are books of the same sort if you do not know that psychology and geometry are both theoretic sciences; nor will you further be able to distinguish them as different unless you know that there are different kinds of science. Similarly, in the case of Aristotle's *Politics* and Adam Smith's *The Wealth of Nations,* you can tell how these books are alike and different only if you know what a practical problem is, and what different kinds of practical problems are.

Titles sometimes make the grouping of books easy. Anyone would know that Euclid's *Elements,* Descartes' *Geometry,* and Hilbert's *Foundations of Geometry* were three mathematical books, more or less closely related in subject matter. This is not always the case. It might not be so easy to tell from the titles that St. Augustine's *City of God,* Hobbes' *Leviathan,* and Rousseau's *Social Contract* were political treatises, although a careful perusal of their chapter headings would reveal the problem common to these three books.

To group books as being of the same kind is not enough, however. To follow this first rule of reading you must know what that kind is. The title will not tell you, nor all the rest of the front matter, nor even the whole book itself sometimes, unless you have some categories you can apply to classify books intelligently. In other words, this rule has to be made a little more intelligible for you if you are to follow it intelligently. This can be done only by a brief discussion of the main kinds of expository books.

Perhaps you read the weekly literary supplements. They classify the books received that week under a series of headings, such as: fiction and poetry, or belles-lettres; history and biography; philosophy and religion; science and psychology; economics and social science; and there is usually a long listing under "miscellaneous." These categories are all right as rough approximations, but they fail to make some basic distinctions and they associate some books which should be separated.

They are not as bad as a sign I have seen in certain bookstores, which indicates the shelves where there are books on "philosophy, theosophy, and new thought." They are not as good as the standard library scheme of classification, which is more detailed, but even that is not quite right for our purposes. We need a scheme of classification which groups books with an eye to the problems of reading, and not for the purpose of selling them or putting them on shelves.

I am going to propose, first, one major distinction, and then, several further distinctions subordinate to the major one. I will not bother you with distinctions which do not matter so far as your skill in reading is concerned.

- 3 -

The major distinction is between theoretical and practical books. Everyone uses the words "theoretical" and "practical," but few know what they mean, least of all the hard-headed practical man who distrusts all theorists, especially if they are in the government. For many, "theoretical" means visionary or even mystical, and "practical" means something that works, something that has an immediate cash return. There is an element of truth in this. The practical has to do with what *works* in some way, at once or in the long run. The theoretical concerns something to be seen or understood. If we polish the rough truth that is here grasped, we come to the distinction between knowledge and action as the two ends a writer may have in mind.

But, you may say, are we not dealing here with books which convey knowledge? How can action come in? You forget that intelligent action depends on knowledge. Knowledge can be used in many ways, not only for controlling nature and inventing useful machines but also for directing human conduct and regulating man's operations in various fields of skill. What I have in mind here is exemplified by the distinction between pure and applied science, or, as it is sometimes inaccurately phrased, science and technology.

Some books and some teachers are interested only in the knowledge itself which they have to communicate. This does not mean that they deny its utility, or that they insist knowledge is good *only* for its own sake. They simply limit themselves to one kind of teaching, and leave the other kind to other men. These others have an interest beyond knowledge for its own sake. They are concerned with the problems of human life which knowledge can be used to solve. They communicate knowledge, too, but always with an emphasis upon its application.

To make knowledge practical we must convert it into rules of operation. We must pass from knowing what is the case to knowing what to do about it if we wish to get somewhere. I can summarize this by reminding you of a distinction you have already met in this book, between knowing *that* and knowing *how*. Theoretic books teach you *that* something *is* the case. Practical books teach you *how* to do something which you think you *should*.

This book is practical, not theoretic. Any "guidebook," to use the student's phrase, is a practical book. Any book which tells you either what you *should* do or *how* to do it is practical. Thus you see that the class of practical books includes all expositions of arts to be learned, all manuals of practice in any field, such as engineering or medicine or cooking, and treatises which are conventionally classified as morals, such as books on economic, ethical, or political problems.

One other instance of practical writing should be mentioned. An oration—a political speech or a moral exhortation—certainly tries to tell you what you should do or how you should feel about something. Anyone who writes practically about anything not only tries to advise you but also tries to get you to follow his advice. Hence there is an element of oratory in every moral treatise. It is also present in books which try to teach an art, such as this one. I, for example, have tried to persuade you to make the effort to learn to read.

Although every practical book is somewhat oratorical— or perhaps, as we would say today, goes in for propaganda—it does not follow that oratory is coextensive with the practical. You know the difference between a political harangue and a treatise on politics, or economic propaganda and an analysis of economic problems. *The Communist Manifesto* is a piece of oratory, but *Das Kapital* is much more than that.

Sometimes you can detect that a book is practical by its title. If it contains such phrases as "the art of" or "how to," you can spot it at once. If the title names fields which you know are practical, such as economics or politics, engineering or business, law or medicine, you can classify the books readily.

There are still other signs. I once asked a student if he could tell from the titles which of two books by John Locke was practical and which was theoretical. The two titles were: *An Essay Concerning Human Understanding* and *An Essay Concerning the Origin, Extent and End of Civil Government.* The student had caught on from the titles. He said that the problems of government were practical, and that the analysis of understanding was theoretical.

He went further. He said he had read Locke's introduction to the book on understanding. There Locke expressed his design as being to inquire into the "origin, certainty, and extent of human knowledge." The phrasing resembled the title of the book on government, with one important difference. Locke was concerned with the *certainty* or validity of knowledge in the one case, and with the *end* of government in the other. Now, said the student, questions about the validity of something are theoretic, whereas to raise questions about the end of anything, the purpose it serves, is practical.

That student had several ways of catching on to the kind of book he was reading and, I may add, he was a better reader than most. Let me use his example to offer you a piece of general advice. Make your first effort to diagnose a book from its title and the rest of the front matter. If that is insufficient, you will have to depend on signs to be found in the main body of the text. By paying attention to the words and keeping the basic categories in mind, you should be able to classify a book without reading very far.

A practical book will soon betray its character by the frequent occurrence of such words as "should" and "ought," "good" and "bad," "ends" and "means." The characteristic statement in a practical book is one that says that something should be done; or that this is the right way of doing something; or that one thing is better than another as an end to be sought, or a means to be chosen. In contrast, a theoretical book keeps saying "is," not "should" or "ought." It tries to show that something is true, that these are the facts; not that things would be better if they were otherwise, and this is the way to make them better.

Before turning now to the subdivision of theoretical books, let me caution you against supposing that the problem is as simple as telling whether you are drinking tea or coffee. I have merely suggested some signs whereby you can begin to make these discriminations. The better you understand everything that is involved in the distinction between the theoretical and the practical, the better you will be able to use the signs.

You will learn to mistrust names and, of course, titles. You will find that although economics is primarily and usually a practical matter, there are, nevertheless, books on economics which are purely theoretical. You will find authors who do not know the difference between theory and practice, just as there are novelists who do not know the difference between fiction and sociology. You will find books that seem to be partly of one sort and partly of another, such as Spinoza's *Ethics*. It remains, nevertheless, to your advantage as a reader to detect the way the author approaches his problem. For this purpose the distinction between theoretical and practical is primary.

- 4 -

You are already familiar with the subdivision of theoretical books into history, science, and philosophy. Everybody, except the professors of those subjects, knows the differences here in a rough way. It is only when you try to refine the obvious, and give the distinctions great precision, that you get into difficulties. Since I do not want you to get as confused as the professors, I shall not try to *define* what history is, or science and philosophy. Rough approximation will suffice for us to be able to distinguish the theoretic books we read as being of one sort or another.

In the case of history, the title usually does the trick. If the word "history" does not appear in the title, the rest of the front matter informs us that this is a book about something which happened in the past, not necessarily in antiquity, for it may have been only yesterday. You remember the schoolboy who characterized the study of arithmetic by the oft-repeated question: "What goes into?" History can be similarly characterized by: "What happened next?" History is knowledge of particular events or things which not only existed in the past but underwent a series of changes in the course of time. The historian narrates these happenings and often colors his narrative with some comment on, or insight into, the significance of the events.

Science is not concerned with the past as such. It treats of matters that can happen at any time or place. Everyone knows that the scientist seeks laws or generalizations. He wants to find out how things happen for the most part or in every case, not, as the historian, how some particular things happened at a given time and place in the past.

The title enables us to tell whether a book offers us instruction in science less frequently than it does in the case of history. The word "science" sometimes appears, but more usually the name of the subject matter occurs, such as psychology or geology or physics. Then we must know whether that subject matter belongs to the scientist, as geology clearly does, or to the philosopher, as metaphysics clearly does. The trouble is with the cases that are not so clear, such as physics and psychology which have been claimed, at various times. by both scientists and philosophers. There is even trouble with the words "philosophy" and "science" themselves, for they have been variously used. Aristotle called his book on *Physics* a scientific treatise, though according to current usage we should regard it as philosophical; and Newton entitled his great work *Mathematical Principles of Natural Philosophy,* though it is for us one of the masterpieces of science.

Philosophy is like science and differs from history in that it seeks general truths rather than an account of particular past events. But the philosopher does not ask the same sort of questions as the scientist, nor does he employ the same kind of method to answer them.

If you are interested in pursuing the matter further, I am going to recommend that you try to read Jacques Maritain's *Degrees of Knowledge* which offers a sound grasp of the method and aim of modern science, as well as a rich apprehension of the scope and nature of philosophy. Only a contemporary writer can treat of this distinction adequately, because it is only in the last hundred years or so that we have fully appreciated what is involved in the problem of distinguishing and relating philosophy and science. And among contemporary writers, Jacques Maritain is rare in being able to do justice to both science and philosophy.

Since titles and subject-matter names are not likely to help us discriminate whether a book is philosophical or scientific, how can we tell? I have one criterion to offer that I think will always work, although you may have to read a great deal of the book before you can apply it. If a theoretic book refers to things which lie outside the scope of your normal, routine, daily experience, it is a scientific work. If not, it is philosophical.

Let me illustrate. Galileo's *Two New Sciences* requires you to imagine, or to see for yourself in a laboratory, the experiment of the inclined plane. Newton's *Opticks* refers to experiences in dark rooms with prisms, mirrors, and specially controlled rays of light. The special experience to which the author refers may not have been obtained by him in a laboratory. You, too, may have to travel far and wide to get that sort of experience. The facts which Darwin reports in *The Origin of Species,* he observed in the course of many years of fieldwork; yet they are facts which can be and have been rechecked by other observers making a similar effort. They are not facts which can be checked in terms of the ordinary daily experience of the average man.

In contrast, a philosophical book appeals to no facts or observations which lie outside the experience of the ordinary man. A philosopher refers the reader to his own normal and common experience for the verification or support of anything he has to say. Thus, Locke's *Essay Concerning Human Understanding* is a philosophical work in psychology, whereas Freud's writings are scientific. Locke makes every point in terms of the experience you have of your own mental processes. Freud can make most of his points only by reporting to you what he observed under the clinical conditions of the psychoanalyst's office—things that most people never dream of, or, if they do, not as the psychoanalyst sees them.

The distinction I have suggested is popularly recognized when we say that science is experimental or depends upon elaborate observational researches, whereas philosophy is really armchair thinking. The contrast is not intended invidiously. There are some problems which can be solved in an armchair by a man who knows how to think about them in the light of common, human experience. There are other problems, of course, that no amount of the best armchair thinking can solve. What is needed is investigation of some sort—experiments or research in the field—to extend experience beyond the normal, everyday routine. Special experience is required.

I do not mean that the philosopher is a pure thinker and that the scientist is merely an observer. Both have to observe and think, but they think about different sorts of observation. One has to make the observations specially, under special conditions, and so forth, before he can think to solve the problem. The other can rely upon his ordinary experience.

This difference in method always reveals itself in philosophical and scientific books, and that is how you can tell which sort of book you are reading. If you note the sort of experience that is being referred to as a condition of understanding what is being said, you will know whether the book is scientific or philosophical. The rules of extrinsic reading are more complicated in the case of scientific books. You may actually have to witness an experiment or go to a museum, unless you can use your imagination to construct

something you have never observed, which the author is
describing as the basis for his most important statements.

Not only are the extrinsic conditions for reading scientific and philosophical books different, but so also are the
rules of intrinsic reading subject to different application in
the two cases. Scientists and philosophers do not think in
exactly the same way. Their styles in arguing are different.
You must be able to find the terms and propositions which
constitute these different sorts of argumentation. That is
why it is important to know the kind of book you are
reading.

The same is true of history. Historical statements are different from scientific and philosophical ones. An historian
argues differently and interprets facts differently. Furthermore, most history books are narrative in form. And a narrative is a narrative, whether it be fact or fiction. The
historian must write poetically, by which I mean he must
obey the rules for telling a good story. The intrinsic rules
for reading a history are, therefore, more complicated than
for science and philosophy, because you must combine the
kind of reading that is appropriate to expository books with
the kind proper for poetry or fiction.

- 5 -

We have discovered one interesting thing in the course
of this discussion. History presents complications for intrinsic reading, because it curiously combines two types of
writing. Science presents complications in the way of extrinsic reading, because it requires the reader somehow to
follow the report of special experiences. I do not mean that
these are the only complications in either intrinsic or

extrinsic reading. We shall find others later. But so far as
the two mentioned are concerned, philosophy would appear to be the simplest type of reading. It is so only in the
sense that a mastery of the rules for reading expository
works is by itself most conducive to mastering philosophical books.

You may object to all this making of distinctions upon
distinctions as of little moment for one who wants to learn
to read. I think I can meet your objections here, though it
may take more than I can say now to convince you fully.
In the first place, let me remind you that you have already
acknowledged the reason for distinguishing between poetry
and science. You realized that one cannot read fiction and
geometry in the same way. The same rules will not work for
both sorts of books, nor will they work in the same way for
different kinds of instructive books, such as histories and
philosophies.

In the second place, let me call your attention to an
obvious fact. If you walked into a classroom in which a
teacher was lecturing or otherwise instructing students, you
could tell very soon, I think, whether the class was one in
history, science, or philosophy. There would be something
in the way the teacher proceeded, the kind of words he used,
the type of arguments he employed, the sort of problems he
proposed, which would give him away as belonging to one
department or another. And it would make a difference to
you to know this, if you were going to try to listen intelligently to what went on. Fortunately, most of us are not as
dull as the boy who sat through half a semester of philoso
phy without knowing that the history course for which he
had registered met elsewhere.

In short, the methods of teaching different kinds of sub-

ject matter are different. Any teacher knows this. Because
of the difference in method and subject matter, the philosopher usually finds it easier to teach students who have not
been previously taught by his colleagues, whereas the scientist prefers the student whom his colleagues have already
prepared. Philosophers generally find it harder to teach one
another than scientists do. I mention these well-known facts
to indicate what I mean by the inevitable difference in
teaching philosophy and science.

Now, if there is a difference in the art of teaching in different fields, there must be a reciprocal difference in the art
of being taught. The activity of the student must somehow
be responsive to the activity of the instructor. The relation
between books and their readers is the same as that between
living teachers and their students. Hence, as books differ
in the kinds of knowledge they have to communicate, they
proceed to instruct us differently; and, if we are to follow
them, we must learn to read each kind in an appropriate
manner.

Having taken all the trouble of this chapter to make the
point, I am now going to let you down. Or, perhaps, you
will be relieved to learn that in the following chapters,
which discuss the remaining rules of reading, I am going to
treat all books which convey knowledge, and which we read
for information and enlightenment, as if they were of the
same sort. They are of the same sort *in the most general
way*. They are all expository rather than poetic. And it is
necessary to introduce you to these rules in the most general way first, before qualifying them for application to the
subordinate kinds of expository literature.

The qualifications will be intelligible only after you have
grasped the rules in general. I shall try, therefore, to post-

pone any further discussion of subordinate kinds until Chapter Fourteen. By that time you will have surveyed all the rules of reading and understood something of their application to any sort of book conveying knowledge. Then it will be possible to suggest how the distinctions we have made in this chapter call for qualifications in the rules.

When you are all done, you may see better than you do now why the first rule of the first reading of any book is to know what kind of book it is. I hope you do, because I am sure that the expert reader is a man of many fine discriminations.

- - - - - -

CHAPTER NINE

Seeing the Skeleton

- I -

EVERY book has a skeleton hidden between its boards. Your job is to find it. A book comes to you with flesh on its bare bones and clothes over its flesh. It is all dressed up. I am not asking you to be impolite or cruel. You do not have to undress it or tear the flesh off its limbs to get at the firm structure that underlies the soft. But you must read the book with X-ray eyes, for it is an essential part of your first apprehension of any book to grasp its structure.

You know how violently some people are opposed to vivisection. There are others who feel as strongly against analysis of any sort. They simply do not like to have things taken apart, even if the only instrument used in cutting up is the mind. They somehow feel that something is being destroyed by analysis. This is particularly true in the case of works of art. If you try to show them the inner structure, the articulation of the parts, the way the joints fit together, they react as if you had murdered the poem or the piece of music.

That is why I have used the metaphor of the X ray. No harm is done to the living organism by having its skeleton lighted up. The patient does not even feel as if his privacy had been infringed upon. Yet the doctor has discovered the disposition of the parts. He has a visible map of the total layout. He has an architect's ground plan. No one doubts the usefulness of such knowledge to help further operations on the living organism.

Well, in the same way, you can penetrate beneath the moving surface of a book to its rigid skeleton. You can see the way the parts are articulated, how they hang together, and the thread that ties them into a whole. You can do this without impairing in the least the vitality of the book you are reading. You need not fear that Humpty-Dumpty will be all in pieces, never to come together again. The whole can remain in animation while you proceed to find out what makes the wheels go round.

I had one experience as a student which taught me this lesson. Like other boys of the same age, I thought I could write lyric poetry. I may have even thought I was a poet. Perhaps that is why I reacted so strongly against a teacher of English literature who insisted that we be able to state the unity of every poem in a single sentence and then give a prosaic catalogue of its contents by an orderly enumeration of all its subordinate parts.

To do this with Shelley's *Adonais* or with an ode by Keats seemed to me nothing short of rape and mayhem. When you got finished with such cold-blooded butchery, all the "poetry" would be gone. But I did the work I was asked to do and, after a year of analysis, I found otherwise. A poem was not destroyed by such tactics in reading. On the contrary, the greater insight which resulted seemed to make the poem more like a vital organism. Instead of its being an ineffable blur, it moved before one with the grace and proportion of a living thing.

That was my first lesson in reading. From it I learned two rules, which are the second and third rules for the first reading of any book. I say "any book." These rules apply to science as well as poetry, and to any sort of expository work. Their application will be somewhat different, of course,

according to the kind of book they are used on. The unity
of a novel is not the same as the unity of a treatise on politics; nor are the parts of the same sort, or ordered in the
same way. But every book which is worth reading at all has
a unity and an organization of parts. A book which did not
would be a mess. It would be relatively unreadable, as bad
books actually are.

• 2 •

I am going to state these two rules as simply as possible.
Then I shall explain them and illustrate them. (The first
rule, which we discussed in the last chapter, was: *Classify
the book according to kind and subject matter*.)

The second rule—I say "second" because I want to keep
the numbering of the four rules which comprise the first
way of reading—can be expressed as follows: *State the unity
of the whole book in a single sentence, or at most in several
sentences (a short paragraph).*

This means that you must be able to say what the whole
book is about as briefly as possible. To say what the
whole book is about is not the same as saying what kind of
book it is. The word "about" may be misleading here. In one
sense, a book is *about* a certain type of subject matter, which
it treats in a certain way. If you know this, you know what
kind of book it is. But there is another and perhaps more
colloquial sense of "about." We ask a person what he is
about, what he is up to. So we can wonder what an author is
trying to do. To find out what a book is *about* in this sense
is to discover its *theme* or main *point*.

Everyone, I think, will admit that a book is a work of
art. Furthermore, they will agree that in proportion as it is

good, as a book and as a work of art, it has a more perfect
and pervasive unity. They know this to be true of music
and paintings, novels and plays. It is no less true of books
which convey knowledge. But it is not enough to acknowledge this fact vaguely. You must apprehend the unity with
definiteness. There is only one way that I know of being
sure you have succeeded. You must be able to tell yourself
or anybody else what the unity is and in a few words. Do
not be satisfied with "feeling the unity" which you cannot
express. The student who says, "I know what it is, but I
just can't say it," fools no one, not even himself.

The third rule can be expressed as follows: *Set forth the
major parts of the book, and show how these are organized
into a whole, by being ordered to one another and to the
unity of the whole.*

The reason for this rule should be obvious. If a work of
art were absolutely simple, it would, of course, have no
parts. But that is not the case. None of the sensible, physical things man knows is simple in this absolute way, nor is
any human production. They are all complex unities. You
have not grasped a complex unity if all you know about it
is how it is one. You must also know how it is many, not a
many which consists of a lot of separate things, but an
organized many. If the parts were not organically related,
the whole which they composed would not be one. Strictly
speaking, there would be no whole at all but merely a
collection.

You know the difference between a heap of bricks, on the
one hand, and the single house they can constitute, on the
other. You know the difference between one house and a
collection of houses. A book is like a single house. It is a
mansion of many rooms, rooms on different levels, of differ-

ent sizes and shapes, with different outlooks, rooms with different functions to perform. These rooms are independent, in part. Each has its own structure and interior decoration. But they are not absolutely independent and separate. They are connected by doors and arches, by corridors and stairways. Because they are connected, the partial function which each performs contributes its share to the usefulness of the whole house. Otherwise the house would not be genuinely livable.

The architectural analogy is almost perfect. A good book, like a good house, is an orderly arrangement of parts. Each major part has a certain amount of independence. As we shall see, it may have an interior structure of its own. But it must also be connected with the other parts—that is, related to them functionally—for otherwise it could not contribute its share to the intelligibility of the whole.

As houses are more or less livable, so books are more or less readable. The most readable book is an architectural achievement on the part of the author. The best books are those that have the most intelligible structure and, I might add, the most apparent. Though they are usually more complex than poorer books, their greater complexity is somehow also a great simplicity, because their parts are better organized, more unified.

That is one of the reasons why the great books are most readable. Lesser works are really more bothersome to read. Yet to read them well—that is, as well as they can be read— you must try to find some plan in them. They would have been better if the author had himself seen the plan a little more clearly. But if they hang together at all, if they are a complex unity to any degree, there must be a plan and you must find it.

⁃ 3 ⁃

Let me return now to the second rule which requires you to state the unity. A few illustrations of this rule in operation may guide you in putting it into practice. I begin with a famous case. Many of you probably read Homer's *Odyssey* in school. Certainly most of you know the story of Ulysses, the man who took ten years to return from the siege of Troy only to find his faithful wife Penelope herself besieged by suitors. It is an elaborate story as Homer tells it, full of exciting adventures on land and sea, replete with episodes of all sorts and many complications of plot. Being a good story, it has a single unity of action, a main thread of plot which ties everything together.

Aristotle, in his *Poetics*, insists that this is the mark of every good story, novel, or play. To support his point, he shows you how the unity of the *Odyssey* can be summarized in a few sentences.

A certain man is absent from home for many years; he is jealously watched by Neptune, and left desolate. Meanwhile his home is in a wretched plight; suitors are wasting his substance and plotting against his son. At length, tempest-tost, he himself arrives; he makes certain persons acquainted with him; he attacks the suitors with his own hand, and is himself preserved while he destroys them.

"This," says Aristotle, "is the essence of the plot; the rest is episode."

After you know the plot in this way, and through it the unity of the whole narrative, you can put the parts into their proper places. You might find it a good exercise to try this with some novels you have read. Try it on some great ones, such as *Tom Jones* or *Crime and Punishment* or the mod⁃

ern *Ulysses.* Once when Mr. Clifton Fadiman was visiting Chicago, Mr. Hutchins and I asked him to lead our class in the discussion of Fielding's *Tom Jones.* He reduced the plot to the familiar formula: boy meets girl, boy wants girl, boy gets girl. This is the plot of every romance. The class learned what it means to say that there are only a small number of plots in the world. The difference between good and bad fiction having the same essential plot lies in what the author does with it, how he dresses up the bare bones.

For another illustration—a more appropriate one because it deals with nonfiction—let us take the first six chapters of this book. You have read them once by this time, I hope. Treating them *as if* they were a complete whole, can you state their unity? If I were asked to, I would do it in the following manner. This book is about the nature of reading in general, the various kinds of reading, and the relation of the art of reading to the art of being taught in school and out. It considers, therefore, the serious consequences of the neglect of reading in contemporary education, suggesting as a solution that books can be substituted for living teachers if individuals can help themselves learn how to read. There is the unity as I see it in two sentences. I hesitate to ask you to reread the first six chapters to see whether I am right.

Sometimes an author obligingly tells you on the title page what the unity is. In the eighteenth century, writers had the habit of composing elaborate titles which told the reader what the whole book was about. Here is a title by Jeremy Collier, an English divine who attacked the obscenity of the Restoration drama much more learnedly than the Legion of Decency has recently attacked the movies: *A Short View of the Immorality and Profaneness of the Eng-*

lish Stage, together with the Sense of Antiquity upon this Argument. You know from this that Collier recites many flagrant instances of the abuse of public morals and that he is going to support his protest by quoting texts from those ancients who argued, as Plato did, that the stage corrupts youth, or, as the early Church fathers did, that plays are seductions of the flesh and the devil.

Sometimes the author tells you the unity of his plan in his preface. In this respect, expository books differ radically from fiction. A scientific or philosophical writer has no reason to keep you in suspense. In fact, the less suspense such an author keeps you in, the more likely you are to sustain the effort of reading him through. Like a newspaper story, an expository book may summarize itself in its first paragraph.

Do not be too proud to accept the author's help if he proffers it, but do not rely too completely on what he says in the preface. The best-laid plans of authors, like those of other mice and men, gang aft aglcy. Be somewhat guided by the prospectus the author gives you, but always remember that the obligation of finding the unity belongs to the reader, as much as having one belongs to the writer. You can discharge that obligation honestly only by reading the whole book.

The opening paragraph of Herodotus' history of the war between the Greeks and the Persians provides an excellent summary of the whole. It runs:

> These are the researches of Herodotus of Halicarnassus, in order that the actions of men may not be effaced by time, nor the great and wondrous deeds displayed by Greeks and barbarians be deprived of renown; and for the rest, for what cause they waged war upon one another.

That is a good beginning for you as a reader. It tells you succinctly what the whole book is about.

But you had better not stop there. After you have read the nine parts through, you will probably find it necessary to elaborate on that statement to do justice to the whole. You may want to mention the Persian kings—Cyrus, Darius, and Xerxes—the Greek heroes of Salamis and Thermopylae, and the major events—the crossing of the Hellespont and the decisive battles of the war.

All the rest of the fascinating details, with which Herodotus richly prepares you for his climax, can be left out of the plot. Note, here, that the unity of a history is a single thread of plot, very much as in fiction. That is part of what I meant in the last chapter by saying that history is an amalgam of science and poetry. So far as unity is concerned, this rule of reading elicits the same kind of answer in history and fiction. But there are other rules of reading which require the same kind of analysis in history as in science and philosophy.

A few more illustrations should suffice. I shall do a practical book first. Aristotle's *Ethics* is an inquiry into the nature of human happiness and an analysis of the conditions under which happiness may be gained or lost, with an indication of what men must do in their conduct and thinking in order to become happy or to avoid unhappiness, the principal emphasis being placed on the cultivation of the virtues, moral and intellectual, although other necessary goods are also recognized, such as wealth, health, friends, and a just society in which to live.

Another practical book is Adam Smith's *Wealth of Nations*. Here the reader is aided by the author's own statement of "the plan of the work" at the very beginning. But that takes several pages. The unity can be more briefly stated as follows: this is an inquiry into the sources of national wealth in any economy which is built on a division of labor, considering the relation of the wages paid labor, the profits returned to capital, and the rent owed the landowner, as the prime factors in the price of commodities. It discusses the various ways in which capital can be more or less gainfully employed, and relates the origin and use of money to the accumulation and employment of capital. Examining the development of opulence in different nations and under different conditions, it compares the several systems of political economy, and argues for the beneficence of free trade. If a reader grasped the unity of *The Wealth of Nations* in this way, and did a similar job for Karl Marx's *Das Kapital,* he would be well on the way toward seeing the relation between two of the most influential books in modern times.

Darwin's *Origin of Species* will provide us with a good example of the unity of a theoretic book in science. I would state it thus: this is an account of the variation of living things during the course of countless generations and the way in which it results in new groupings of plants and animals; it treats both of the variability of domesticated animals and of variability under natural conditions, showing how such factors as the struggle for existence and natural selection operate to bring about and sustain such groupings; it argues that species are not fixed and immutable groups, but that they are merely varieties in transition from a less to a more marked and permanent status, supporting this argument by evidences from extinct animals found in the earth's crust, from the geographical distribution of living things, and from comparative embryology and anatomy. That may seem like a big mouthful to you, but the book was an even bigger one for the nineteenth century to swallow in many gulps.

Finally, I shall take Locke's *Essay Concerning Human Understanding* as a theoretic book in philosophy. You may recall from the last chapter that Locke himself summarized his work by saying that it was "an inquiry into the origin, certainty and extent of human knowledge, together with the grounds and degrees of belief, opinion and assent." I would not quarrel with so excellent a statement of plan by the author, except to add two subordinate qualifications to do justice to the first and third parts of the essay: it will be shown, I would say, that there are no innate ideas but that all human knowledge is acquired from experience; and language will be discussed as a medium for the expression of thought, its proper uses and most familiar abuses to be indicated.

There are two things I want you to note before we proceed. The first is how frequently you can expect the author, especially a good one, to help you state the plan of his book. Despite that fact, most students are almost at a total loss when you ask them to say briefly what the whole book is about. Partly that may be due to their general inability to speak concise English sentences. Partly it may be due to their neglect of this rule in reading. But it certainly indicates that they pay as little attention to the author's introductory words as they do to his title. I do not think it rash to conclude that what is true of students in school is true also of most readers in any walk of life. Readers of this sort, if they can be called readers at all, seem to want to keep a book as, according to William James, the world appears to a baby: a big, buzzing, blooming confusion.

The second point is a plea that I make in self-defense.

Please do not take the sample summaries I have given you as if I meant them, in each case, to be a final and absolute formulation of the book's unity. A unity can be variously stated. There is no simple criterion of right and wrong in this business. One statement is better than another, of course, in proportion as it is brief, accurate, and comprehensive. But quite different statements may be equally good, or equally bad.

I have often stated the unity of a book quite differently from the author's expression of it, and without apologies to him. You may differ similarly from me. After all, a book is something different to each reader. It would not be surprising if that difference expressed itself in the way the reader stated its unity. This does not mean that anything goes. Though readers be different, the book is the same, and there can be an objective check upon the accuracy and fidelity of the statements anyone makes about it.

- 4 -

Now we can turn to the other structural rule, the rule which requires us to set forth the major parts of the book in their order and relation. This third rule is closely related to the second which we have just discussed. You may have noticed already how a well-stated unity indicates the major parts that compose the whole. You cannot apprehend a whole without somehow seeing its parts. But it is also true that unless you grasp the organization of its parts, you cannot know the whole comprehensively.

You may wonder, therefore, why I have made two rules here instead of one. It is primarily a matter of convenience. It is easier to grasp a complex and unified structure in two steps rather than in one. The second rule directs your attention toward the unity, and the third toward the complexity, of a book. There is another reason for the separation. The major parts of a book may be seen at the moment when you grasp its unity. But these parts are usually themselves complex and have an interior structure you must see. Hence the third rule involves more than just an enumeration of the parts. It means treating the parts as if they were subordinate wholes, each with a unity and a complexity of its own.

I can write out the formula for operating according to this third rule. Because it is a formula, it may guide you in a general way. According to the second rule, you will remember, we had to say: the whole book is about so and so and such and such. That done, we can proceed as follows: (1) the author accomplished this plan in five major parts, of which the first part is about so and so, the second part is about such and such, the third part is about this, the fourth part about that, and the fifth about still another thing. (2) The first of these major parts is divided into three sections, of which the first considers X, the second considers Y, and the third considers Z. Each of the other major parts is then similarly divided. (3) In the first section of the first part, the author makes four points, of which the first is A, the second B, the third C, and the fourth D. Each of the other sections is then similarly analyzed, and this is done for each of the sections of each of the other major parts.

Terrifying? I can see why it might be. All this to do, you say, and on what is only the first reading of a book. It would take a lifetime to read a book that way. If you feel this way, I can also see that all my warnings have done no good. When put down this way in a cold and exacting formula, the rule looks as if it required an impossible amount of work from you. But you have forgotten that the good reader does this sort of thing habitually, and hence easily and naturally. He may not write it all out. He may not even at the time of reading have made it all verbally explicit. But if he were called upon to give an account of the structure of a book, he would do something that approximated the formula I have suggested.

The word "approximation" should relieve your anxiety. A good rule always describes the ideal performance. But a man can be skilled in an art without being the ideal artist. He can be a good practitioner if he merely approximates the rule. I have stated the rule here for the ideal case. I would be satisfied, and so should you be with yourself, if you made a very rough approximation to what is required. Even when you become more skilled, you will not wish to read every book with the same degree of effort. You will not find it profitable to expend all your skill on some books.

I have tried to make a close approximation to the requirements of this rule in the case of relatively few books. In other instances, which means for the most part, I am satisfied if I have a fairly rough notion of the book's structure. You will find, as I have, that the degree of approximation you wish to make varies with the character of the book and your purpose in reading it. Regardless of this variability, the rule remains the same. You must know how to follow it, whether you follow it closely and strictly or only in a rough fashion.

The forbidding aspect of the formula for setting forth the order and relation of the parts may be somewhat lessened by a few illustrations of the rule in operation. Unfortunately, it is more difficult to illustrate this rule than the other one about stating the unity. A unity, after all, can be stated in a sentence or two, at most a short paragraph. But in the case of any large and complex book, a careful and adequate recital of the parts, and their parts, and *their* parts down to the least structural units, would take a great many pages to write out.

Some of the greatest medieval commentaries on the works of Aristotle are longer than the originals. They include, of course, more than a structural analysis, for they undertake to interpret the author sentence by sentence. The same is true of certain modern commentaries, such as the great ones on Kant's *The Critique of Pure Reason*. I suggest that you look into a commentary of this sort if you want to see this rule followed to perfection. Aquinas, for instance, begins each section of his commentary with a beautiful outline of the points that Aristotle has made in that part of his work; and he always says explicitly how that part fits into the structure of the whole, especially in relation to the parts that come before and after.

On second thought, perhaps you had better not look at masterly commentaries. A beginner in reading might be depressed by their perfection. He might feel as the beginner in climbing feels at the bottom of the Jungfrau. A poor and slight sample of analysis by me might be more encouraging, though certainly less uplifting. It is all right to hitch your wagon to a star, but you had better be sure it is well lubricated before you take the reins.

- 5 -

There is one other difficulty about illustrating this rule. I must choose something that I can be relatively sure most of you have read. Otherwise you will not be able to profit very much from the sample analysis as a guide. As a starter, therefore, let me take again the first six chapters of this book. I must warn you at once that this is not a very good book. Its author is not what I should call a great mind. The book has a very loose structure. Its chapter divisions do not correspond to basic divisions of the whole treatment. And within the chapters the progression of points is often disorderly and interrupted by rambling digressions. You may have thought it was an easy book to read, but analysis will show that it is really not very readable.

Here is an analysis of the first six chapters, comprising Part I, treated as a whole:

1. This book (*i.e.*, Part I) is divided into three major parts:
   A. The first treats of the nature and kinds of reading, and the place of reading in education.
   B. The second treats of the failure of contemporary education with respect to reading.
   C. The third attempts to show how the contemporary educational situation can be remedied.
2. The first part (A) is divided into the following sections:
   a. A first dealing with the varieties and degrees of reading ability;
   b. A second dealing with the major distinctions between reading for amusement and reading for instruction;
   c. A third dealing with the distinction, in reading for instruction, between information and understanding;

d. A fourth dealing with the relation of this last distinction to one between active and passive reading;

e. A fifth which defines the sort of reading to be discussed as the reception of communications conveying knowledge;

f. A sixth which relates reading to learning, by distinguishing between learning by discovery and learning by instruction;

g. A seventh which treats of the relation of books and teachers, distinguishing them as dead and alive, and shows that reading is learning from dead teachers;

h. An eighth which distinguishes between primary and secondary teachers, living or dead, and defines the great books as original communications, and hence primary teachers.

The second part (B) is divided into the following sections:

a. A first in which various evidences are recited, giving the writer's personal experiences with the inability of students to read;

b. A second in which the relation of reading to such other skills as writing and speaking are discussed with respect to current educational defects;

c. A third in which the results of scientific educational measurements are reported to show the lack of these skills in the graduates of our schools;

d. A fourth in which other evidences, especially

from book publishers, are offered as corroborating these findings;

e. A fifth in which an attempt is made to explain why the schools have failed.

The third part (C) is divided into the following sections:

a. A first in which it is shown that any art or skill can be acquired by those who will practice according to rules;

b. A second in which it is indicated how the art of reading might be acquired by those who did not learn how in school;

c. A third in which it is suggested that, by learning how to read, people can compensate for the defects of their education;

d. A fourth in which it is hoped that if people generally understood what an education should be, through having learned to read and having read, they would take serious steps to reform the failing school system.

3. In the first section of the first part, the following points are made:

(1) That the readers of this book must be able to read in one sense, though perhaps not in another;

(2) That individuals differ in their abilities to read, both according to their natural endowments and their educational benefits;

(3) That most people do not know what is involved in the art of reading. . . .

And so forth and so on.

I stop here because you see how many pages it might take if I proceeded to do the job in detail. I would have to enumerate the points made in each of the sections of each of the major parts. You will notice that I have numbered the three main steps of analysis here to correspond to the three parts of the formula I gave you some pages back. The first is the statement of the major parts; the second is their division into sections; the third is the enumeration of points in each section. I completed the first two stages of the analysis, but not the third.

You will notice, furthermore, if you glance back over the six chapters I have thus analyzed, that they are not as well structured, not as orderly and clear, as I have made them out to be. Some of the points occur out of order. Some of the chapters overlap in their consideration of the same point or their treatment of the same theme. Such defects in organization are what I meant by saying this is not a very good book. If you try to complete the analysis I have started, you will find that out for yourself.

I may be able to give you a few more examples of applying this rule if I do not try to carry the process out in all its details. Take the Constitution of the United States. That is an interesting, practical document, and a very well-organized piece of writing, indeed. You should have no difficulty in finding its major parts. They are pretty clearly indicated, though you have to do some analysis to make the main divisions. I suggest the following:

> *First:* The preamble, setting forth the purpose of the Constitution;
> *Second:* The first article, dealing with the legislative department of the government;

Third: The second article, dealing with the executive department of the government;

Fourth: The third article, dealing with the judicial department of the government;

Fifth: The fourth article, dealing with the relationship between state and Federal governments;

Sixth: The fifth, sixth, and seventh articles, dealing with the amendment of the Constitution, its status as the supreme law of the land, and provisions for its ratification;

Seventh: The first ten amendments, constituting the Bill of Rights;

Eighth: The remaining amendments up to the present day.

This is only one way of doing the job. There are many others. The first three articles could be grouped together in one division, for instance; or instead of two divisions with respect to the amendments, more divisions could be introduced, grouping the amendments according to the problems they dealt with. I suggest that you try your hand at making your own division of the Constitution into its main parts. Go further than I did, and try to state the parts of the parts as well. You may have read the Constitution many times before this, but if you exercise this rule on it for another reading, you will find a lot there you never saw before.

I am going to attempt one more example, with great brevity. I have already stated the unity of Aristotle's *Ethics*. Now let me give you a first approximation of its structure. The whole is divided into the following main parts: a first, treating of happiness as the end of life, and discussing it in relation to all other practicable goods; a second, treating of the nature of voluntary action, and its relation to the formation of virtuous and vicious habits; a third, discussing the various virtues and vices, both moral and intellectual; a fourth, dealing with moral states which are neither virtuous nor vicious; a fifth, treating of friendship, and a sixth and last, discussing pleasure, and completing the account of human happiness begun in the first.

These divisions obviously do not correspond to the ten books of the *Ethics*. Thus, the first part is accomplished in the first book; the second part runs through book two and the first half of book three; the third part extends from the rest of book three to the end of the sixth book; the discussion of pleasure occurs at the end of book seven and again at the beginning of book ten.

I mention all this to show you that you need not follow the apparent structure of a book as indicated by its chapter divisions. It may, of course, be better than the blueprint you develop, but it may also be worse; in any case, the point is to make your own blueprint. The author made his in order to write a good book. You must make yours in order to read it well. If he were a perfect writer and you a perfect reader, it would naturally follow that the two would be the same. In proportion as either of you or both fall away from perfection, all sorts of discrepancies will inevitably result.

I do not mean that you should totally ignore chapter headings and sectional divisions made by the author. They are intended to help you, just as titles and prefaces are. But you must use them as guides for your own activity, and not rely on them passively. There are few authors who execute their plan perfectly, but there is often more plan in a great book than meets the eye at first. The surface can be deceiving. You must look beneath to discover the real structure.

- 6 -

In general, these two rules of reading which we have been discussing look as if they were rules of writing also. Of course, they are. Writing and reading are reciprocal, as are teaching and being taught. If authors or teachers did not organize their communications, if they failed to unify them and order their parts, there would be no point in directing readers or listeners to search for the unity and uncover the structure of the whole.

Though there are reciprocal rules in the two cases, they are not followed in the same way. The reader tries to *uncover* the skeleton the book conceals. The author starts with it and tries to *cover it up*. His aim is to conceal the skeleton artistically or, in other words, to put flesh on the bare bones. If he is a good writer, he does not bury a puny skeleton under a mass of fat. The joints should not show through where the flesh is thin, but if flabbiness is avoided, the joints will be detectible and the motion of the parts will reveal the articulation.

I made a mistake several years ago which was instructive on this point. I wrote a book in outline form. I was so obsessed with the importance of structure that I confused the arts of writing and reading. I outlined the structure of a book, and published it. Naturally, it was repulsive to most self-respecting readers who thought that they could do their job, if I did mine. I learned from their reactions that I had given them a reading of a book I had not written. Writers should write books and leave commentaries to readers.

Let me summarize all this by reminding you of the old-fashioned maxim that a piece of writing should have unity, clarity, and coherence. That is a basic maxim of good writing. The two rules we have been discussing in this chapter respond to writing which follows that maxim. If the writing has unity, we must find it. If the writing has clarity and coherence, we must appreciate it by finding the distinction and the order of the parts. What is clear is so by the distinctness of its outlines. What is coherent hangs together in an orderly disposition of parts.

These two rules, I might add, can be used in reading any substantial part of an expository book, as well as the whole. If the part chosen is itself a relatively independent, complex unity, its unity and complexity must be discerned for it to be well read. Here there is a significant difference between books conveying knowledge and poetical works, plays, and novels. The parts of the former can be much more autonomous than the parts of the latter. The student who is supposed to have read a novel and who says he has "read enough to get the idea" does not know what he is talking about. If the novel is any good at all, the idea is in the whole, and cannot be found short of reading the whole. But you can get *the* idea of Aristotle's *Ethics* or Darwin's *The Origin of Species* by reading some parts of it carefully.

- 7 -

So long ago that you may have forgotten it, I mentioned a fourth rule to complete the first way of reading a book.

It can be stated briefly. It needs little explanation and no illustration. It really repeats in another form what you have already done if you have applied the second and third rules. But it is a useful repetition because it throws the whole and its parts into another light.

This fourth rule requires you *to find out what the author's problems were*. This rule is most pertinent, of course, to the great books. If you remember that they are original communications, you will realize that the man who wrote them started out with problems and ended by writing what the solutions were. A problem is a question. The book ostensibly contains one or more answers to it.

The writer may or may not tell you what the questions were as well as give you the answers which are the fruits of his work. Whether he does or does not, and especially if he does not, it is your task as a reader to formulate the problem as precisely as you can. You should be able to state the main problem or problems which the book tries to answer, and you should be able to state the subordinate problems if the main questions are complex and have many parts. You should not only have a fairly adequate grasp of all the questions involved, but you should be able to put the questions in an intelligible order. Which are primary and which secondary? Which questions must be answered first, if others are to be answered later?

You see how this fourth rule duplicates, in a sense, work you have already done in stating the unity and finding its parts. It may, however, actually help you to do that work. In other words, following the fourth rule is a useful procedure in conjunction with obeying the other two.

If you know the kinds of questions *anyone can ask about anything*, you will become adept in detecting an author's problems. They can be briefly formulated. Does something exist? What kind of thing is it? What caused it to exist, or under what conditions can it exist, or why does it exist? What purpose does it serve? What are the consequences of its existence? What are its characteristic properties, its typical traits? What are its relations to other things of a similar sort, or of a different sort? How does it behave? *The foregoing are all theoretical questions. The following are practical.* What ends should be sought? What means should be chosen to a given end? What things must one do to gain a certain objective, and in what order? Under these conditions, what is the right thing to do, or the better rather than the worse? Under what conditions would it be better to do this rather than that?

This list of questions is far from being exhaustive or analytically refined, but it does represent the types of most frequently asked questions in the pursuit of theoretic or practical knowledge. It may help you to discover the problems a book has tried to solve.

When you have followed the four rules stated in this chapter and the previous one, you can put down the book you have in hand for a moment. You can sigh and say: "Here endeth the first reading."

CHAPTER TEN

Coming to Terms

- I -

WHERE are we?

We have seen that any good book deserves three readings. They have to be done separately and consciously when
we are learning to read, though they can be done together
and unconsciously when we are expert. We have discovered
that there are four rules for the first, or analytical, reading.
They are: (1) classify the book according to kind and subject
matter; (2) state what the whole book is about with the
utmost brevity; (3) define its major parts in their order and
relation, and analyze these parts as you have analyzed the
whole; (4) define the problem or problems the author is
trying to solve.

You are now prepared to go on with the second reading,
and its four rules. You are already somewhat acquainted
with the first of these rules. It was stated in the second chapter of this book: spot the important words an author uses
and figure out how he uses them. We then put this rule into
operation by running down the various meanings of such
words as "reading" and "learning." When in any context
you knew precisely what I meant when I used these words,
you had *come to terms* with me.

Coming to terms is nearly the last stage in any successful
business negotiation. All that remains is to sign on the
dotted line. But in the reading of a book, coming to terms
is the first stage of interpretation. Unless the reader comes
to terms with the author, the communication of knowledge

from one to the other does not take place. A term, as you will see shortly, is the basic element of communicable knowledge.

But you can see at once that a *term* is not a *word*—at least, not just a word without any further qualifications. If a term and a word were exactly the same, you would only have to find the important words in a book and you would know its basic terms immediately. But a word can have many meanings, especially an important word. If the author uses a word in one meaning, and the reader reads it in another, words have passed between them, but they have not come to terms. Where there is unresolved ambiguity in communication, there is no communication, or at best it must be incomplete.

Just look at the word "communication" for a moment. Its root is related to the word "common." We speak of a community when people have something in common. Communication is an effort on the part of one man to share something with another: his knowledge, his decisions, his sentiments. It succeeds only when it results in a common something, as an item of knowledge which two men have in common.

Now when there is ambiguity in communication, all that is in common are the words which one man speaks or writes and another hears or reads. So long as ambiguity remains, there are no meanings in common between writer and reader. For the communication to be successfully completed, therefore, it is necessary for the two parties to use the same words with the same meanings. When that happens, communication happens, the miracle of two minds with but a single thought.

A term can be defined as an unambiguous word. That

is not quite accurate, for strictly there are no unambiguous words. What I should have said is that a term is a word *used unambiguously.* The dictionary is full of words. They are almost all ambiguous in the sense that they have many meanings. Look up *any* word and find this out for yourself, if you think there are many exceptions to this generalization. But a word which has several meanings can be used in one sense at a time. When you and I together, as writer and reader, somehow manage for a time to use a given word with one meaning, then, during that time of unambiguous usage, we have come to terms. I think we did manage to come to terms in the matter of reading and learning, for instance.

You cannot find terms in dictionaries, though the materials for making them are there. Terms occur only in the process of communication. They occur when a writer tries to avoid ambiguity and a reader helps him by trying to follow his use of words. There are, of course, many degrees of success in this business. Coming to terms is the ideal limit toward which writer and reader should strive. Since this is one of the primary achievements of the art of writing and reading, we can think of terms as an artistic use of words, a skilled use of words for the sake of communicating knowledge.

Let me restate the rule for you. As I phrased it originally, it was: spot the important words and figure out how the author is using them. Now I can make that a little more precise and elegant: *find the important words and through them come to terms with the author.* Note that the rule has two parts. The first step is to locate the words which make a difference. The second is to determine their meanings, as used, with precision.

This is the first rule for the second way of reading, the interpretative reading. The other rules, to be discussed in the next chapter, are like this first one in an important respect. They, also, require you to take two steps: a step dealing with the language as such, and a step beyond the language to the thought which lies behind it.

If language were a pure and perfect medium for thought, these steps would not be separate. If every word had only one meaning, if words could not be used ambiguously, if, in short, each word was an ideal term, language would be a diaphanous medium. The reader would see straight through the writer's words to the content of his mind. If that were the case, there would be no need at all for this second way of reading. *Interpretation would be unnecessary.*

But you know that that is far from being the case. There is no use in crying about it, no use in faking up impossible schemes for an ideal language, as the philosopher Leibnitz and some of his followers have tried to do. The only thing to do is to make the best of language as it is, and the only way to do that is to use language as skillfully as possible.

Because language is imperfect as a medium, it also functions as an obstacle to communication. The rules of interpretative reading are directed to overcoming that obstacle. We can expect a good writer to do his best to reach us through the barrier language inevitably sets up, but we cannot expect him to do it all. In fact, we must meet him halfway. We, as readers, must try to tunnel through from our side. The chance of a meeting of minds *through* language depends on the willingness of both reader and writer to work toward each other. Just as teaching will not avail unless there is a reciprocal activity of being taught, so no author, regardless of his skill in writing, can achieve communication without a reciprocal skill on the part of readers. The reciprocity here is founded on the fact that the rules of good reading and writing are ultimately the same in principle. If that were not so, the diverse skills of writing and reading would not bring minds together, however much effort was expended, any more than the men who tunnel through from opposite sides of a mountain would ever meet unless they made their calculations according to the same principles of engineering.

You have noted that each of the rules of interpretative reading involves two steps. Let me shift from the engineering analogy to explain how they are related. They can be likened to the two steps a detective takes in pursuing the murderer. Of all the things which lie around the scene of the crime, he must pick out those he thinks are likely to be *clues*. He must then use these clues in running down the culprit. Interpreting a book is a kind of detective work. Finding the important words is locating the clues. Coming to terms through them is running down the author's thought.

If I were to get technical for a moment, I should say that these rules have a grammatical and a logical aspect. The grammatical step is the one which deals with words. The logical step deals with their meanings or, more precisely, with terms. So far as communication is concerned, both steps are indispensable. If language is used without thought, nothing is being communicated. And thought or knowledge cannot be communicated without language. As arts, grammar and logic are concerned with language in relation to thought and thought in relation to language. That is why I said earlier that skill in reading and writing is gained through these liberal arts, especially grammar and logic.

This business of language and thought—especially the distinction between words and terms—is so important that I am going to risk being repetitious to be sure you understand the main point. The main point is that *one* word can be the vehicle for *many* terms. Let me illustrate this schematically in the following manner. The word "reading" has been used in many senses in the course of our discussion. Let us take three of the meanings: (1) reading in the sense of getting amusement; (2) reading in the sense of getting information, and (3) reading in the sense of gaining insight.

Now let us symbolize the word "reading" by the letter X, and the three meanings by the letters a, b, and c. What is symbolized, then by Xa, Xb, and Xc, are not three words, for X remains the same throughout. But they are three terms, on the condition, of course, that you and I know when X is being used in one definite sense, and not another. If I write Xa in a given place, and you read Xb, we are writing and reading the same word, but not in the same way. The ambiguity prevents communication. Only when you think the word as I think it do we have one thought between us. Our minds cannot meet in X, but only in Xa or Xb or Xc. Thus we come to terms.

- 2 -

You are prepared now, I hope, to consider the rule which requires a reader to come to terms. How does he go about taking the first step? How does he find the important words in a book?

You can be sure of one thing. Not all the words an author uses are important. Better than that, you can be sure that most of his words are not. Only those words which he uses in a special way are important for him, and for us as readers. This is not an absolute matter, of course, but one of degree. Words may be more or less important. Our only concern is with the fact that some words in a book are more important than others. At one extreme are the words which the author uses as the proverbial man in the street does. Since the author is using these words as ordinary men do in ordinary discourse, the reader should have no trouble with them. He is familiar with their ambiguity and he has grown accustomed to the variation in their meanings as they occur in this context or that.

For example, the word "reading" occurs in Sir Arthur Eddington's fine book on *The Nature of the Physical World*. He speaks of "pointer-readings," the readings of dials and gauges on scientific instruments. He is using the word "reading" in one of its ordinary senses. It is not for him a technical word. He can rely on ordinary usage to convey what he means to the reader. Even if he used the word "reading" in a different sense somewhere else in his book— in a phrase, let us say, such as "reading nature"—he could be confident that the reader would note the shift to another of the word's ordinary meanings. The reader who could not do this could not talk to his friends or carry on his daily business.

But Sir Arthur cannot use the word "cause" so light-heartedly. That may be a word of common speech, but Sir Arthur is using it in a definitely special sense when he discusses the theory of causation. How that word is to be understood makes a difference which both he and the reader must bother about. For the same reason, the word "reading" is important in this book. We cannot get along with using it in an ordinary way.

I repeat that an author uses most words as men ordinarily do in conversation, with a range of meanings, and trusting to context to indicate the shifts. Knowing this fact should be of some help to you in detecting the more important words. There is one qualification here. We must not forget that at different times and places the same words are not equally familiar items in daily usage. A contemporary like Eddington or me will employ most words as they are ordinarily used *today*, and you will know what these are because you are alive today. But in reading the great books of the past, it may be more difficult to detect the words the author is using as most men did at the time and place he was writing. The translation of books from foreign languages complicates the matter further.

You can see, therefore, why eliminating the ordinary words may be a rough discrimination. Nevertheless, it remains true that most of the words in any book can be read just as one would use them in talking to one's friends. Take any page of this book and count the words which we are using that way: all the prepositions, conjunctions, and articles, and certainly most of the verbs, nouns, and adjectives. In this chapter so far, I would say that there have been only a few important words: "word," "term," "ambiguity," "communication," "important"; of these, "term" is clearly the most important. All the others are important in relation to it.

You cannot locate the important words without making an effort to understand the passage in which they occur. This situation is somewhat paradoxical. If you do under-

stand the passage, you will, of course, know which words
in it are the most important. If you do not fully understand the passage, it is probably because you do not know
the way the author is using certain words. If you mark the
words that trouble you, you may hit the very ones the author
is using specially. That this is likely to be so follows from
the fact that you should have no trouble with the words
the author uses in an ordinary way.

From your point of view as a reader, the most important
words are those which give you trouble. As I have said, it
is likely that these words are important for the author as
well. The opposite is possible, of course. They may not be.

It is also possible that words which are important for the
author do not bother you, and precisely because you understand them. In that case, you have already come to terms
with the author. Only where you fail to come to terms have
you work still to do.

- 3 -

So far we have been proceeding negatively by eliminating
the ordinary words. You discover some of the important
words by the fact that they are *not ordinary for you.* That
is why they bother you. But is there any other way of spotting the important words? Are there any positive signs
which point to them?

There are several positive signs I can suggest. The first
and most obvious sign is the explicit stress an author places
upon certain words and not others. He may do this in many
ways. He may use such typographical devices as quotation
marks or italics to mark the word for you. He may call your
attention to the word by explicitly discussing its various
senses and the way he is going to use it here and there. Or

he may emphasize the word by defining the thing which the word is used to name.

No one can read Euclid without knowing that such words as "point," "line," "plane," "angle," "figure," "parallel," and so forth are of the first importance. These are the words which name geometrical entities that Euclid defines. There are other important words, such as "equals," "whole," and "part," but these do not name anything which is defined. You know that they are important from the fact that they occur in the axioms. Euclid helps you here by making his primary propositions explicit at the very beginning. You can guess that the terms which compose such propositions are basic, and that underlines for you the words which express these terms. You may have no difficulty with these words, because they are words of common speech, and Euclid appears to be using them that way.

If all authors wrote as Euclid did, you may say, this business of reading would be much easier. Unfortunately, that is not possible, although some men have thought that any subject matter can be expounded in the geometrical manner. I shall not try to explain why the procedure—the method of exposition and proof—which works in mathematics is not applicable in other fields of knowledge. For our purposes, it is sufficient to note what is common to every sort of exposition. Every field of knowledge has its own technical vocabulary. Euclid makes his plain right at the beginning. The same is true of any writer, such as Newton or Galileo, who writes in the geometrical manner. In books differently written or in other fields, the technical vocabulary must be discovered by the reader.

If the author has not pointed out the words himself, the reader may locate them through having some prior knowledge of the subject matter. If he knows something about biology or economics before he begins to read Darwin or Adam Smith, he certainly has some leads toward discerning the technical words. The various steps of the first reading may be helpful here. If you know what kind of book it is, what it is about as a whole, and what its major parts are, you are greatly aided in separating the technical vocabulary from the ordinary words. The author's title, chapter headings, and preface may be useful in this connection.

Now you know that "wealth" is a technical word for Adam Smith, and "species" is one for Darwin. And as one technical word leads to another, you cannot help but discover other technical words in a similar fashion. You can soon make a list of the important words used by Adam Smith: labor, capital, land, wages, profits, rent, commodity, price, exchange, productive, unproductive, money, and so forth. And here are some you cannot miss in Darwin: variety, genus, selection, survival, adaptation, hybrid, fittest, creation.

Where a field of knowledge has a well-established technical vocabulary, the task of locating the important words in a book treating that subject matter is relatively easy. You can spot them *positively* through having some acquaintance with the field, or *negatively* by knowing what words must be technical, because they are not ordinary. Unfortunately, there are many fields in which a technical vocabulary is not well established.

Philosophers are notorious for having private vocabularies. There are some words, of course, which have a traditional standing in philosophy. Though they may not be used by all writers in the same sense, they are nevertheless technical words in the discussion of certain problems. But philosophers often find it necessary to coin new words, or to take some word from common speech and make it a technical word. This last procedure is likely to be most misleading to the reader who supposes that he knows what the word means, and therefore treats it as an ordinary word.

In this connection, one clue to an important word is that the author quarrels with other writers about it. When you find an author telling you how a particular word has been used by others, and why he chooses to use it differently, you can be pretty sure that that word makes a great difference to him.

I have emphasized the notion of technical vocabulary, but you must not take this too narrowly. The relatively small set of words which express the author's main ideas, his leading concepts, constitutes his special vocabulary. They are the words which carry his analysis. If he is making an original communication, some of these words are likely to be used by him in a very special way, although he may use others in a fashion which has become traditional in that field. In either case, these are the words which are most important *for him*. They should be important *for you* as a reader also, but in addition any other word whose meaning is not clear is important for you.

- 4 -

The trouble with most readers is that they simply do not pay enough attention to words to locate their difficulties. They fail to distinguish the words they do not understand sufficiently from those they do. All the things I have suggested to help you find the important words in a book will be of no avail unless you make a deliberate effort to note the words you must work on to find the terms they convey. The reader who fails to ponder, or at least to mark, the words he does not understand is likely to end up as badly as the locomotive engineer who drives past red signals in the hope that the traffic congestion will straighten itself out.

If you are reading a book that can increase your understanding, it stands to reason that all its words will not be equally intelligible. If you proceed as if they were all ordinary words, all on the same level of general intelligibility as the words of a newspaper article, you will not make the first step toward an interpretative reading. You might just as well be reading a newspaper, for the book cannot enlighten you if you do not try to understand it.

I know how inveterately most of us are addicted to passive reading. The outstanding fault of the passive reader is his inattention to words, and his consequent failure to come to terms with the author. Some years ago Professor Malcolm Sharp, of the University of Chicago Law School, and I gave a special course for students who were planning to study law. One of our primary aims was to teach them how to read and write. A lawyer should possess these abilities. The faculty of the Law School had come to suspect that the colleges could not be counted on to develop these skills. Our experience with these students, who had reached their junior year, showed their suspicion to be well founded.

We soon discovered how passively they read. John Locke's second essay *Of Civil Government* had been assigned, and they had had several weeks in which to read about a hundred pages. The class met. Mr. Sharp and I asked relatively simple, leading questions about Locke's views on government, the relation of natural and civil rights, the nature

of liberty, and so forth. They answered these questions, but
not in a way which showed any acquaintance with Locke.
They could have made the same replies if they had never
opened Locke's essay.

Had they read the book? They assured us they had. We
even inquired whether they had make the mistake of reading the first essay, rather than the second. There was no
mistake, it seemed. The only thing left to do was to show
them that, though they may have *looked* at every page, they
had not *read* the book.

I went to the board and asked them to call out the most
important words in the essay. I said I wanted either those
words which were most important for Locke or those which
they had trouble in understanding. At first there was no
response. Only after I put such words as "natural," "civil,"
"property," and "equality," on the board was I able to get
them to contribute. We finally did get a list which included
"liberty," "despotism," "consent (of the governed),"
"rights," "justice," and so forth.

Before I went further, I paused to ask whether these
words were utterly strange to them. No, they were all
familiar and ordinary words, they said. One student pointed
out that some of these words occurred in the Declaration
of Independence. It was said there to be self-evident that
all men are created *equal,* that they are endowed with certain inalienable *rights,* that the *just* powers of government
are derived from the *consent* of the governed. They found
other words, such as "despotism," "usurpation," and "liberty," which they thought Locke and the founding fathers
probably used in a similar way.

That was our cue. We agreed that the writers of the
Declaration and the framers of the Constitution had made

these words extremely popular in the tradition of American political discussion. Mr. Sharp added that many of them had probably read Locke's essay and had followed his usage of them. How did Locke use them? What were their meanings, not in general, not in popular speech, but in Locke's political theory, and in the great American documents which may have been influenced by Locke?

I went to the board again to write down the meanings of the words as they suggested them. But few suggestions were forthcoming, and seldom did a student offer a set of meanings. Few had discovered the fundamental ambiguity of the important words. Mr. Sharp and I then listed the meanings of the words, not one meaning for each, but several. By contrasting the meanings of "natural" and "civil," we tried to show them Locke's distinctions between *natural* and *civil* equality, *natural* and *civil* liberty, and *natural* and *civil* rights.

At the end of the hour, I asked them whether they still thought that they had read the book. A little sheepishly now they admitted that perhaps they hadn't. They had, of course, read it in the way they read the newspaper or a textbook. They had read it passively, without any attention to words and meanings. For the purpose of understanding what Locke had to say that was just the same as not reading it at all. Here were a group of future lawyers who did not know the meaning of the leading words in the Declaration of Independence or the preamble to the Constitution.

My point in telling this story is to show that until passive reading is overcome, the reader proceeds as if he knew what all the words meant, especially if he is reading something in which the important words also happen to be words in

popular usage. Had these students developed the habit of
active reading, they would have noted the words I have
mentioned. They would have known, in the first place,
that such words are not only popular but belong to the
technical vocabulary of political theory. Recognizing that,
they would, in the second place, have wondered about their
technical meanings. And finally, if they had tried to determine their significance, they would have found Locke using
these words in several senses. Then they might have realized
the need to come to terms with the author.

I should add that the lesson was learned. With these same
students, we subsequently read more difficult books than
Locke's essay. They came to class better prepared for discussion, because they had marked the words that made a
crucial difference. They had pursued important words
through their shifts of meaning. What is more, they were
beginning to enjoy a new experience—the active reading of
a book. It came a little late in their college life, but most
of them gratefully acknowledged that it was better late
than never.

- 5 -

Remember that spotting the important words is only the
beginning of the task. It merely locates the places in the
text where you have to go to work. There is another step
in carrying out this first rule of interpretative reading. Let
us turn to that now. Let us suppose that you have marked
the words that trouble you. What next?

There are two major possibilities. Either the author is
using these words in a single sense throughout or he is using
them in two or more senses, shifting his meaning from place

to place. In the first alternative, the word stands for a single term. A good example of the use of important words so that they are restricted to a single meaning is found in Euclid. In the second alternative, the word stands for several terms. This is the more usual case. It is illustrated by the usage in Locke's essay.

In the light of these alternatives, your procedure should be as follows. First, try to determine whether the word has one or many meanings. If it has many, try to see whether they are related and how. Finally, note the places where the word is used in one sense or another, and see if the context gives you any clue to the reason for the shift in meaning. This last will enable you to follow the word in its change of meanings with the same flexibility that characterizes the author's usage.

But, you may complain, everything is clear except the main thing. How does one find out what the meanings are? There is only one answer to the question. I fear you may not think it a very satisfactory one. But patience and practice will show you otherwise. The answer is that you have to discover the meaning of a word you do not understand by using the meanings of all the other words in the context which you do understand. This must be the way, however merry-go-roundish it may seem at first.

The simplest way to illustrate this is to consider a definition. A definition is stated in words. If you do not understand any of the words used in the definition, you obviously cannot understand the meaning of the word which names the thing being defined. The word "point" is a basic word in geometry. You may think you know what it means, but Euclid wants to be sure you use it in only one way. He tells you what he means by first defining the thing which he is later going to use the word to name. He says: "A point is that which has no parts."

How does that bring you to terms with him? You know, he assumes, what every other word in the sentence means with sufficient precision. You know that whatever has parts is a complex whole. You know that the opposite of complex is simple. To be simple is the same as to lack parts. You know that the use of the words "is" and "that which" means that the thing referred to must be an entity of some sort. You may even know that there are no physical things without parts, and hence that a point, as Euclid speaks of it, cannot be physical.

This illustration is typical of the process by which you acquire meanings. You operate with meanings you already possess. If every word that was used in a definition had itself to be defined, nothing could ever be defined. If every word in a book you were reading were entirely strange to you, as it is in the case of a book in a totally foreign lan guage, you could make no progress at all.

I suppose that is what people mean when they say of a book that it's all Greek to them. They simply have not tried to understand it. Most of the words in any English book are familiar words. These words surround the strange words, the technical words, the words that may cause the reader some trouble. The surrounding words are the *context* for the words to be interpreted. The reader has all the materials he needs to do the job.

I am not pretending the job is an easy one. I am only insisting that it is not an impossible one. If it were, no one could read a book to gain in understanding. The fact that a book can give you new insights or enlighten you indicates that it probably contains words you may not readily understand. If you could not come to understand these words by your own efforts, then the kind of reading we are talking about would be impossible. It would be impossible to pass from understanding less to understanding more by your own operations on a book.

If it is not impossible—*and it is not*—then the only solution is the one I have indicated. Because you understand something to begin with, you can employ your fund of meanings to interpret the words that challenge you. When you have succeeded, you have elevated yourself in understanding. You have approached or reached the understanding with which the author began.

There is no rule of thumb for doing this. The process is something like the trial-and-error method of putting a jigsaw puzzle together. The more parts you put together, the more easily the remaining parts fit. A book comes to you with a large number of words already in place. A word in place is a term. It is definitely located by the meaning which you and the author share in using it. The remaining words must be put into place. You do this by trying to make them fit this way or that. The better you understand the picture which the words so far in place incompletely reveal, the easier it is to complete the picture by making terms of the remaining words. Each word put into place makes the next adjustment easier.

You will make errors, of course, in the process. You will think you have managed to find where a word belongs and how it fits, only to discover later that the placement of another word requires you to make a whole series of readjustments. The errors will get corrected because, so long as they are not found out, the picture cannot be completed. Once you have had any experience at all in this work of coming to terms, you will soon be able to check yourself. You will know whether you have succeeded or not. You will not blithely think you understand when you do not.

In comparing a book to a jigsaw puzzle, I have made one assumption that is not simply or universally true. A good puzzle is, of course, one all of whose parts fit. The picture can be perfectly completed. The same is true of the ideally good book. But there are few books of this sort. In proportion as they are good, their terms will be so well made and put together by the author that the reader can do the work of interpretation fruitfully. Here, as in the case of every other rule of reading, bad books are less readable than good ones. The rules do not work on them, except to show you how bad they are. If the author uses words ambiguously, you cannot find out precisely what he is trying to say. You can only find out that he has not been precise.

But, you may ask, doesn't an author who uses a word in more than a single sense use it ambiguously? And didn't you say that the usual practice is for authors to use words in several senses, especially their most important words?

The answer to the second question is Yes, to the first, No. To use a word ambiguously is to use it in several senses without distinguishing or relating these meanings. (For example, I have probably used the word "important" ambiguously in this chapter, never quite clear as to whether I mean important for the author or important for you.) The author who does that has not made terms which the reader can come to. But the author who distinguishes the several senses in which he is using a critical word and enables the reader to make a responsive discrimination is offering terms.

You must not forget that one word can represent several

terms. One way to remember this is to distinguish between the author's technical *vocabulary* and his analytical *terminology*. If you make a list in one column of the important words, and in another of their various meanings, you will see the relation between the vocabulary and the terminology.

- 6 -

There are several further complications. In the first place, a word which has several distinct meanings can be used either in a single sense or in a combination of senses. Let me take the word "reading" again as an example. In some places, I have used it to stand for reading any kind of book. In others, I have used it to stand for reading books which instruct rather than amuse. In still others, I have used it to stand for reading which enlightens rather than informs.

Now if we symbolize here, as we did before, the three distinct meanings of "reading" by Xa, Xb, and Xc, you can see that the first usage just mentioned is $Xabc$, the second is Xbc, and the third Xc. In other words, if three meanings are related, one can use a word to stand for all of them, for some of them, or for only one of them at a time. So long as each usage is definite, the word so used is a term.

In the second place, there is the problem of synonyms. You know in general that synonyms are words which have the same meaning or closely related shades of meaning. A pair of synonyms is exactly the opposite of a single word used in two ways. Synonyms are two words used in the same way. Hence one and the same term can be represented by two or more words used synonymously.

We can indicate this symbolically as follows. Let X and Y

be two different words, such as "enlightenment" and "insight." Let the letter a stand for the same meaning which
each can express, namely, a gain in understanding. Then
Xa and Ya represent the same term, though they are distinct as words. When I speak of reading "for insight" and
reading "for enlightenment," I am referring to the same
kind of reading, because the two phrases are being used
with the same meaning. The words are different, but there
is only one term here for you as a reader to grasp.

You can see why this is important. If you supposed that
every time an author changed his words, he was shifting
his terms, you would make as great an error as to suppose
that every time he used the same words, the terms remained
the same. Keep this in mind when you list the author's
vocabulary and terminology in separate columns. You will
find two relationships. On the one hand, a single word may
be related to several terms. On the other, a single term
may be related to several words.

That this is generally the case results from the nature of
language in relation to thought. A dictionary is a record of
the usage of words. It shows how men have used the same
word to refer to different things, and different words to
refer to the same thing. The reader's problem is to know
what the author is doing with words at any place in the
book. The dictionary may help sometimes, but if the writer
departs in the least from common usage, the reader is on
his own.

In the third place, and finally, there is the matter of
phrases. A phrase, as you know, is a group of words which
does not express a complete thought as a sentence does. If
the phrase is a unit, that is, if it is a whole which can be
the subject or predicate of a sentence, it is like a single

word. Like a single word, it can refer to something being talked about in some way.

It follows, therefore, that a term can be expressed by a phrase as well as by a word. And all the relations which exist between words and terms hold also between terms and phrases. Two phrases may express the same terms, and one phrase may express several terms, according to the way its constituent words are used.

In general, a phrase is less likely to be ambiguous than a word. Because it is a group of words, each of which is in the context of the others, the single words are more likely to have restricted meanings. That is why a writer is likely to substitute a fairly elaborate phrase for a single word if he wants to be sure that you get his meaning.

One illustration should suffice. To be sure that you come to terms with me about reading, I substitute the phrase "reading for enlightenment" for the single word "reading." To make doubly sure, I may even substitute a more elaborate phrase, such as "the process of passing from understanding less to understanding more by the operation of your mind upon a book." There is only one term here, namely, the reference to a kind of reading which I am trying to talk about. But that one term has been expressed by a single word, a short phrase, and a longer one.

This has probably been the hardest chapter for you to read so far. I know it has been the hardest for me to write. I think I know the reason why. The rule of reading we have been discussing cannot be made fully intelligible without going into all sorts of grammatical and logical explanations about words and terms.

I assure you I have done very little explaining. To give an adequate account of these matters would take many chapters. I say this to warn you that I have merely touched the most essential points. I hope I have said enough to make the rule a useful guide in practice. The more you put it into practice, the more you will appreciate the intricacies of the problem. You will want to know something about the literal and metaphorical use of words. You will want to know about the distinction between abstract and concrete words, or between proper and common names. You will become interested in the whole business of definitions: the difference between defining words and defining things; why some words are indefinable, and yet have definite meanings, and so forth. You will seek light on what is called "the emotive use of words," that is, the use of words to arouse emotions, to move men to action or change their minds, as distinct from the communication of knowledge.

If the practice of reading elicits these further interests, you will be in a position to satisfy them by reading books on these special subjects. And you will profit more from reading such books, because you will go to them with questions born of your own experience in reading. The study of grammar and logic, the sciences which underlie these rules of interpretation, is practical only to the extent you can relate it to practice.

CHAPTER ELEVEN

What's the Proposition and Why

• I •

NOT only coming to terms but making propositions occurs among traders as well as in the world of books. What a buyer or seller means by a proposition is some sort of proposal, some sort of offer or acceptance. In honest dealings, the man who makes a proposition in this sense is declaring his intention to act in a certain way. More than honesty is needed for successful negotiations. The proposition should be clear and, of course, attractive. Then the traders can come to terms.

A proposition in a book is also a declaration. It is an expression of the author's judgment about something. He affirms something he thinks true, or denies something he judges to be false. He asserts this or that to be a fact. A proposition of this sort is a declaration of knowledge, not intentions. The author may tell us his intentions at the beginning in a preface. In an expository book, he usually promises to instruct us about something. To find out whether he keeps those promises, we must look for his propositions.

The order of reading reverses the order of business somewhat. Businessmen come to terms after they find out what the proposition is. But the reader must usually come to terms with an author first, before he can find out what the author is proposing, what judgments he is declaring. That is why the first rule of interpretation concerns words and terms, and the second, which we are about to discuss, concerns sentences and propositions.

There is a third rule of interpretation closely related to the second. The author may be honest in declaring himself on matters of fact or knowledge. We usually proceed in that trust. But honesty is not enough. Unless we are exclusively interested in the author's personality, we should not be satisfied with knowing what his opinions are. His propositions are nothing but expressions of opinion unless there is some reason for them. If it is the subject matter of the book we are interested in, and not just the author, we want to know not merely what the propositions are, but why.

The third rule, therefore, deals with arguments of all sorts. There are many kinds of reasoning, many ways of supporting what one says. Sometimes it is possible to argue that something is true; sometimes no more than a probability can be defended. But every sort of argument consists of a number of statements related in a certain way. This is said *because* of *that*. The word "because" here signifies a reason being given.

The presence of arguments is indicated by other words which relate statements, such as: *if* this is so, *then* that; or, *since* this, *therefore* that; or, it *follows* from this, that that is the case. In the course of earlier chapters, such sequences occurred. If thinking, I said, is the use of our minds to gain knowledge, and if we use our minds to gain knowledge only in two ways, either in being taught or in investigating, then, I said, we must conclude that all the thinking we do occurs in the course of one or the other of these two activities.

An argument is always a set or series of statements of which some provide the grounds or reasons for what is to be concluded. It, therefore, takes a paragraph, or at least a collection of sentences, to express an argument. The premises or principles of an argument may not always be stated first, but they are the *source* of the conclusion, nevertheless. If the argument is valid, the conclusion follows from the premises. That does not necessarily mean that the conclusion is true, because the premises which support it may be false, one or all.

Perhaps you have already observed something about the sequence of these three rules. We go from terms to propositions to arguments, by going from words (and phrases) to sentences to collections of sentences or paragraphs.

When grammar was still taught in the schools, everyone was acquainted with these units. A schoolboy knew that an orderly sequence of sentences made up a paragraph. My experience with college students in the last ten years makes me doubt that this simple knowledge is common any longer. They do not seem able to write or speak sentences and paragraphs, and that has made me wonder whether they can recognize them in the books they read.

You will notice, furthermore, that we are now moving in the direction of building up from simpler to more complex units. The smallest significant element in a book is, of course, a single word. It would be true but not adequate to say that a book consists of words. It also consists of groups of words, taken as a unit, and similarly groups of sentences, taken as a unit. The reader, who is active rather than passive, is attentive not only to the words but to the sentences and paragraphs. There is no other way of discovering the author's terms, propositions, and arguments.

The movement of this second or interpretative reading seems to be in the opposite direction to the movement of the first or structural reading. There we went from the book as a whole to its major parts, and then to their subordinate divisions. As you might suspect, the two movements meet somewhere. The major parts of a book and even their principal divisions contain many propositions and usually several arguments. But if you keep on dividing the book into its parts, you at last have to say: "In this part, the following points are made." Now each of these points is likely to be a proposition, and some of them taken together probably form an argument.

Thus, the two processes, which we have called the first and the second reading, meet. You work down to propositions and arguments by dividing the book into its parts. You work up to arguments by seeing how they are composed of propositions and ultimately of terms. When you have completed these two readings, you can really say you know the contents of a book.

- 2 -

There is one other thing to be noticed about the rules we are going to discuss in this chapter. As in the case of the rule about words and terms, we are here also dealing with the relation of language and thought. Sentences and paragraphs are grammatical units. They are units of language. Propositions and arguments are logical units, or units of thought and knowledge.

If you remember what our main problem was in the last chapter, you will be prepared to face a similar one here. Because language is not a perfect medium for the expression of thought, because one word can have many meanings and two or more words can have the same meaning, we saw how complicated was the relation between an author's *vocabulary* and his *terminology*. One word may represent several terms, and one term may be represented by several words.

Mathematicians describe the relation between the buttons and buttonholes on a well-made coat as a perfect one-to-one relationship. There is a button for every buttonhole, and a hole for every button. Well, the point is that words and terms do *not* stand in a one-to-one relation. The greatest error you can make in applying these rules is to suppose that a one-to-one relationship exists between the elements of language and those of thought or knowledge.

Let me show you this at once in the case of sentences and propositions. Not every sentence in a book expresses a proposition. For one thing, some sentences express questions. They state problems rather than answers. Propositions are the answers to questions. They are declarations of knowledge or opinion. That is why we call sentences which express them declarative, and distinguish sentences which ask questions as interrogative. Other sentences express wishes or intentions. They may give us some knowledge of the author's purpose, but they do not convey the knowledge he is trying to expound.

Moreover, not all the declarative sentences can be read as if each expressed one proposition. There are at least two reasons for this. The first is the fact that words are ambiguous and can be used in various senses. Hence it is possible for the same sentence to express different propositions if there is a shift in the terms the words express. "Reading is learning" is certainly a simple sentence. But if at one place I mean by "learning" the acquisition of information, and at another I mean the development of understanding, the proposition is not the same, because the terms are different. Yet the sentence is verbally the same.

The second reason is that all sentences are not as simple as "reading is learning." You may remember from grammar school, if you belonged to a more fortunate generation, the distinction between simple sentences, on the one hand, and complex or compound sentences, on the other. When its words are used unambiguously, a simple sentence usually expresses a single proposition. But even when its words are used unambiguously, a compound sentence expresses two or more propositions. A compound sentence is really a collection of sentences, connected by such words as "and," or "if" and "then," or "not only" and "but also." You may rightly conclude that the line between a long compound sentence and a short paragraph may be difficult to draw. A compound sentence can express a number of propositions related in the form of an argument.

Complex sentences are the most difficult to interpret. There is no question that compound sentences express several propositions somehow related. But a complex sentence may express either one proposition or several. Let me take an interesting sentence from Machiavelli's *The Prince* to show you what I mean:

> A prince ought to inspire fear in such a way that, if he does not win love, he avoids hatred; because he can endure very well being feared whilst he is not hated, which will always be as long as he abstains from the property of his citizens and from their women.

That is grammatically a *single* sentence, though it is both compound and complex. The semicolon and the "because" indicate the major break which makes the sentence compound. The first proposition is that a prince ought to inspire fear in a certain way.

Beginning with the word "because," we have a complex sentence. It could be made independent by saying: "The reason for this is that he can endure," and so forth. This complex sentence expresses two propositions at least: (1) the reason why the prince ought to inspire fear in a certain way is that he can endure being feared so long as he is not hated; (2) he can avoid being hated only by abstaining from the property of his citizens and their women.

You can see why it is important to distinguish the various propositions that a long compound and complex sentence contains. In order to agree or disagree with Machiavelli, you must first understand what he is saying. But he is saying three things in this one sentence. You may disagree with one of them and agree with the others. You may think Machiavelli is wrong in recommending terrorism to a prince on any grounds; but you may acknowledge his shrewdness in saying that the prince had better not arouse hatred along with fear, and you may also agree that keeping his hands off their property and women is an indispensable condition of not being hated. Unless you recognize the distinct propositions in a complicated sentence, you cannot make a discriminating judgment on what the writer is saying.

Lawyers know this fact very well. They have to examine sentences carefully to see what is being alleged by the plaintiff or denied by the defendant. The single sentence, "John Doe signed the lease on March 24," looks simple enough, but still it says several things, one of which may be true and the other false. John Doe may have signed the lease, but not on March 24, and that fact may be important. In short, even a grammatically simple sentence sometimes expresses two or more propositions.

- 3 -

I have said enough to indicate what I mean by the difference between sentences and propositions. They are not related as one to one. Not only may a single sentence express several propositions, either through ambiguity or complexity, but one and the same proposition can be expressed by two or more different sentences. If you grasp my terms through the words and phrases I use synonymously, you will know that I am saying the same thing when I say, "Teaching and being taught are correlative functions," and "Initiating and receiving communication are related processes."

I am going to stop explaining the grammatical and logical points involved, and turn to the rules. The difficulty in this chapter, as in the last, is to stop explaining. Perhaps I had better assume that the school you went to taught some grammar. If it did, you may see now why all that business of syntax, of parsing and diagramming sentences, was not a meaningless routine invented by old-fashioned teachers to crush the spirit of the young. It all helps toward skill in writing and reading.

In fact, I should say it is almost indispensable. You cannot begin to deal with terms, propositions, and arguments—the elements of thought—until you can penetrate beneath the surface of language. So long as words, sentences, and paragraphs are opaque and unanalyzed, they are a barrier to, rather than a medium of, communication. You will read words but not receive knowledge.

Here are the rules. The first rule, you will recall from the last chapter, is: *Find the important words and come to terms.* The second rule is: *Mark the most important sentences in a book and discover the propositions they contain.* The third rule is: *Locate or construct the basic arguments in the book by finding them in the connection of sentences.* You will see later why I did not say "paragraphs" in the formulation of this rule.

You have already been introduced to the second and third rules. In the early chapters, we marked the sentence "reading is learning" as important, because it expressed a basic proposition in this discussion. We also noted several different kinds of argument: a proof that the great books are most readable, and a marshaling of evidence to show that the schools have failed to teach the arts of reading and writing.

Our task now is to get further light on how to operate according to the rules. How does one locate the most important sentences in a book? How, then, does one interpret them to discover the one or more propositions they contain?

Again, there is this emphasis on what is *important.* To say that there is only a relatively small number of important sentences in a book does not mean that you need pay no attention to all the rest. Obviously you have to understand every sentence. But most of the sentences, like most of the words, will cause you no difficulty. From your point of view as a reader, the sentences important *for you* are those which require an effort of interpretation because, at first sight, they are not perfectly intelligible. You understand them just well enough to know there is more to understand. These may not be the sentences which are most important *for the author,* but they are likely to be, because you are likely to have the greatest difficulty with the most important things the author has to say.

From the author's point of view, the important sentences are those which express the judgments on which his whole argument rests. A book usually contains much more than the bare statement of an argument, or a series of arguments. The author may explain how he came to the point of view he now holds, or why he thinks his position has serious consequences. He may discuss the words he has to use. He may comment on the work of others. He may indulge in all sorts of supporting and surrounding discussion. But the heart of his communication lies in the major affirmations and denials he is making, and the reasons he gives for so doing. To come to grips, therefore, you have to see the main sentences as if they were raised from the page in high relief.

Some authors help you do this. They underline the sentences for you. They either tell you that this is an important point when they make it, or they use one or another typographical device to make their leading sentences stand out. Of course, nothing helps those who will not keep awake while reading. I have met many students who paid no attention to such signs. They preferred to read on rather than stop and examine the important sentences carefully. They somehow knew unconsciously that the author was not just being helpful. He was trying to get them to do some mental work where it was most needed.

There are a few books in which the leading propositions are set forth in sentences which occupy a special place in the order and style of the exposition. Euclid, again, gives us the most obvious example of this. He not only states his definitions, his postulates, and axioms—his principal propositions—at the beginning, but he labels every proposition to be proved. You may not understand his statements. You may not follow his arguments. But, if you have eyes in your head, you cannot miss the important sentences or the grouping of sentences for the statement of the proofs. That is all done for you.

The *Summa Theologica* of St. Thomas Aquinas is another book whose style of exposition puts the leading sentences into high relief. It proceeds by raising questions. Each section is headed by a question. There are many indications of the answer which St. Thomas is trying to defend. A whole series of objections opposing the answer is stated. The place where St. Thomas begins to argue his point is marked by the words, "I answer that." There is no excuse for not being able to locate the important sentences in such a book, those expressing the reasons as well as the conclusions, yet I must report that it is all a blur for students who treat everything they read as equally important. That usually means that everything is equally unimportant.

- 4 -

Apart from books whose style or format calls attention to what most needs interpretation by the reader, the spotting of sentences is a job the reader must perform for himself. There are several things he can do. I have already mentioned one. If he is sensitive to the difference between passages he can understand readily and those he cannot, he will probably be able to locate the sentences which carry the main burden of meaning. Perhaps you are beginning to see how essential a part of reading it is to be perplexed and know it. Wonder is the beginning of wisdom in learning from books as well as from nature. If you never ask yourself any questions about the meaning of a passage, you cannot expect the book to give you any insight you do not already possess.

Another clue to the important sentences is found in the words which compose them. If you have already marked the important words, they should lead you to the sentences which deserve further attention. Thus the first step in interpretative reading prepares for the second. But the reverse may also be the case. It may be that you will mark certain words only after you have become puzzled by the meaning of a sentence. The fact that I have stated these rules in a fixed order does not mean that you have to follow them in that order. Terms constitute propositions. Propositions contain terms. If you know the terms the words express, you have caught the proposition in the sentence. If you understand the proposition conveyed by a sentence, you have arrived at the terms also.

This suggests one further clue to the location of the principal propositions. They must belong to the main arguments of the book. They must be either premises or conclusions. Hence, if you can detect those sentences which seem to form a sequence, a sequence in which there is a beginning and an end, you probably have put your finger on sentences which are important.

I said a sequence in which there is a beginning and an end. Every argument which men can express in words takes time to state, more obviously so than a single sentence. You may speak a sentence in one breath, but there are pauses in an argument. You have to say one thing first, then another, and still another. An argument begins somewhere, goes somewhere, gets somewhere. It is a movement of

thought. It may begin with what is really the conclusion
and then proceed to give the reasons for it. Or it may start
with the evidences and reasons and bring you to the conclusion which follows therefrom.

Of course, here as elsewhere, the clue will not work
unless you know how to use it. You have to recognize an
argument when you see one. Despite some disappointing
experiences in teaching, I still persist in my opinion that
the human mind is as naturally sensitive to arguments as
the eye is to colors. The eye will not see if it is not kept open,
and the mind will not follow an argument if it is not awake.
I explain my disappointment with students in this connection by saying that they are mostly asleep while they read a
book or listen to what goes on in class.

Several years ago, Mr. Hutchins and I began to read some
books with a new group of students. They had had almost
no training in reading and had read very little when we first
met them. One of the first books we read was Lucretius'
account of *The Nature of Things*. We thought this would
be interesting for them. Most of our students are extreme
materialists to begin with. And this work by Lucretius is
a powerful exposition of the extreme materialistic position.
It is the most extensive statement we have of the position
of the ancient Greek atomists.

Because they were beginners in reading (though most
of them were college juniors and seniors), we read the book
slowly, at the rate of about thirty pages a time. Even so,
they had difficulty in knowing what words to mark, what
sentences to underline. Everything Lucretius said seemed
to them of equal importance. Mr. Hutchins decided that
it would be a good exercise for them to write out *just* the

conclusions which Lucretius reached or tried to prove in the next part. "Don't tell us," he said, "what Lucretius thinks about the gods or women, or what you think about Lucretius. We want the argument in a nutshell, and that means finding the conclusions first."

The main argument in the section they had to read was an attempt to show that the atoms differ only in shape, size, weight, and speed of motion. They have no qualities at all, no colors or smells or textures. All the qualities we experience are entirely subjective—in us rather than in things.

The conclusions could have been written down in a few propositions. But they brought in statements of every sort. Their failure to extract conclusions from everything else was not due to lack of training in logic. They had no difficulty in following the line of an argument once it was presented to them. But they had to have the argument lifted out of the text for them. They were not good enough readers yet to do that for themselves. When Mr. Hutchins did the job, they saw how the statements written on the board formed an argument. They could see the difference between the premises—the reasons or evidences—and the conclusions they supported. In short, they had to be taught how to read, not how to reason.

I repeat, we did not have to teach them logic or explain in detail what an argument was. They could recognize one as soon as it was put on the board in a few simple statements. But they could not find arguments in a book because they had not yet learned to read *actively,* to disengage the important sentences from all the rest, and to observe the connections the author made. Reading Lucretius as they read the newspaper, they naturally did not make such discriminations.

- 5 -

Now let us suppose that you have located the leading sentences. Another step is required by the rule. You must discover the proposition or propositions each of these sentences contains. This is just another way of saying that you must know what the sentence means. You discover terms by discovering what a word means in a given usage. You discover propositions similarly by interpreting all the words that make up the sentence, and especially its principal words.

Obviously, you cannot do this unless you know a little grammar. You must know the role which adjectives and adverbs play, how verbs function in relation to nouns, how modifying words and clauses restrict or amplify the meaning of the words they modify, and so forth. You must be able to dissect a sentence according to the rules of syntax. I said before that I was going to assume you knew this much grammar. I cannot believe you do not, though you may have grown a little rusty from lack of practice in the rudiments of the art of reading.

There are only two differences between finding the terms which words express and the propositions in sentences. One is that you employ a larger context in the latter case. You bring all the surrounding sentences to bear on the sentence in question, just as you used the surrounding words to interpret a particular word. In both cases, you proceed from what you do understand to the gradual elucidation of what is at first relatively unintelligible.

The other difference lies in the fact that complicated sentences usually express two or more propositions. You have not completed your interpretation of an important sentence until you have separated out of it all the different,

though perhaps related, propositions it contains. Skill in
doing this is easily exercised. Take some of the complicated
sentences in this book and try to state in your own words
each of the things that is being asserted. Number them and
relate them.

"State in your own words!" That suggests the best test I
know for telling whether you have understood the proposition or propositions in the sentence. If, when you are asked
to explain what the author means by a particular sentence,
all you can do is to repeat his very words, with some minor
alterations in order, you had better suspect that you do not
know what he means. Ideally, you should be able to say the
same thing in totally different words. The ideal can, of
course, be approximated in degrees. But if you cannot get
away at all from the author's words, it shows that *only words*
have passed from him to you, *not thought* or *knowledge*.
You know his words, not his mind. He was trying to communicate knowledge, and all you received were words.

The process of translation from a foreign language into
English is relevant to the test I have suggested. If you cannot state in an English sentence what a French sentence
says, you know you do not understand the meaning of the
French. Such translation is entirely on the verbal level, because even when you have formed a faithful English
replica, you still may not know what the writer of the
French sentence was trying to convey. I have read a lot of
translations which reveal such ignorance.

The translation of one English sentence into another,
however, is not merely verbal. The new sentence you have
formed is not a verbal replica of the original. If accurate,
it is faithful to the thought alone. That is why the making of
such translations is the best test you can apply to yourself,

if you want to be sure you have caught the proposition, not merely swallowed the words. I have tried it countless times on students. It never fails to detect the counterfeit of understanding. The student who says he knows what the author means, but can only repeat the author's sentence to show that he does, would not be able to recognize the author's proposition if it were presented to him in other words.

The author may himself express the same proposition in different words in the course of his writing. The reader who has not seen through the words to the proposition they convey is likely to treat the equivalent sentences as if they were statements of different propositions. Imagine a person who did not know that "$2 + 2 = 4$" and "$4 - 2 = 2$" were different notations for the same arithmetic relationship— the relationship of four as the double of two, or two as the half of four.

You would have to conclude that that person simply did not understand the equation. The same conclusion is forced on you concerning yourself or anybody else who cannot tell when equivalent statements of the same proposition are being made, or who cannot himself offer an equivalent statement when he claims to understand the proposition a sentence contains.

These remarks have a bearing on the problem of reading two books about the same subject matter. Different authors frequently say the same thing in different words, or different things using almost the same words. The reader who cannot see through the language to the terms and propositions will never be able to compare such related works. Because of their verbal differences, he is likely to misread the authors as disagreeing, or to ignore their real differences because of verbal resemblances in their statements. I would

go further and say that a person who cannot read two related books in a discriminating way cannot read either of
them by itself.

There is one other test of whether you understand the
proposition in a sentence you have read. Can you point to
some experience you have had which the proposition describes or to which the proposition is in any way relevant?
Can you exemplify the general truth which has been enun-
ciated by referring to a particular instance of it? To imagine
a possible case is often as good as reporting an actual one.
If you cannot do anything at all to exemplify or illustrate the
proposition, either imaginatively or by reference to actual
experiences, you should suspect that you do not know what
is being said.

All propositions are not equally susceptible to this test.
It may be necessary to have the special experience which
only a laboratory can afford to be sure you have grasped
certain scientific propositions. We shall return to this point
later in the discussion of reading scientific books. But here
the main point is clear. Propositions do not exist in a
vacuum. They refer to the world in which we live. Unless
you can show some acquaintance with actual or possible
facts to which the proposition refers or is relevant somehow, you are *playing with words,* not dealing with thought
and knowledge.

Let me give you one illustration. A basic proposition in
metaphysics is expressed by the following words: "Nothing
acts except what is actual." I have had many students repeat
these words to me with an air of satisfied wisdom. They have
thought they were discharging their duty to me and to the
author by so perfect a verbal repetition. But the sham was
too obvious I would first ask them to state the proposition

in other words. Seldom could they say, for instance, that if something does not exist, it cannot do anything. Yet this is an immediately apparent translation—apparent, at least, to anyone who understood the proposition in the original sentence.

Failing to get a translation, I would then ask for an ex-emplification of the proposition. If any one of them told me that people do not run away from what is merely possible —that a baseball game is not postponed on account of *possible* showers—I would know at once that the proposition had been grasped.

The vice of "verbalism" can be defined as the bad habit of using words without regard for the thoughts they should convey and without awareness of the experiences to which they should refer. It is playing with words. As the two tests I have just suggested indicate, "verbalism" is the besetting sin of those who fail to read interpretatively. Such readers never get beyond the words. They possess what they read as a verbal memory which they can recite emptily. Strangely enough, one of the charges made by progressive educators against the liberal arts is that they tend to verbalism, when the facts clearly show that it is progressive education's neglect of the three R's which does exactly that. The failure in reading—the vicious verbalism—of those who have not been trained in the arts of grammar and logic shows how lack of such discipline results in slavery to words rather than mastery of them.

- 6 -

We have spent enough time on propositions. Let us now turn to the third rule, which requires the reader to deal with collections of sentences. I said before that there was a reason for not formulating this third rule by saying that the reader should find the most important paragraphs. The reason is that there are no settled conventions among writers about how to construct paragraphs. Some great writers, such as Montaigne and Locke, write extremely long paragraphs; others, such as Machiavelli and Hobbes, write relatively short ones. In recent times, under the influence of newspaper and magazine style, most writers tend to cut their paragraphs to fit quick and easy reading. I must confess to you that in the course of writing this book I have often made two para-graphs out of what seemed to me to be naturally one, be-cause I have been told that most readers like short para-graphs. This paragraph, for instance, is probably too long. If I had wanted to coddle my readers, I should have started a new one with the words, "Some great writers."

It is not merely a matter of length. The point that is troublesome here has to do with the relation between lan-guage and thought. The logical unit to which the third rule directs our attention is the argument—a sequence of propo-sitions, some of which give reasons for another. This logical unit is not uniquely related to any recognizable unit of writing, as terms are related to words and phrases, and propositions to sentences. An argument, as we have seen, may be expressed in a single complicated sentence. Or it may be expressed in a number of sentences that are only part of one paragraph. Sometimes an argument may coincide with a paragraph, but it may also happen that an argument runs through several paragraphs.

There is one further difficulty. There are many para-graphs in any book which do not express an argument at all—perhaps not even part of one. They may consist of col-lections of sentences that detail evidence or report how the evidence has been gathered. As there are sentences that are of secondary importance, because they are merely digressions or side remarks, so also can there be paragraphs of this sort.

Because of all this, I suggest the following rule: *Find if you can the paragraphs in a book which state its important arguments; but if the arguments are not thus expressed, your task is to* construct *them, by taking a sentence from this paragraph, and one from that, until you have gathered together the sequence of sentences which state the propositions that compose the argument.*

After you have discovered the leading sentences, the construction of paragraphs should be relatively easy. There are various ways of doing this. You can do it by actually writing out on a pad the propositions that together form an argument. Or you can put a number in the margin to indicate the place where the sentences occur that should be tied together in a sequence.

Authors are more or less helpful to their readers in this matter of making the arguments plain. Good authors try to reveal, not conceal, their thought. Yet not even all good authors do this in the same way. Some, such as Euclid, Galileo, Newton (authors who write in a geometrical or mathematical style), come close to the ideal of making a single paragraph an argumentative unit. With the exception of Euclid, there are almost none who make every paragraph an argument. The style of most writing in non-mathematical fields of science tends to present two or more arguments in a single paragraph or to have an argument run through several.

In proportion as a book is more loosely constructed, the paragraphs tend to become more diffuse. You often have to

search through all the paragraphs of a chapter to find the
sentences you can construct into the statement of a single
argument. I have read some books which make you search
in vain, and some which do not even encourage the search.

A good book usually summarizes itself as its arguments
develop. If the author summarizes his arguments for you at
the end of a chapter, or at the end of an elaborate section,
you should be able to look back over the preceding pages
and find the materials he has brought together in the summary. In *The Origin of Species,* Darwin summarizes his
whole argument for the reader in a last chapter, entitled
"Recapitulation and Conclusion." The reader who has
worked through the book deserves that help. The one who
has not, cannot use it.

Another difference between a good and a bad writer is
the omission of steps in an argument. Sometimes they can
be omitted without damage or inconvenience, because the
propositions left out can be generally supplied from the
common knowledge of readers. But sometimes their omission is misleading, and may even be intended to mislead.
One of the most familiar tricks of the orator or propagandist
is to leave certain things unsaid, things which are highly
relevant to the argument, but which might be challenged
if made explicit. While we do not expect such devices in an
honest author whose aim is to instruct us, it is nevertheless
a sound maxim of careful reading to make every step in an
argument explicit.

Whatever kind of book it is, your obligation as a reader
remains the same. If the book contains arguments, you
must know what they are, and in a nutshell. Any good argument can be put into a nutshell. There are, of course, arguments built upon arguments. In the course of an elaborate

analysis, one thing may be proved in order to prove another, and this may be used in turn to make a still further point. The units of reasoning, however, are single arguments. If you can find these in any book you are reading, you are not likely to miss the larger sequences.

This is all very well to say, you may object, but unless one knows the structure of argument as a logician does, how can one be expected to find them in a book, or worse, to construct them when the author doesn't state them compactly in a single paragraph?

I can answer you by pointing out why it must be obvious that you do not have to know about arguments "as a logician does." There are relatively few logicians in the world, for better or for worse. Most of the books which convey knowledge and can instruct us contain arguments. They are intended for the general reader, not for the specialists in logic.

I, for one, do not believe that great logical competence is needed to read these books. I repeat what I said before, that the nature of the human mind is such that if it works at all during the process of reading, if it comes to terms with the author and reaches his propositions, it will see his arguments as well.

There are, however, a few things I can say which may be helpful to you in carrying out this third rule. In the first place, remember that every argument must involve a number of statements. Of these, some give the reasons why you should accept a conclusion the author is proposing. If you find the conclusion first, then look for the reasons. If you find the reasons first, see what they lead to.

In the second place, discriminate between the kind of argument which points to one or more particular facts as evidence for some generalization and the kind which offers a series of general statements to prove some further generalization. General propositions which are called self-evident, or axioms, are propositions we know to be true as soon as we understand their terms. Such propositions are ultimately derived from our experience of particulars.

For example, when you understand what any *physical* whole is, and when you understand what it means for anything to be a part of *such* a whole, you know at once that the whole is greater than any of its parts. Through understanding three terms—whole, part, and greater than—you at once know a true proposition. The most important step in getting to that truth is restricting the meaning of the word "whole" by the qualification *physical*. The proposition that the whole is greater than a part is not true for every sort of whole. But when you use these words with restricted meanings, you reach terms which are evidently related in a certain way. What becomes evident in this way is a familiar axiom, a proposition which men have commonly recognized to be true for many centuries.

Sometimes such propositions are called tautologies. The name makes very little difference except to indicate how you feel about the proposition whose truth is clear without proof—a generalization which is argued directly from particulars. When in modern times self-evident truths have been called "tautologies," the feeling behind it is sometimes one of contempt for the trivial, or a suspicion of legerdemain. Rabbits are being pulled out of the hat. You put the truth in by defining your words, and then pull it out as if you were surprised to find it there. Notice, however, that that is not the case. To restrict the meaning of a word is not to define a thing. Wholes and parts are things, not words. We did not define them. In fact, we cannot. What we did do was to limit our words so that they referred to a certain type of thing with which we are acquainted. Once that was done we found we knew something that our restricted words could express.

In the literature of science, the distinction is observed between the proof of a proposition by reasoning and its establishment by experiment. Galileo, in his *Two New Sciences*, speaks of illustrating by experiment conclusions which had already been reached by mathematical demonstration. And in a concluding chapter, the great physiologist Harvey writes: "It has been shown by reason and experiment that blood by the beat of the ventricles flows through the lungs and heart and is pumped to the whole body." Sometimes it is possible to support a proposition both by reasoning from other general truths and by offering experimental evidence. Sometimes only one method of argument is available.

In the third place, observe what things the author says he must assume, what he says can be proved or otherwise evidenced, and what need not be proved because it is self-evident. He may honestly try to tell you what all his assumptions are, or he may just as honestly leave you to find them out for yourself. Obviously, everything cannot be proved, just as everything cannot be defined. If every proposition had to be proved, there would be no beginning to any proof. Such things as axioms, or propositions somehow drawn directly from experience, and assumptions, or postulates, are needed for the proof of other propositions. If these others are proved, they can, of course, be used as premises in further proofs.

- 7 -

These three rules of reading—about terms, propositions, and arguments—can be brought to a head in a fourth and final rule. This fourth rule governs the last step in the second reading of a book. More than that, it ties the second reading together with the first.

You may remember that the last step in the first reading was the discovery of the major problems which the author tried to answer in the course of his book. Now, after you have come to terms with him and grasped his propositions and arguments, you can check what you have found by answering the following questions. Which of the problems that the author *tried* to solve did he *succeed* in solving? In the course of solving these, did he get into any new ones? Of the problems he failed to solve, old or new, which did the author himself know he failed on? A good writer, like a good reader, should know whether a problem has been solved or not, though I can see how it might cost the reader less pain to acknowledge the failure.

When you are able to answer these questions, you can feel reasonably assured that you have managed to understand the book. If you started with a book that was above you—and one, therefore, that was able to teach you something—you have come a long way. More than that, you are now able to complete your reading of the book.

The third and last stage of the job will be relatively easy. You have been keeping your eyes and mind open and your mouth shut. Up to this point, you have been following the author. From this point on, you are going to get a chance to argue with the author and express yourself.

‑‑‑‑‑‑

CHAPTER TWELVE

The Etiquette of Talking Back

‑ I ‑

AND where are we now?

I said at the end of the last chapter that we have come a long way. We have learned what is required of us in the first reading of a book. That is the reading in which we analyze the book's structure. We have also learned four rules for doing a second reading of the same book—an interpretative reading. The four rules are: (1) come to terms with an author by interpreting his basic words; (2) grasp the author's leading propositions through finding his important sentences; (3) know the author's argu‑ ments by finding them in, or constructing them out of, sequences of sentences; (4) determine which of his problems the author solved and which he did not, and, of the latter, decide which the author knew he failed to solve.

You are now ready for the third way of reading the same book. Here you will reap the reward of all your previous efforts.

Reading a book is a kind of conversation. You may think it is not conversation at all, because the author does all the talking and you have nothing to say. If you think that, you do not realize your opportunities and obligations as a reader.

As a matter of fact, the reader has the last word. The author has had his say, and then it is the reader's turn. The conversation between a book and its reader would appear to be an orderly one, each party talking in turn, no interruptions, and so forth. If, however, the reader is undisciplined and impolite, it may be anything but orderly. The poor author cannot defend himself. He cannot say, "Here, wait till I've finished, before you start disagreeing." He cannot protest that the reader has missed his point.

Ordinary conversations between persons who confront each other are good only when they are carried on decently. I am not thinking merely of the decencies according to conventions of social politeness. There is, in addition, an intellectual etiquette one should observe. Without it, conversation is bickering rather than profitable communication. I am assuming here, of course, that the conversation is about a serious matter on which men can agree or disagree. Then it becomes important that they conduct themselves well. Otherwise, there is no profit in the enterprise. The profit in good conversation is something learned.

What is true of ordinary conversation is even more true of the rather special situation in which a book has talked to a reader and the reader answers back. That the author is well disciplined, we shall take for granted temporarily. That he has conducted his part of the conversation well can be assumed in the case of great books. What *can* the reader do to reciprocate? What *must* he do to hold up his end well?

The reader has an obligation as well as an opportunity to talk back. The opportunity is clear. Nothing can stop a reader from pronouncing judgment. The roots of the obligation, however, lie a little deeper in the nature of the relation between books and readers.

If a book is of the sort which conveys knowledge, the author's aim was to instruct. He has tried to teach. He has tried to convince or persuade his reader about something. His effort is crowned with success only if the reader finally says, "I am taught. You have convinced me that such and such is true, or persuaded me that it is probable." But even if the reader is not convinced or persuaded, the author's intention and effort should be respected. The reader owes him a considered judgment. If he cannot say, "I agree," he should at least have grounds for disagreeing or even for suspending judgment on the question.

I am saying no more than that a good book deserves an active reading. The activity of reading does not stop with the work of understanding what a book says. It must be completed by the work of criticism, the work of judging. The passive reader sins against this requirement, probably even more than against the rules of analysis and interpretation. He not only makes no effort to understand; he dismisses a book simply by putting it down or forgetting it. Worse than faint praise, he damns it by no critical consideration whatsoever.

- 2 -

What I mean by talking back, you now can see, is not something apart from reading. It is the third way in which a book must be read. There are rules here as in the case of the other two readings. Some of these are general maxims of intellectual etiquette. We shall deal with them in this chapter. Others are more specific criteria for defining the points of criticism. They will be discussed in the next chapter.

There is a tendency to think that a good book is above the criticism of the average reader. The reader and the author are not peers. The author is subject to trial only by a jury of his peers. Remember Bacon's recommendation to the reader: "Read not to contradict and confute; not to believe and take for granted; nor to find talk and discourse; but to weigh and consider." Sir Walter Scott casts even more direful aspersions on those "who read to doubt or read to scorn."

There is a certain truth here, as we shall see, but I do not like the aura of impeccability with which books are thus surrounded, and the false piety it breeds. Readers may be like children, in the sense that great authors can teach them, but that does not mean they must not be heard from. I am not sure Cervantes was right in saying, "There is no book so bad but something good may be found in it." I do think, however, that there is no book so good that fault cannot be found with it.

It is true that a book which can enlighten its readers, and is in this sense their better, should not be criticized by them until they understand it. When they do, they have elevated themselves almost to peerage with the author. Now they are fit to exercise the rights and privileges of their new position. Unless they exercise their critical faculties now, they are doing the author an injustice. He has done what he could to make them his equal. He deserves that they act like his peers, that they engage in conversation with him, that they talk back.

As I pointed out before, docility is generally confused with subservience. (We tend to forget that the word "docile" is derived from the Latin root which means to teach or be taught.) A person is wrongly thought to be docile if he is passive and pliable. On the contrary, docility is the extremely active virtue of being teachable. No one is really teachable who does not freely exercise his power of independent judgment. The most docile reader is, therefore, the most critical. He is the reader who finally responds to a book by the greatest effort to make up his own mind on the matters the author has discussed.

I say "finally" because docility requires that a teacher be fully heard and, more than that, understood, before he is judged. I should add also that sheer amount of effort is not an adequate criterion of docility. The reader must know how to judge a book, just as he must know how to arrive at an understanding of its contents. This third group of rules for reading is a guide to the last stage in the disciplined exercise of docility.

We have everywhere found a certain reciprocity between the art of teaching and the art of being taught, between the skill of the author which makes him a considerate writer and the skill of the reader which makes him handle a book considerately. We have seen how the same principles of grammar and logic underlie rules of good writing as well as rules of good reading. The rules we have so far discussed concern the achievement of intelligibility on the part of the writer and the achievement of understanding on the part of the reader. This last set of rules goes beyond understanding to critical judgment. Here is where rhetoric comes in.

There are, of course, many uses of rhetoric. We usually think of it in connection with the orator or propagandist. But in its most general significance, rhetoric is involved in every situation in which communication takes place among men. If we are the talkers, we wish not only to be understood but to be agreed with in some sense. If our purpose in trying to communicate is serious, we wish to convince or persuade—more precisely, to convince about theoretical matters and to persuade about matters that ultimately affect action or feeling.

To be equally serious in receiving such communication, one must be not only a responsive but a responsible listener. You are responsive to the extent that you follow what has been said and note the intention which prompts it. But you also have the responsibility of taking a position. When you take it, it is yours, not the author's. To regard anyone except yourself as responsible for your judgment is to be a slave, not a freeman.

On the part of the speaker or writer, rhetorical skill is knowing how to convince or persuade. Since this is the ultimate end in view, all the other aspects of communication must serve it. Grammatical and logical skill in writing clearly and intelligibly has virtue in itself, but it is also a means to an end. Reciprocally, on the part of the reader or listener, rhetorical skill is knowing how to react to anyone who tries to convince or persuade us. Here, too, grammatical and logical skill, which enables us to understand what is being said, prepares the way for a critical reaction.

- 3 -

Thus you see how the three arts of grammar, logic, and rhetoric co-operate in regulating the elaborate processes of writing and reading. Skill in the first two readings comes from a mastery of grammar and logic. Skill in the third depends on the remaining art. The rules of this third reading rest on the principles of rhetoric, conceived in the broadest sense. We shall consider them as a code of etiquette to make the reader not only polite but effective in talking back.

You probably also see what the first rule is going to be. It has been intimated several times already. It is simply that you must not begin to talk back until you have listened carefully and are sure you understand. Not until you are honestly satisfied that you have accomplished the first two readings should you feel free to express yourself. When you have, you not only can justifiably turn critic, but you should.

This means that the third reading must always follow the other two in time. You have already seen how the first two readings interpenetrate each other. They are separate in time only for the beginner, and even he may have to combine them somewhat. Certainly, the expert reader can discover the contents of a book by analyzing the whole into its parts and, at the same time, constructing the whole out of its elements of thought and knowledge, its terms, propositions, and arguments. But the expert no less than the beginner must wait until he understands before he is justified in criticizing.

Let me restate this first rule of critical reading in the following form. *You must be able to say, with reasonable certainty, "I understand," before you can say any one of the following things: "I agree," or "I disagree," or "I suspend judgment."* These three remarks exhaust all the critical positions you can take. I hope you have not made the error of supposing that to criticize is always to disagree. That is an unfortunate, popular misconception. To agree is just as much an exercise of critical judgment on your part as to disagree. You can be just as wrong in agreeing as in disagreeing. To agree without understanding is inane. To disagree without understanding is impudent.

Though it may not be so obvious at first, suspending judgment is also an act of criticism. It is taking the position that something has not been shown. You are saying that you are not convinced or persuaded one way or the other.

This rule seems to be such obvious common sense that you may wonder why I have bothered to state it so explicitly. I have two reasons. In the first place, many people make the error I mentioned above of identifying criticism with disagreement. In the second place, though this rule seems obviously sound, my experience has been that few people observe it in practice. Like the golden rule, it elicits more lip service than intelligent obedience.

I have had the experience, shared by all authors, of suffering book reviews by critics who did not feel obliged to do the first reading first. The critic too often thinks he does not have to be a reader as well as a judge. I have also had the experience of lecturing, both in the university and on the public platform, and of having critical questions asked which were not based on any understanding of what I had said. (By a "critical question" here, I mean that rhetorical device by which someone in the audience tries to show the speaker up.) And you may remember an occasion where someone said to a speaker, in one breath or at most two, "I don't know what you mean, but I think you're wrong."

I have gradually learned that there is no point in answering critics of this sort. The only polite thing to do is to ask them to state your position for you, the position they claim to be challenging. If they cannot do it satisfactorily, if they cannot repeat what you have said *in their own words,* you know that they do not understand, and you are entirely justified in ignoring their criticisms. They are irrelevant, as all criticism must be which is not solidly based on understanding. When you find the rare person who shows that he understands what you are saying as well as you do, then you can delight in his agreement or be seriously disturbed by his dissent.

In years of reading books with students, I have found this rule more honored in the breach than in the observance. Students who plainly do not know what the author is saying seem to have no hesitation in setting themselves up as his judges. They not only disagree with something they do not understand but, what is equally bad, they often agree to a position they cannot express intelligibly in their own way. Their discussion, like their reading, is all words, words, words. Where understanding is not present, affirmations and denials are equally meaningless and unintelligent. Nor is a position of doubt or detachment any more intelligent in a reader who does not know what he is suspending judgment about.

There are several further points to note concerning the observance of this first rule. If you are reading a great book, you ought to hesitate before you say, "I understand." The presumption certainly is that you have a lot of work to do before you can make that declaration honestly and with assurance. You must, of course, be a judge of yourself in this matter, and that makes the responsibility even more severe.

To say "I don't understand" is, of course, a critical judgment, but only after you have tried your hardest does it reflect on the book rather than yourself. If you have done everything that can be expected of you and still do not understand, it may be because the book is unintelligible. The presumption, however, is in favor of the book, especially if it be a great one. In reading great books, failure to understand is usually the reader's fault. Hence he is obligated to stay with the task of the first two readings a long time before entering on the third. When you say "I don't understand" watch your tone of voice. Be sure it concedes the possibility that it may not be the author's fault.

There are two other conditions under which the rule requires especial care. If you are reading only part of a book, it is more difficult to be sure that you understand, and hence you should be more hesitant to criticize. And sometimes a book is related to other books by the same author, and depends upon them for its full significance. In this situation, also, you should be more circumspect about saying "I understand," and slower to raise your critical lance.

The best example of brashness in this last respect is furnished by literary critics who have agreed or disagreed with Aristotle's *Poetics* without realizing that the main principles in Aristotle's analysis of poetry depend in part on points made in other of his works, his treatises on psychology and logic and metaphysics. They have agreed or disagreed without understanding what it is all about.

The same is true of other writers, such as Plato and Kant, Adam Smith and Karl Marx, who have not been able to say everything they thought or knew in a single work. Those who judge Kant's *Critique of Pure Reason* without reading his *Critique of Practical Reason,* or Adam Smith's *Wealth of Nations* without reading his *Theory of the Moral Sentiments,* or *The Communist Manifesto* without Marx's *Das Kapital,* are more likely than not to be agreeing or disagreeing with something they do not fully understand.

- 4 -

The second general maxim of critical reading is as obvious as the first, but needs explicit statement, nevertheless, for the same reason. It is that *there is no point in winning an argument if you know or suspect you are wrong.* Practically, of course, it may get you ahead in the world for a short time. But honesty is the better policy in the slightly longer run.

As thus stated, I learned the maxim from Mr. Beardsley Ruml, at the time he was dean of the Social Science Division in Chicago. He formulated it in the light of many sad experiences, both in the academic world and out. He has since become a leader in the mercantile world, and he still finds it true that many people think a conversation is an occasion for personal aggrandizement. They think that winning the argument is what matters, not learning the truth.

He who regards conversation as a battle can win only by being an antagonist, only by disagreeing successfully, whether he is right or wrong. The reader who approaches a book in this spirit reads it only to find something he can disagree with. For the disputatious and contentious, a bone can always be found to pick on. It makes no difference whether the bone is really a chip off the other man's shoulder. What is sought is a *casus belli*—like an incident in the Far East or in middle Europe.

Now in a conversation which a reader has with a book in the privacy of his own study, there is nothing to prevent the reader from winning the argument. He can dominate the situation. The author is not there to defend himself. If all he wants is the empty satisfaction of seeming to show the author up, he can get it readily. He scarcely has to read the book through to get it. Glancing at the first few pages will suffice.

But if he realizes that the only profit in conversation, with live or dead teachers, is what one can learn from them, if he realizes that you win only by gaining knowledge, not by knocking the other fellow down, he may see the futility of mere contentiousness. I am not saying that a reader should not ultimately disagree and try to show where the author is wrong. I am saying only that he should be as prepared to agree as to disagree. Whichever he does should be motivated by one consideration alone—the facts and the truth about them.

More than honesty is required here. It goes without saying that a reader should admit a point when he sees it. But he also should not *feel* whipped by having to agree with an author, instead of dissenting. If he feels that way, he is chronically disputatious. In the light of this second maxim, I would advise him to go to a psychoanalyst before he tries to do much serious reading.

- 5 -

The third maxim is closely related to the second. It states another condition prior to the undertaking of criticism. It recommends *that you regard disagreements as capable of being resolved.* Where the second maxim urged you not to disagree *disputatiously,* this one warns you against disagreeing *hopelessly.* One is hopeless about the fruitfulness of discussion if one does not recognize that all rational men can agree. Note that I said *"can* agree." I did not say all rational men *do* agree. I am saying that even when they do not agree, they can. And the point I am trying to make is that disagreement is futile agitation unless it is undertaken with the hope that it may lead to the resolution of an issue.

These two facts, that men do disagree and can agree, arise from the complexity of human nature. Men are rational animals. Their rationality is the source of their power to agree. Their animality, and the imperfections of their reason which it entails, is the cause of most of the disagreements that occur. They are creatures of passion and prejudice. The language they must use to communicate is an imperfect medium, clouded by emotion and colored by interest as well as inadequately transparent for thought. Yet to the extent that men are rational, these obstacles to their understanding one another can be overcome. The sort of disagreement which is only apparent, resulting from misunderstanding, is certainly curable.

There is, of course, another sort of disagreement, which is due to inequalities of knowledge. The ignorant often foolishly disagree with the learned about matters exceeding their knowledge. The more learned, however, have a right to be critical of errors made by those who lack relevant knowledge. Disagreements of this sort can also be corrected. Inequality in knowledge is always curable by instruction.

In other words, I am saying that all human disagreements can be resolved by the removal of misunderstanding or of ignorance. Both cures are always possible, though sometimes difficult. Hence the man who, at any stage of a conversation, disagrees, should at least hope to reach agreement in the end. He should be as much prepared to have his own mind changed as seek to change the mind of another. He should always keep before him the possibility that he misunderstands or that he is ignorant on some point. No one who looks upon disagreement as an occasion for teaching another should forget that it is also an occasion for being taught.

But the trouble is that many people regard disagreement as unrelated to either teaching or being taught. They think that everything is just a matter of opinion. I have mine. You have yours. Our right to our opinions is as inviolable as our right to private property. On such a view, communication cannot be profitable if the profit to be gained is an increase in knowledge. Conversation is hardly better than a ping-pong game of opposed opinions, a game in which no one keeps score, no one wins, and everyone is satisfied because he ends up holding the same opinions he started with.

I cannot take this view. I think that knowledge can be communicated and that discussion can result in learning. If knowledge, not opinion, is at stake, then either disagreements are apparent only—to be removed by coming to terms and a meeting of minds; or, if they are real, then the genuine issues can always be resolved—in the long run, of course—by appeals to fact and reason. The maxim of rationality concerning disagreements is to be patient for the long run. I am saying, in short, that disagreements are arguable matters. And argument is both empty and vicious unless it is undertaken on the supposition that there is attainable truth which, when attained by reason in the light of all the relevant evidence, resolves the original issues.

How does this third maxim apply to the conversation between reader and author? It deals with the situation in which the reader finds himself disagreeing with something in a book. It requires him first to be sure that the disagreement is not due to misunderstanding. Suppose that the reader has been careful to observe the rule that he must not begin a critical reading until he understands, and is therefore satisfied that there is no misunderstanding here. What then?

This maxim then requires him to distinguish between knowledge and opinion, and to regard an issue concerning knowledge as one which can be resolved. If he pursues the matter further he may be instructed by the author on points which will change his mind. If that does not happen, he may be justified in his criticism, and, metaphorically at least, be able to instruct the author. He can at least hope that were the author alive and present, his mind could be changed.

You may remember something that was said in the previous chapter. If an author does not give reasons for his propositions, they can be treated only as expressions of opinion on his part. The reader who does not distinguish between the reasoned statement of knowledge and the flat expression of opinion is not reading to learn. He is at most interested in the author's personality and is using the book as a case history. Such a reader will, of course, neither agree nor disagree. He does not judge the book but the man.

If, however, the reader is primarily interested in the book and not the man—if, seeking to learn, he looks for knowledge not opinion—he should take his critical obligations seriously. The distinction between knowledge and opinion applies to him as well as to the author. The reader must do more than make judgments of agreement or disagreement. He must give reasons for them. In the former case, of course, it suffices if he actively share the author's reasons for the point on which they agree. But when he disagrees, he must give his own grounds for doing so. Otherwise, he is treating a matter of knowledge as if it were opinion.

Let me summarize now the three general maxims I have discussed. The three together state the conditions of a critical reading and the manner in which the reader should proceed to talk back.

The first requires the reader to complete the task of understanding before rushing in. The second adjures him not to be disputatious or contentious. The third asks him to view disagreement about matters of knowledge as remediable. It goes further. It commands him to give reasons for his disagreements so that issues are not merely stated but defined. In that lies all hope for resolution.

- ◆◆◆◆◆ -

CHAPTER THIRTEEN

The Things the Reader Can Say

- I -

THE first thing a reader can say is that he understands or that he does not. In fact, he must say he understands, in order to say more. If he does not understand, he should keep his peace and go back to work on the first two readings of the book.

There is one exception to the harshness of the second alternative. "I don't understand" may be itself a critical remark. To make it so, the reader must be able to support it. If the fault is with the book rather than himself, the reader must locate the sources of trouble. He should be able to show that the structure of the book is disorderly, that its parts do not hang together, that some of it lacks relevance. Or, perhaps, the author equivocates in the use of important words, with a whole train of consequent confusions. To the extent that a reader can support his charge that the book is unintelligible, he has no further critical obligations.

Let us suppose, however, that you are reading a good book. That means it is a relatively intelligible one. And let us suppose that you are finally able to say, "I understand." If in addition to understanding the book, you agree thoroughly with what the author says, the work is over. The reading is completely done. You have been enlightened, and convinced or persuaded. It is clear that we have additional steps to consider only in the case of disagreement or suspended judgment. The former is the more usual case. We shall deal mainly with it in this chapter.

To the extent that authors argue with their readers— and expect their readers to argue back—the good reader must be acquainted with the principles of argument. He must be able to carry on polite, as well as intelligent, controversy. That is why there is need for a chapter of this sort in a book on reading. Not simply by *following* an author's arguments, but only by *meeting* them as well, can the reader ultimately reach significant agreement or disagreement with his author.

The meaning of agreement and disagreement deserves a moment's further consideration. The reader who comes to terms with an author, and grasps his propositions and reasoning, is *en rapport* with the author's mind. In fact, the whole process of interpretation is directed toward a meeting of minds through the medium of language. Understanding a book can be described as a kind of agreement between writer and reader. They agree about the use of language to express ideas. Because of that agreement, the reader is able to see through the author's language to the ideas he is trying to express.

If the reader understands a book, then how can he disagree with it? Critical reading demands that he make up his own mind. But his mind and the author's have become as one through his success in understanding the book. What mind has he left to make up independently?

There are some people who make the error which causes this apparent difficulty. They fail to distinguish between two senses of "agreement." In consequence, they wrongly suppose that where there is understanding between men.

disagreement is impossible. They say that all disagreement is simply due to misunderstanding.

The error is corrected as soon as we remember that the author is making judgments about the world in which we live. He claims to be giving us theoretic knowledge about the way things exist and behave, or practical knowledge about what should be done. Obviously, he can be either right or wrong. His claim is justified only to the extent that he speaks truly, or says what is probable in the light of evidence. Otherwise, his claim is unfounded.

If you say, for instance, that "all men are equal," I may take you to mean that all men are equally endowed at birth with intelligence, strength, and other abilities. In the light of the facts as I know them, I disagree with you. I think you are wrong. But suppose I have misunderstood you. Suppose you meant by these words that *all men should have equal political rights.* Because I misapprehended your meaning, my disagreement was irrelevant. Now suppose the mistake corrected. Two alternatives still remain. I can agree or disagree, but now if I disagree, there is a real issue between us. I understand your political position but hold a contrary one.

Issues about matters of fact or policy—issues about the way things are or should be—are real only when they are based on a common understanding of what is being said. Agreement about the use of words is the absolutely indispensable condition for genuine agreement or disagreement about the facts being discussed. It is because of, not in spite of, your meeting the author's mind through a sound interpretation of his book that you are able to make up your own mind as concurring in or dissenting from the position he has taken.

- 2 -

Now let us consider the situation in which, having said you understand, you proceed to disagree. If you have tried to abide by the maxims stated in the previous chapter, you disagree because you think the author can be shown to be wrong on some point. You are not simply voicing your prejudice or expressing your emotions.

What seems to me now like many years ago, I wrote a book called *Dialectic*. It was my first book, and wrong in many ways, but at least it was not as pretentious as its title. It was about the art of intelligent conversation, the etiquette of controversy.

My chief error was in thinking that there are two sides to every question, that is, two sides both of which could be equally right. I did not know then how to distinguish between knowledge and opinion. Despite this error, I think I rightly suggested three conditions which must be satisfied in order for controversy to be well conducted.

Since men are animals as well as rational, it is necessary to acknowledge the emotions you bring to a dispute, or those which arise in the course of it. Otherwise you are likely to be giving vent to feelings, not stating reasons. You may even think you have reasons, when all you have are strong feelings.

Furthermore, you must make your own assumptions explicit. You must know what your prejudices—that is, your *prejudgments*—are. Otherwise you are not likely to admit that your opponent may be equally entitled to different assumptions. Good controversy should not be a quarrel about assumptions. If an author, for example, explicitly asks you to take something for granted, the fact that the opposite can also be taken for granted should not prevent you from honoring his request. If your prejudices lie on the opposite side, and if you do not acknowledge them to be prejudices, you cannot give the author's case a fair hearing.

Finally, I suggested that an attempt at impartiality is a good antidote for the blindness that is inevitable in partisanship. Controversy without partisanship is, of course, impossible. But to be sure that there is more light in it, and less heat, each of the disputants should at least try to take the other fellow's point of view. If you have not been able to read a book sympathetically, your disagreement with it is probably more contentious than judicial.

I still think that these three conditions are the *sine qua non* of intelligent and profitable conversation. They are obviously applicable to reading, in so far as that is a kind of conversation between reader and author. Each of them contains sound advice for readers who are willing to respect the decencies of disagreement.

But I have grown older since I wrote *Dialectic*. And I am a little less optimistic about what can be expected of human beings. I am sorry to say that most of my disillusionment arises from a knowledge of my own defects. I have so frequently violated all of my own rules about good intellectual manners in controversy. I have so often caught myself *attacking* a book rather than *criticizing* it, knocking straw men over, denouncing where I could not support denials, proclaiming my prejudices, as if mine were any better than the author's.

- 3 -

I am still naïve enough, however, to think that conversation and critical reading can be well disciplined. Only now, twelve years later, I am going to substitute for the rules of *Dialectic* a set of prescriptions which may be easier to follow. They indicate the four ways in which a book can be *adversely* criticized. My hope is that if a reader confine himself to making these points, he will be less likely to indulge in expressions of emotion or prejudice.

The four points can be briefly summarized by conceiving the reader as conversing with the author, as talking back. After he has said, "I understand but I disagree," he can make the following remarks: (1) *"You are uninformed"*; (2) *"You are misinformed"*; (3) *"You are illogical, your reasoning is not cogent"*; (4) *"Your analysis is incomplete."*

These may not be exhaustive, though I think they are. In any case, they are certainly the principal points a reader who disagrees can make. They are somewhat independent. Making one of these remarks does not prevent you from making another. Each and all can be made, because the defects they refer to are not mutually exclusive.

But, I should add, the reader cannot make any of these remarks without being definite and precise about the respect in which the author is uninformed or misinformed or illogical. A book cannot be uninformed or misinformed about *everything*. It cannot be totally illogical. Furthermore, the reader who makes any of these remarks must not only make it definitely, by specifying the respect, but he must always support his point. He must give reasons for saying what he does.

The first three remarks are somewhat different from the

fourth, as you will presently see. Let us consider each of them briefly, and then turn to the fourth.

(1) To say that an author is *uninformed* is to say that he lacks some piece of knowledge which is *relevant* to the problem he is trying to solve. Notice here that unless the knowledge, if possessed by the author, would have been relevant, there is no point in making this remark. To support the remark, you must be able yourself to state the knowledge which the author lacks and show how it is relevant, how it makes a difference to his conclusions.

A few illustrations here must suffice. Darwin lacked the knowledge of genetics which the work of Mendel and later experimentalists now provides. His ignorance of the mechanism of inheritance is one of the major defects in *The Origin of Species*. Gibbon lacked certain facts which later historical research has shown to have a bearing on the fall of Rome. Usually, in science and history, the lack of information is discovered by later researches. Improved techniques of observation and prolonged investigation make this the way things happen for the most part. But in philosophy, it may happen otherwise. There is just as likely to be loss as gain with the passage of time. The ancients, for example, clearly distinguished between what men can sense and imagine and what they can understand. Yet, in the eighteenth century, David Hume revealed his ignorance of this distinction between images and ideas, even though it had been so well established by the work of earlier philosophers.

(2) To say that an author is *misinformed* is to say that he asserts what is not the case. His error here may be due to lack of knowledge, but the error is more than that. Whatever its cause, it consists of assertions contrary to fact. The

author is proposing as true or more probable what is in fact false or less probable. He is claiming to have knowledge he does not possess. This kind of defect should be pointed out, of course, only if it is relevant to the author's conclusions. And to support the remark you must be able to argue the truth or greater probability of a position contrary to the author's.

For example, in a political treatise, Spinoza appears to say that democracy is a more primitive type of government than monarchy. This is contrary to well-ascertained facts of political history. Spinoza's error in this respect has a bearing on his argument. Aristotle was misinformed about the role which the male factor played in animal reproduction, and consequently came to unsupportable conclusions about the processes of procreation. Thomas Aquinas erroneously supposed that the heavenly bodies changed only in position, that they were otherwise unalterable. Modern astrophysics corrects this error and thereby improves on ancient and medieval astronomy. But here is an error which has limited relevance. Making it does not affect St. Thomas's metaphysical account of the nature of all sensible things as composed of matter and form.

These first two points of criticism are somewhat related. Lack of information, as we have seen, may be the cause of erroneous assertions. Further, whenever a man is misinformed, he is also uninformed of the truth. But it makes a difference whether the defect be simply negative or positive as well. Lack of relevant knowledge makes it impossible to solve certain problems or support certain conclusions. Erroneous suppositions, however, lead to wrong conclusions and untenable solutions. Taken together, these two points charge an author with defects in his premises.

He needs more knowledge than he possesses. His evidences and reasons are not good enough in quantity or quality.

(3) To say that an author is *illogical* is to say that he has committed a fallacy in reasoning. In general, fallacies are of two sorts. There is the *non sequitur,* which means that what is drawn as a conclusion simply does not follow from the reasons offered. And there is the occurrence of *inconsistency,* which means that two things the author has tried to say are incompatible. To make either of these criticisms, the reader must be able to show the precise respect in which the author's argument lacks cogency. One is concerned with this defect only to the extent that the major conclusions are affected by it. A book may lack cogency in irrelevant respects.

It is more difficult to illustrate this third point, because few great books make obvious slips in reasoning. When they do occur, they are usually elaborately concealed, and it requires a very penetrating reader to discover them. But I can show you a patent fallacy which I found in a recent reading of Machiavelli's *Prince:*

> The chief foundations of all states, new as well as old, are good laws. As there cannot be good laws where the state is not well armed, it follows that where they are well armed they have good laws.

Now it simply does not *follow from* the fact that good laws depend on an adequate police force, *that* where the police force is adequate, the laws will necessarily be good. I am ignoring the highly questionable character of the first fact. I am only interested in the *non sequitur* here. It is truer to say that happiness depends on health (than that good laws depend on an effective police force), but it does not follow that all who are healthy are happy.

In his *Elements of Law,* Hobbes argues in one place that all bodies are nothing but quantities of matter in motion. The world of bodies, he says, has no qualities whatsoever. Then, in another place, he argues that man is himself nothing but a body, or a collection of atomic bodies in motion. Yet, admitting the existence of sensory qualities—colors, odors, tastes, and so forth—he concludes that they are nothing but the motions of atoms in the brain. This conclusion is inconsistent with the position first taken, namely, that the world of bodies in motion is without qualities. What is said of *all* bodies in motion must apply to any particular group of them, including the atoms of the brain.

This third point of criticism is related to the other two. An author may, of course, fail to draw the conclusions which his evidences or principles imply. Then his reasoning is incomplete. But we are here concerned primarily with the case in which he reasons poorly from good grounds. It is interesting, but less important, to discover lack of cogency in reasoning from premises that are themselves untrue, or from evidences that are inadequate.

A person who from sound premises reaches a conclusion invalidly is, in a sense, misinformed. But it is worth while to distinguish the kind of erroneous statement which is due to bad reasoning from the kind previously discussed, due to other defects, especially insufficient knowledge of relevant details.

- 4 -

The first three points of criticism, which we have just considered, deal with the soundness of the author's statements and reasoning. Let us turn now to the fourth adverse remark a reader can make. It deals with the completeness of the author's execution of his plan—the adequacy with which he discharges the task he has chosen.

Before we proceed to this fourth remark, one thing should be observed. Since you have said you understand, your failure to support any of these first three remarks obligates you to agree with the author as far as he has gone. You have no freedom of will about this. It is not your sacred privilege to decide whether you are going to agree or disagree.

Since you have not been able to show that the author is uninformed, misinformed, or illogical on relevant matters, you simply cannot disagree. You must agree. You cannot say, as so many students and others do, "I find nothing wrong with your premises, and no errors in reasoning, but I don't agree with your conclusions." All you can possibly mean by saying something like that is that you do not *like* the conclusions. You are not disagreeing. You are expressing your emotions or prejudices. If you have been convinced, you should admit it. (If, despite your failure to support one or more of these three critical points, you still *honestly feel* unconvinced, perhaps you should not have said you understood in the first place.)

The first three remarks are related to the author's terms, propositions, and arguments. These are the elements he used to solve the problems which initiated his efforts. The fourth remark—that the book is *incomplete*—bears on the structure of the whole.

(4) To say that an author's analysis is *incomplete* is to say that he has not solved all the problems he started with, or that he has not made as good a use of his materials as possible, that he did not see all their implications and ramifications, or that he has failed to make distinctions which are

relevant to his undertaking. It is not enough to say that a book is incomplete. Anyone can say that of any book. Men are finite, and so are their works, every last one. There is no point in making this remark, therefore, unless the reader can define the inadequacy precisely, either by his own efforts as a knower or through the help of other books.

Let me illustrate this point briefly. The analysis of types of government in Aristotle's *Politics* is incomplete. Because of the limitations of his time and his erroneous acceptance of slavery, Aristotle fails to consider, or for that matter even to conceive, the truly democratic constitution which is based on universal manhood suffrage; nor can he imagine either representative government or the modern kind of federated state. His analysis would have to be extended to apply to these political realities. Euclid's *Elements of Geometry* is an incomplete account because he failed to consider other postulates about the relation of parallel lines. Modern geometrical works, making these other assumptions, supply the deficiencies. Dewey's *How We Think*, I pointed out earlier, is an incomplete analysis of thinking because it fails to treat the sort of thinking which occurs in reading or learning by instruction in addition to the sort which occurs in investigation and discovery. To a Christian, believing in personal immortality, Aristotle's *Ethics* is an incomplete account of human happiness because it is limited to happiness in this life.

This fourth point is strictly not a basis for disagreement. It is critically adverse only to the extent that it marks the limitations of the author's achievement. A reader who agrees with a book in part—because he finds no reason to make any of the other points of adverse criticism—may, nevertheless, suspend judgment on the whole, in the light of this fourth point about the book's incompleteness. Suspended judgment on the reader's part responds to an author's failure to solve his problems perfectly.

Related books in the same field can be critically compared by reference to these four criteria. One is better than another in proportion as it speaks more truth and makes fewer errors. If we are reading for knowledge, that book is best, obviously, which most adequately treats a given subject matter. One author may lack information which another possesses; one may make erroneous suppositions from which another is free; one may be less cogent than another in reasoning from similar grounds. But the profoundest comparison is made with respect to the completeness of the analysis which each presents. The measure of such completeness is to be found in the number of valid and significant distinctions which the accounts being compared contain. You may see now how useful it is to have a grasp of the author's terms. The number of distinct terms is correlative with the number of distinctions.

You may also see how the fourth critical remark ties together the three readings of any book. The last step in the first reading is to know the problems which the author is trying to solve. The last step in the second reading is to know which of these problems the author solved and which he did not. The final step of criticism is the point about completeness. It touches the first reading in so far as it considers how adequately the author stated his problems, and the second reading in so far as it measures how satisfactorily he solved them.

- 5 -

We have now completed, in a general way, the enumeration and discussion of the rules of reading. When you have read a book according to these rules, you have done something. I need not tell you. You will feel that way about it yourself. But perhaps I should remind you that these rules describe an ideal performance. Few people have ever read any book in this ideal manner, and those who have, probably read very few books this way. The ideal remains, however, the measure of achievement. You are a good reader in the degree to which you approximate it.

When we speak of someone as "well read," we should have this ideal in mind. Too often, I fear, we use that phrase to mean the quantity rather than the quality of reading. A person who has read widely but not well deserves to be pitied rather than praised, for so much effort has been misguided and profitless.

The great writers have always been great readers, but that does not mean that they read *all* the books which, in their day, were listed as the great and indispensable ones. In many cases, they read fewer books than are now required in some of our better colleges, but what they did read, they read well. Because they had mastered these books, they became peers with their authors. They were entitled to become authorities in their own right. In the natural course of events, a good student frequently becomes a teacher, and so, too, a good reader becomes an author.

My intention here is not to lead you from reading to writing. It is rather to remind you that one approaches the ideal of good reading by applying the rules I have described in the reading of a single book, and not by trying to become superficially acquainted with a large number. There are, of course, many books worth reading well. There is a much larger number which should be only scanned and skimmed. To become well read, in every sense of the word, one must know how to use whatever skill one possesses with discrimination—by reading every book according to its merits.

CHAPTER FOURTEEN

And Still More Rules

- I -

SAITH the Preacher: "Of making many books there is no end, and much study is weariness of the flesh." You probably feel that way about the reading of books by now, and the rules for doing so. I hasten to say, therefore, that this chapter is not going to increase the number of rules you have to worry about. All the basic rules have now been stated in general.

Here I am going to try to be more particular by considering the rules in application to different kinds of books. And I shall return briefly to the problem of extrinsic reading. So far we have kept our nose in the book. There are a few points to make about the utility of looking outside the book you are reading, in order to read it well.

Before I undertake either of these matters, it may be helpful to present all the rules in a single table, each written in the form of a simple prescription.

I. THE ANALYSIS OF A BOOK'S STRUCTURE
   1. *Classify the book according to kind and subject matter.*
   2. *State what the whole book is about with the utmost brevity.*
   3. *Enumerate its major parts in their order and relation, and analyze these parts as you have analyzed the whole.*

    4. *Define the problem or problems the author is trying to solve.*

II. THE INTERPRETATION OF A BOOK'S CONTENTS
    1. *Come to terms with the author by interpreting his basic words.*
    2. *Grasp the author's leading propositions through dealing with his most important sentences.*
    3. *Know the author's arguments, by finding them in, or constructing them out of, sequences of sentences.*
    4. *Determine which of his problems the author solved, and which he did not; and of the latter, decide which the author knew he failed to solve.*

III. THE CRITICISM OF A BOOK AS A COMMUNICATION OF KNOWLEDGE
  A. General Maxims
    1. *Do not begin criticism until you have completed analysis and interpretation. (Do not say you agree, disagree, or suspend judgment, until you can say, "I understand.")*
    2. *Do not disagree disputatiously or contentiously.*
    3. *Respect the difference between knowledge and opinion, by having reasons for any critical judgment you make.*
  B. Specific Criteria for Points of Criticism
    1. *Show wherein the author is uninformed.*
    2. *Show wherein the author is misinformed.*
    3. *Show wherein the author is illogical.*
    4. *Show wherein the author's analysis or account is incomplete.*

Note: Of these, the first three are criteria for disagreement. Failing in all of these, you must agree, in part at least, though you may suspend judgment on the whole, in the light of the fourth point.

In any art or field of practice, rules have a disappointing way of being too general. The more general, of course, the fewer, and that is an advantage. But it is also true that the more general, the more remote they are from the intricacies of the actual situation in which you try to follow them.

I have stated rules generally enough to apply to any instructive book. But you cannot read a book in general. You read this book or that, and every particular book is of a particular sort. It may be a history or a book in mathematics, a political tract or a work in natural science. Hence you must have some flexibility and adaptability in following these rules. I think you will gradually get the feel of how they work on different kinds of books, but I may be able to speed the process somewhat by a few indications of what to expect.

In Chapter Seven we excluded from consideration all belles-lettres—novels, plays, and lyrics. I am sure you see now that *these* rules of reading do not apply to fiction. (There is, of course, a parallel set of rules which I shall try to suggest in the following chapter.) Then, in Chapter Eight we saw that the basic division of expository books is into the practical and the theoretical—books that are concerned with problems of action and books that are concerned only with something to be known. I propose now that we examine the nature of practical books a little further.

- 2 -

The most important thing about any practical book is that it can never *solve* the practical problems with which it is concerned. A theoretical book can solve its own problems. Questions about the nature of something can be answered completely in a book. But a practical problem can only be solved by action itself. When your practical problem is how to earn a living, a book on how to make friends and influence people cannot solve it, though it may suggest things to do. Nothing short of the doing solves the problem. It is solved only by earning a living.

Take this book, for example. It is a practical book. If your interest in it is practical, you want to solve the problem of learning to read. You would not regard that problem as solved and done away with until you did learn. This book cannot solve the problem for you. It can only help. You must actually go through the activity of reading, not merely this book, but others. That is what I mean by saying that nothing but action solves practical problems, and action occurs only in the world, not in books.

Every action takes place in a particular situation, always in the here and now and under these special circumstances. You cannot act in general. The kind of practical judgment which immediately precedes action must be highly particular. It can be expressed in words, but it seldom is. It is almost never found in books, because the author of a practical book cannot envisage the concrete practical situations in which his readers may have to act. Try as he will to be helpful, he cannot give them really concrete practical advice. Only another person in exactly the same situation could do that.

Practical books can, however, state more or less general rules which apply to a lot of particular situations of the same general sort. Whoever tries to use such books must apply the rules to particular cases and, therefore, must exercise practical judgment in doing so. In other words, the reader himself must add something to the book to make it applicable in practice. He must add his knowledge of the particular situation, and his judgment of how the rule applies to the case.

Any book which contains rules—prescriptions, maxims, or any sort of general directions—you will readily recognize as a practical book. But a practical book may contain more than rules. It may try to state the principles which underlie the rules and make them intelligible. For example, in this practical book about reading, I have tried here and there to explain the rules by brief expositions of grammatical and logical principles. The principles which underlie rules are usually in themselves scientific, that is, they are items of theoretic knowledge. Taken together, they are the theory of the thing. Thus, we talk about the theory of bridge building or the theory of bridge whist. We mean the theoretical principles which make the rules of good procedure what they are.

Practical books fall into two main groups. Some, like this one and the cookbook and the driver's manual, are primarily presentations of rules. Whatever other discussion they contain is for the sake of the *rules*. I know of no great book of this sort. The other kind of practical book is primarily concerned with the *principles which generate rules*. All the great books in economics, politics, and morals are of this sort.

I do not mean that the distinction is sharp and absolute.

Both principles and rules may be found in the same book. The point is only one of relative emphasis. You will have no difficulty in sorting books into these two piles. The book of rules in any field will always be immediately recognizable as practical. The book of practical principles may look at first like a theoretical book. In a sense it is, as we have seen. It deals with the theory of a particular kind of practice. You can always tell it is practical, however. The nature of its problems gives it away. It is always about a field of human behavior in which men can do better or worse.

In reading a book which is primarily a rulebook, the major propositions to look for, of course, are the rules. A rule is most directly expressed by an imperative rather than a declarative sentence. It is a command. It says: "Save nine, by taking a stitch in time." It can also be expressed declaratively, as when we say, "A stitch in time saves nine." Both forms of statement suggest—the imperative a little more emphatically—that it is worth while to be prompt in order to save nine stitches.

Whether it is stated declaratively or in the form of direct command, you can always recognize a rule because it recommends something as worth doing to gain a certain end. Thus, the rule of reading which commands you to come to terms can also be stated as a recommendation: good reading involves coming to terms. The word "good" is the giveaway here. That such reading is worth doing is implied.

The arguments in a practical book of this sort will be attempts to show you that the rules are sound. The writer may have to appeal to principles to persuade you that they are, or he may simply illustrate their soundness by showing you how they work in concrete cases. Look for both sorts of arguments. The appeal to principles is usually less persuasive, but it has one advantage. It can explain the reason for the rules better than examples of their use can.

In the other kind of practical book, dealing mainly with the principles underlying rules, the major propositions and arguments will, of course, look exactly like those in a purely theoretical book. The propositions will say that something is the case, and the arguments will try to show that it is so.

But there is an important difference between reading such a book and a purely theoretical one. Since the ultimate problems to be solved are practical—problems of action— an intelligent reader of such books about "practical principles" always reads between the lines or in the margins. He tries to see the rules which may not be expressed but can, nevertheless, be derived from the principles. He may go even further. He may try to figure out how the rules should be applied in practice.

Unless it is so read, a practical book is not read *as practical.* To fail to read a practical book *as practical* is to read it poorly. You really do not understand it, and you certainly cannot criticize it properly in any other way. If the intelligibility of rules is to be found in principles, it is no less true that the significance of practical principles is to be found in the rules they lead to, the actions they recommend.

This indicates what you must do to understand either sort of practical book. It also indicates the ultimate criteria for critical judgment. In the case of purely theoretical books, the criteria for agreement or disagreement relate to the truth of what is being said. But practical truth is different from theoretic truth. A rule of conduct is practically true on two conditions: one is that it works; the other is that its working leads you to the right end, an end you rightly desire.

Suppose that the end which an author thinks you should

seek does not seem like the right one to you. Even though his recommendations may be practically sound, in the sense of getting you to that end, you will not agree with him ultimately. And your judgment of his book as practically true or false will be made accordingly. If you do not think careful and intelligent reading is worth doing, this book has little practical truth for you, however sound my rules may be.

Notice what this means. In judging a theoretic book, the reader must observe the identity of, or the discrepancy between, his own basic principles or assumptions and those of the author. In judging a practical book, everything turns on the ends or goals. If you do not share Karl Marx's fervor about economic justice, his economic doctrine and the reforms it suggests are likely to seem practically false or irrelevant. You may think that preserving the *status quo* is a more desirable objective than removing the iniquities of capitalism. In that case, you are likely to think that revolutionary documents are preposterously false. Your main judgment will always be in terms of the ends, not the means. We have no practical interest in even the soundest means to reach ends we do not care about.

- 3 -

This brief discussion gives you a clue to the two major questions you must ask yourself in reading any sort of practical book. The first is: What are the author's objectives? The second is: What means is he proposing? It may be more difficult to answer these questions in the case of a book about principles than in the case of one about rules. The ends and means are likely to be less obvious. Yet answering them in either case is necessary for the understanding and criticism of a practical book.

It also reminds you of one aspect of practical writing we noted earlier. There is an admixture of oratory or propaganda in every practical book. I have never read a political book—however theoretical it may appear, however "abstract" the principles with which it deals—that did not try to persuade the reader about "the best form of government." Similarly, moral treatises try to persuade the reader about "the good life" as well as recommend ways of leading it.

You can see why the practical author must always be something of an orator or propagandist. Since your ultimate judgment of his work is going to turn on your acceptance of the goal for which he is proposing means, it is up to him to win you to his ends. To do this, he has to argue in a way that appeals to your heart as well as your mind. He may have to play on your emotions and gain direction of your will. That is why I call him an orator or propagandist.

There is nothing wrong or vicious about this. It is of the very nature of practical affairs that men have to be persuaded to think and act in a certain way. Neither practical thinking nor action is an affair of the mind alone. The guts cannot be left out. No one makes serious practical judgments or engages in action without being moved somehow from below the neck. The writer of practical books who does not realize this will be ineffective. The reader of them who does not is likely to be sold a bill of goods without his knowing it.

The best protection against propaganda of any sort is the complete recognition of it for what it is. Only hidden and undetected oratory is insidious. What reaches the heart without going through the mind is likely to bounce back and put the mind out of business. Propaganda taken in that way is like a drug you do not know you are swallowing. The effect is mysterious. You do not know afterwards why you feel or think the way you do. But putting alcohol in your drink in a recognized dosage can give you a lift you need and know how to use.

The person who reads a practical book intelligently, who knows its basic terms, propositions, and arguments, will always be able to detect its oratory. He will spot the passages which make an "emotive use of words." Aware that he must be subject to persuasion, he can do something about weighing the appeals. He has sales resistance. But do not make the error of supposing that sales resistance must be one hundred per cent. It is good when it prevents you from buying hastily and thoughtlessly. But it should not withdraw you from the market entirely. The reader who supposes he should be totally deaf to all appeals might just as well not read practical books.

There is one further point here. Because of the nature of practical problems and because of the admixture of oratory in all practical writing, the "personality" of the author is more important in the case of practical books than theoretical. Both in order to understand and to judge a moral treatise, a political tract, or an economic discussion, you should know something about the character of the writer, something about his life and times. In reading Aristotle's *Politics,* it is highly relevant to know that Greek society was based on slavery. Similarly, much light is thrown on *The Prince* by knowing the Italian situation at the time of Machiavelli, and his relation to the Medicis; or, in the case of Hobbes' *Leviathan,* to know that Hobbes lived during the English civil wars and was pathologically distressed by social violence and disorder.

Sometimes the author tells you about himself, his life, and times. Usually he does not do so explicitly, and when he does, his deliberate revelation of himself is seldom adequate or dependable. Hence reading his book and nothing else may not suffice. To understand it and to judge it, you may have to read other books, books about him and his times, or books which he himself read and reacted to.

Any aid to reading which lies outside the book being read is extrinsic. You may remember that I distinguished between intrinsic rules and extrinsic aids in Chapter Seven. Well, the reading of *other* books is one of the most obvious extrinsic aids in reading a particular book. Let me call this aid "extrinsic reading." I can summarize my point here simply by saying that extrinsic reading about the author is much more important for interpreting and criticizing practical books than theoretical ones. Remember this as an additional rule to guide you in reading practical books.

- 4 -

Now let us turn to the large class of theoretic books and see if there are any additional rules there. I must break this large class up into three major divisions, which I have already named and discussed in Chapter Eight: *history, science,* and *philosophy.* In order to deal briefly with a complicated matter, I shall discuss only two things in connection with each of these types of books. I shall first consider whatever is peculiar to the problems of that type of book— its terms, propositions, and arguments—and then discuss whatever extrinsic aids are relevant.

You already know the point about a history book being a combination of knowledge and poetry. All of the great historical works are narratives. They tell a story. Any story must have a plot and characters. It must have episodes, complications of action, a climax, and an aftermath. These are the elements of a history, viewed as a narrative—not terms, propositions, and arguments. To understand a history in its poetic aspect, therefore, you must know how to read fiction. I have not yet discussed the rules for doing that, but most people can do this sort of reading with some skill anyway. They know how to follow a story. They also know the difference between a good and a bad story. History may be stranger than fiction, but the historian has to make what happened appear plausible, nevertheless. If he does not, he tells a bad story, a dull one, or even a preposterous one.

I shall discuss in the next chapter the rules for reading fiction. Such rules may help you to interpret and criticize histories in their poetic dimension as narratives. Here I shall confine myself to the logical rules we have already discussed. Applied to histories, they require you to distinguish two kinds of statement you will find. In the first place, there are all the propositions about particular things—events, persons, or institutions. These are, in a sense, the matter of the history, the substance of what is being narrated. In so far as such statements are subject to argument, the author may try to give you, in his text or footnotes, the evidences for believing that things happened this way rather than otherwise.

In the second place, the historian may have some general interpretation of the facts he is narrating. This may be expressed poetically in the way he tells the story—whom he makes the hero, where he places the climax, how he develops the aftermath. But it may also be expressed in certain generalizations he enunciates. You must look for general propositions of this sort. Herodotus, in his history of the Persian wars, tells you early what his major insight is.

> The cities which were formerly great, have most of them become insignificant; and such as are at present powerful, were weak in olden time. I shall therefore discourse equally of both, convinced that *prosperity never continues long in one place.*

I have italicized the generalization which Herodotus exemplifies again and again in the course of his story. He does not try to prove the proposition. He is satisfied with showing you countless instances in which it appears to be true. That is usually the way historians argue for their generalizations.

There are some historians who try to argue for their general insights about the course of human affairs. The Marxist historian not only writes in such a way that the class struggle is always clearly exemplified; he frequently argues that this must be the case in terms of his "theory of history." He tries to show that the economic interpretation is the only one. Another historian, such as Carlyle, tries to show that human affairs are controlled by the action of leaders. This is the "great man" theory of history.

To read a history critically, therefore, you must discover the interpretation a writer places on the facts. You must know his "theory," which means his generalizations and, if possible, the reasons for them. In no other way can you tell why certain facts are selected and others omitted, why stress is placed on this and not on that. The easiest way to catch on is to read two histories of the same thing, written from different points of view. (One of the things which distinguishes history from science is that there can be two or more good histories of the same events—sharply divergent though equally persuasive and creditable. Of a given matter, there is at any time only one good scientific account.)

Extrinsic reading is thus an aid to understanding and judging history books. You may go to other histories, or to reference books, to check on the facts. You may even get interested enough to look into the original documents from which the historian gathered evidence. Reading other books is not the only extrinsic aid to understanding a history. You can also visit the places where things happened, or look at monuments and other relics of the past. The experience of walking around the battlefield at Gettysburg made me realize how much better I should understand the account of Hannibal's invasion had I ever crossed the Alps on the back of an elephant.

I want to stress the reading of other great histories of the same events as the best way to get a line on the bias of a great historian. But there is often more than bias in a history. There is propaganda. A history of something remote in time or place is also often a tract or diatribe for the home folks, as was Tacitus' account of the Germans, and Gibbon's explanation of why Rome fell. Tacitus exaggerated the primitive virtues of the Teutonic tribes to shame the decadence and effeminacy of his fellow Romans. Gibbon stressed the part a rising Christianity had played in a falling Rome to support the freethinkers and anticlericals of his day against the established churchmen.

Of all theoretical books, a history is most like practical books in this respect. Therefore, the advice to a reader is the same. Find out something about the character of the historian. and the local conditions which may have motivated him. Facts of this sort will not only explain his bias but prepare you for the moral lessons he tells you history teaches.

- 5 -

The additional rules for reading scientific works are the easiest to state. By a scientific work, I mean the report of findings or conclusions in some field of research, whether carried on experimentally in a laboratory or by observations of nature in the raw. The scientific problem is always to describe the phenomena as accurately as possible, and to trace the interconnections among different kinds of phenomena.

In the great works of science, there is no oratory or propaganda, though there may be bias in the sense of initial presuppositions. You detect this, and take account of it, by distinguishing what the author assumes from what he establishes through argument. The more "objective" a scientific author is, the more he will explicitly beg you to take this or that for granted. Scientific objectivity is not the absence of initial bias. It is attained by frank confession of it.

The leading terms in a scientific work are usually expressed by uncommon or technical words. They are relatively easy to spot, and through them you can readily grasp the propositions. The main propositions are always general ones. A scientist, unlike a historian, tries to get away from locality in time and place. He tries to say how things are generally, how they generally behave.

The only point of difficulty is with respect to the arguments. Science, as you know, is primarily inductive. This means that its primary arguments are those which establish a general proposition by reference to observable evidence—

a single case created by an experiment, or a vast array of cases collected by patient inquiry. There are other arguments of the sort which are called deductive. These are arguments in which a proposition is *proved* by other propositions already somehow established. So far as proof is concerned, science does not differ much from philosophy. But the inductive argument is peculiar to science.

To understand and judge the inductive arguments in a scientific book, you must be able to follow the evidence which the scientist reports as their basis. Sometimes the scientist's description of an experiment performed is so vivid and clear that you have no trouble. Sometimes a scientific book contains illustrations and diagrams which help to acquaint you with the phenomena described.

If these things fail, the reader has only one recourse. He must get the necessary special experience for himself at first hand. He may have to witness a laboratory demonstration. He may have to look at and handle pieces of apparatus similar to those referred to in the book. He may have to go to a museum and observe specimens or models.

That is the reason why St. John's College in Annapolis, where all students read the great books, also requires four years of laboratory work for all students. The student must not only learn how to employ apparatus for precise measurements and laboratory constructions, but he must also become acquainted, through direct experience, with the crucial experiments in the history of science. There are classical experiments as well as classical books. The scientific classics become more intelligible to those who have seen with their own eyes and done with their own hands what a great scientist describes as the procedure by which he reached his insights.

Thus you see how the major extrinsic aid in the reading of scientific books is not the reading of other books but rather getting a direct acquaintance with the phenomena involved. In proportion as the experience to be obtained is highly specialized, it is both more indispensable and more difficult to get.

I do not mean, of course, that extrinsic reading may not be helpful, too. Other books about the same subject matter may throw light on the problems, and help us to be critical of the book we are reading. They may locate points of misinformation, lack of evidence, incompleteness of analysis. But I still think that the primary aid is the one which throws direct light on the inductive arguments that are the heart of any scientific book.

– 6 –

The reading of philosophical works has special aspects which relate to the difference between philosophy and science. I am considering here only theoretic works in philosophy, such as metaphysical treatises or books about the philosophy of nature, because ethical and political books have already been treated. They are practical philosophy.

The philosophical problem is to explain, not to describe, the nature of things. It asks about more than the connection of phenomena. It seeks to penetrate to the ultimate causes and conditions of things, as existing and changing. Such problems are solved only when the answers to them are clearly demonstrated.

The major effort of the reader here must be with respect to the terms and the initial propositions. Although the philosopher also has a technical terminology, the words which express his terms are often taken from common speech and used in a very special sense. This demands special care from the reader. If he does not overcome the tendency to use familiar words in a familiar way, he will probably make gibberish and nonsense of the book. I have seen many people throw a philosophical book away in disgust or irritation, when the fault was theirs, not the author's. They did not even try to come to terms.

The basic terms of philosophical discussion are, of course, abstract. But so are those of science. No general knowledge is expressible except in abstract terms. There is nothing peculiarly difficult about abstractions. We use them every day of our lives and in every sort of conversation. If you substitute the distinction between the particular and the general for that between the concrete and the abstract, you will have less fear of abstractions.

Whenever you talk generally about anything, you are using abstractions. What you can perceive through your senses is concrete and particular. What you think with your mind is always abstract and general. To understand an "abstract word" is to have the idea it expresses. "Having an idea" is just another way of saying that you know a general aspect of something, to which the mind can refer. You cannot see or touch or even imagine the aspect thus referred to. If you could, there would be no difference between the senses and the mind. People who try to *imagine* what ideas refer to befuddle themselves, and end up with that hopeless feeling about all abstractions.

Just as the inductive arguments should be the reader's main focus in the case of scientific books, so here you must pay closest attention to the philosopher's principles. The word "principle" means a beginning. The propositions with which a philosopher begins are his principles. They may be either things he asks you to assume with him, or matters which he calls self-evident.

There is no problem about assumptions. Make them to see what follows, even if you yourself have contrary presuppositions. The clearer you are about your own prejudgments, the more likely you are not to misjudge those made by others.

It is the other sort of principle, however, which may cause you trouble. I know of no philosophical book which does not have some initial propositions the author regards as self-evident. These propositions are like the scientist's inductions in one respect. They are drawn directly from experience rather than proved by other propositions.

The difference lies in the experience from which they are drawn. The philosopher appeals to the common experience of mankind. He does no work in laboratories or research in the field. Hence to understand and test a philosopher's leading principles you do not need the extrinsic aid of special experience. He refers you to your own common sense and daily observation of the world in which you live.

Once you have grasped a philosopher's terms and principles, the rest of your task in reading his book raises no special difficulties. You must follow the proofs, of course. You must note every step he takes in the progress of his analysis—his definitions and distinctions, his ordering of terms. But the same is true in the case of a scientific book. Acquaintance with the evidence, in the one case, and acceptance of the principles, in the other, are the indispensable conditions for following all the remaining arguments.

A good *theoretic* work in philosophy is as free from oratory and propaganda as a good scientific treatise. You do not have to be concerned about the "personality" of the author, or investigate his social and economic backgrounds. There is utility, nevertheless, in doing extrinsic reading in connection with a philosophical book. You should read the works of other great philosophers who dealt with the same problems. The philosophers have carried on a long conversation with one another in the history of thought. You had better listen in on it before you make up your mind about what any one of them says.

The fact that philosophers disagree does not make them different from other men. In reading philosophical books, you must remember, above all, the maxim to respect the difference between knowledge and opinion. The fact of disagreement must not lead you to suppose that everything is just a matter of opinion. Persistent disagreements sometimes locate the great unsolved and, perhaps, insoluble problems. They point to the mysteries. But where problems are genuinely answerable by knowledge, you must not forget that men *can* agree if they will talk to one another long enough.

Do not worry about the disagreement of others. Your responsibility is only for making up your own mind. In the presence of the long conversation which the philosophers have had through their books, you must judge what is true and false. When you have read a philosophical book well —and that means sufficient extrinsic reading as well as skillful interpretation—you are in a position to judge.

The most distinctive mark of philosophical questions is that every man must answer them for himself. Taking the *opinions* of others is not solving them, but evading them. They are answered only by knowledge, and it must be your knowledge. You cannot depend on the testimony of the experts, as you may have to in the case of science.

There are two further points about extrinsic reading in connection with philosophical books. Do not spend all your time reading books about the philosophers, their lives and opinions. Try reading the philosophers themselves, in rela- tion to one another. And in reading ancient and medieval philosophers, or even the early moderns, do not be dis- turbed by the errors or inadequacies of scientific knowledge which their books reveal.

Philosophical knowledge rests directly on common ex- perience and not on the findings of science, not on the re- sults of specialized research. You will see, if you follow the arguments carefully, that the misinformation or lack of in- formation about scientific matters is irrelevant.

This second point makes it important to note the date of the philosopher you are reading. That will not only place him properly in the conversation with those who came be- fore and after, but prepare you for the sort of scientific imagery he will employ to illustrate some of his points. The same urbanity which makes you indulgent of those who speak a foreign tongue should lead you to cultivate a toler- ance for men of wisdom who did not know all the facts we now possess. Both may have something to say that we would be fools not to listen to, simply because of our provincialism.

- 7 -

There are two classes of books I have failed to mention specially. One is mathematics, the other theology. My reason is that at one level of reading, they do not present special problems. And at another, the problems they present are much too complicated and difficult for me to handle here. Perhaps I can say a few simple things about them, however.

In general, the type of proposition and the type of argument in a mathematical book are philosophical rather than scientific. The mathematician like the philosopher is an armchair thinker. He does no experiments. He undertakes no special observations. From principles, which are either self-evident or assumed, he proves his conclusions, and solves his problems.

The difficulty in reading mathematical books arises in part from the kind of symbols the mathematician uses. He writes in a special language, not that of ordinary speech. It has a special grammar, a special syntax, and special rules of operation. In part, also, the precise method of mathematical demonstration is peculiar to this one subject matter. We have already seen many times that Euclid and others who write mathematically have a distinctly different style from that of other authors.

You must know the special grammar and logic of mathematics if you are to become an accomplished reader of mathematical books. The general rules we have discussed can be applied intelligently to this subject matter only through understanding them in the light of special principles. I might add that the logic of scientific argument and of philosophical proof are also different, not only from mathematics, but from each other. The insight I would like you to get here is that there are as many special grammars and logics as there are specifically different applications of the rules of reading to different kinds of books and subject matters.

A word about theology. It differs from philosophy in that its first principles are articles of faith adhered to by the communicants of some religion. Reasoning which rests on premises to which reason can itself attain is philosophi-

cal, not theological. A theological book always depends
upon dogmas and the authority of a church which proclaims
them. If you are not of the faith, if you do not belong to
the church, you can nevertheless read a theological book
well by treating its dogmas with the same respect you treat
the assumptions of the mathematician. But you must remember that an article of faith is not something which the
faithful *assume*. Faith, for those who have it, is the most
certain form of knowledge, not a tentative opinion.

There is one kind of extrinsic reading peculiar to theological works. Those who have faith believe in the revealed
word of God, as that is contained in a sacred scripture.
Thus, Jewish theology requires that its readers be acquainted with the Old Testament, Christian theology with
the New as well, Mohammedan theology with the Koran,
and so forth.

Here I must stop. The problem of reading the Holy
Book—if you have faith that it is the Word of God—is the
most difficult problem in the whole field of reading. There
have been more books written about how to read Scripture
than about all other aspects of the art of reading together.
The Word of God is obviously the most difficult writing
men can read. The effort of the faithful has been duly proportionate to the difficulty of the task. I think it would be
true to say that, in the European tradition at least, the Bible
is *the* book in more senses than one. It has been not only
the most widely read but the most carefully.

- 8 -

Let me close this chapter with a brief summary of the
extrinsic aids to reading. What lies beyond the book you

are reading? Three things, it seems to me, which are especially relevant: experience—common or special; other books; and live discussion. The role of experience as an extrinsic factor is, I think, sufficiently clear. Other books may be of various sorts. They may be reference books, secondary books, and commentaries, or other great books, dealing with the same or with related matters.

Following all the rules of intrinsic reading is seldom sufficient to read any book well, either interpretatively or critically. Experience and other books are indispensable extrinsic aids. In reading books with students, I am as frequently impressed by the fact that they do not employ these aids as that they do not know how to read the book by itself.

Under the elective system, a student takes a course as if it were something quite apart. One course has no connection with another, and no course seems to have any connection with his ordinary affairs, his vital problems, his daily experience. Students who take courses this way read books in the same way. They make no effort to connect one book with another, even when they are most obviously related, or to refer what the author is saying to their own experience. They read about Fascism and Communism in the newspapers. They hear defenses of democracy over the radio. But it never seems to occur to most of them that the great political treatise they may be reading deals with the same problems, though the language it speaks is a little more elegant.

Only last year Mr. Hutchins and I read a series of political works with some students. At first, they tended to read each book as if it existed in a vacuum. Despite the fact that the various authors were plainly arguing about the same thing, they did not seem to think that it was worth while to mention one book in discussing another. But the good students could make all these connections when called upon to do so. We had one of our most exciting class hours after Mr. Hutchins had asked whether Hobbes would have defended Hitler for keeping Pastor Niemöller in a concentration camp. Would Spinoza have tried to get him out? What would Locke have done, and John Stuart Mill?

The problems of free speech and free conscience found dead authors talking about living issues. The students took sides on the Niemöller question, and so did the books— Mill against Hobbes, and Locke against Spinoza. Even if the students could not help Pastor Niemöller, his case had helped them focus the opposition of political principles in the light of their practical consequences. Students who before had seen nothing wrong with Hobbes and Spinoza now began to doubt their prior judgments.

The utility of extrinsic reading is simply an extension of the value of context in reading a book by itself. We have seen how the context must be used to interpret words and sentences to find terms and propositions. Just as the whole book is a context for any of its parts, so related books provide an even larger context that helps you interpret the one you are reading.

I like to think of the great books as involved in a prolonged conversation about the basic problems of mankind. The great authors were great readers, and one way to understand them is to read the books they read. As readers, they carried on a conversation with other authors, just as each of us carries on a conversation with the books we read, though we may not write other books.

To get into this conversation, we must read the great

books in relation to one another, and in an order that somehow respects chronology. The conversation of the books takes place in time. Time is of the essence here and should not be disregarded. The books can be read from the present into the past or from the past into the present. Though I think the order from past to present has certain advantages, through being more natural, the fact of chronology can be observed in either way.

The conversational aspect of reading (the authors conversing with one another, and any reader conversing with his author) explains the third extrinsic factor I mentioned above, namely, live discussion. By live discussion, I mean no more than the actual conversation you and I may have together about a book we have read in common.

While this is not an indispensable aid to reading, it is certainly a great help. That is why Mr. Hutchins and I conduct our course in reading books by meeting with the students to discuss them. The reader who learns to discuss a book well with other readers may come thereby to have better conversations with the author when he has him alone in his study. He may even come to appreciate better the conversation which the authors had with one another.

PART III

THE REST OF
THE READER'S
LIFE

CHAPTER FIFTEEN

- - - - -

The Other Half

◆ I ◆

THIS is only half a book on reading, or perhaps I should say
that so far it has been concerned with only half the reading that most people do. Even that might be too liberal an
estimate. I am not so naïve as to suppose that most of the
reader's life will be spent in reading the great books. Probably the greater part of anybody's reading time is spent on
newspapers and magazines. And so far as books are concerned, most of us read more fiction than nonfiction. True,
the best-seller lists are usually divided in half: fiction and
nonfiction. But although the nonfiction books often reach
large audiences, their total audience is somewhat less than
the audience of fiction, good and bad. Of the nonfiction
books, the most popular are frequently those which, like
the newspapers and magazines, deal with matters of contemporary interest.

I have not deceived you about the rules set forth in preceding chapters. In Chapter Seven, before undertaking a
detailed discussion of the rules, I explained that we would
have to limit ourselves to the business of reading serious
nonfiction books. To expound the rules for reading imaginative and expository literature *at the same time* would be
confusing, and an adequate treatment of the reading of
fiction or poetry could not be managed in less space than
it took to discuss the nonfiction rules. I seemed to be faced
with the choice of writing a much longer book, perhaps

even another one, or ignoring half the reading people do. For the sake of clarity, I took the second alternative while writing the preceding part of this book. But now, when I consider the rest of the reader's life, I cannot ignore the other types of reading any longer. I shall try to make up for these deficiencies, even though I know that a single chapter devoted to all other kinds of reading must be inadequate.

I would be far from frank if I let you think that lack of space was my only shortcoming. I must confess that I have much less competence for the task this chapter undertakes, though I might add, in extenuation, that the problem of knowing how to read imaginative literature is inherently much more difficult. Nevertheless, you may think that the need to formulate rules for reading fiction is less urgent, because more people seem to know how to read fiction and get something out of it than nonfiction.

Observe the paradox here. On the one hand, I say that skill in reading fiction is more difficult to analyze; on the other, it seems to be a fact that such skill is more widely possessed than the art of reading science and philosophy, politics, economics, and history. It may be, of course, that people deceive themselves about their ability to read novels intelligently. If that is not the case, I think I can explain the paradox another way. Imaginative literature delights primarily rather than instructs. It is much easier to be delighted than instructed, but much harder to know *why* one is delighted. Beauty is more elusive, analytically, than truth.

From my teaching experience, I know how tongue-tied people become when asked to say what they liked about a novel. That they enjoyed it is perfectly clear to them, but they cannot give much account of their enjoyment or tell what the book contained which caused them pleasure. This indicates, you may say, that people can be good readers of fiction without being good critics. I suspect this is, at best, a half-truth. A critical reading of anything depends upon the fullness of one's apprehension. Those who cannot say what they like about a novel probably have not read it below its most obvious surfaces.

To make this last point clear would require an explicit formulation of all the rules for reading imaginative literature. Lacking both space and competence to do that, I shall offer you two short cuts. The first proceeds by the *way of negation,* stating the obvious "don'ts" instead of the constructive rules. The second proceeds by the *way of analogy,* briefly translating the rules for reading nonfiction into their equivalents for reading fiction. I shall use the word "fiction" to name all of imaginative literature, including lyric poetry as well as novels and plays. Lyric poetry really deserves a separate and elaborate discussion. In fact, just as in the case of expository books, where the general rules must be particularized for history, science, and philosophy, so here an adequate treatment would have to consider the special problems involved in reading the novel, the drama, and the lyric. But we shall have to be satisfied with much less.

- 2 -

In order to proceed by the way of negation, it is first of all necessary to grasp the basic differences between expository and imaginative literature. These differences will explain why we cannot read a novel as if it were a philosophical argument, or a lyric as if it were a mathematical demonstration.

The most obvious difference, already mentioned, relates to the purposes of the two kinds of writing. Expository books aim primarily to instruct, imaginative ones to delight. The former try to convey knowledge—knowledge about experiences which the reader either has or could have. The latter try to communicate an experience itself—one which the reader can get *only* by reading—and if they succeed they give the reader something to be enjoyed. Because of their diverse intentions, the two sorts of work appeal differently to the intellect and the imagination.

We experience things through the exercise of our senses and imagination. To know anything we must use our powers of judgment and reasoning, which are intellectual. I do not mean that we can think without using our imagination, or that sense experience is ever divorced from some rational reflection. The point is only one of emphasis. Fiction appeals primarily to the imagination. That is the reason for calling it imaginative literature, in contrast to science and philosophy which are intellectual.

We have been considering reading as an activity by which we receive communication from others. If we look a little more deeply now, we shall see that expository books *do* communicate what is eminently and essentially communicable—*abstract knowledge;* whereas imaginative books *try* to communicate what is essentially and profoundly incommunicable—*concrete experience*. There is something mysterious about this. If concrete experience is really incommunicable, by what magic does the poet or novelist hope to convey to you for your enjoyment an experience which he has enjoyed?

Before I answer this question, I must be sure that you fully realize the incommunicability of concrete experience.

Everyone has gone through some intense emotional crisis—
the quick wave of anger, prolonged anxiety about an im-
pending disaster, the cycle of hope and despair in love. Have
you ever tried to tell your friends about it? You can tell
them all the facts without much trouble, because the out-
ward and observable facts are matters of ordinary knowledge and can be easily communicated. But can you give
them the experience itself, in all its concrete inwardness—
the experience which you find difficult even to remember
in its fullness and intensity? If your own memory of it is
pale and fragmentary, how much more so must be the impression you are conveying by your words. As you watch
the faces of your listeners, you can tell that they are not
having the experience you are talking about. And you may
realize then that it takes more narrative art than you possess—an art which is the distinctive possession of the great
imaginative writers.

In one sense, of course, even the greatest writer cannot
communicate his own experiences. They are uniquely his
through all eternity. A man can share his knowledge with
others, but he cannot share the actual pulsations of his life.
Since unique and concrete experience cannot be communicated, the artist does the next best thing. He creates in the
reader what he cannot convey. He uses words to produce
an experience for the reader to enjoy, an experience which
the reader lives through in a manner similar and proportionate to the writer's own. His language so works upon
the emotions and imagination of each reader that each in
turn suffers an experience he has never had before, even
though memories may be evoked in the process. These new
experiences, different for each reader according to his own
individual nature and memories, are nevertheless alike, be-

cause they are all created according to the same model—the incommunicable experiences on which the writer draws. We are like so many instruments for him to play upon, each with its special overtones and resonances, but the music that he plays so differently on each of us follows one and the same score. That score is written into the novel or poem. As we read it, it seems to communicate, but it really creates, an experience. That is the magic of good fiction, which creates imaginatively the similitude of an actual experience.

I cannot substantiate what I have said by quoting a whole novel or play. I can only ask the reader to remember and dwell upon what happened to him while he was reading some fiction which moved him deeply. Did he learn facts about the world? Did he follow arguments and proofs? Or did he suffer a novel experience actually created in his imagination during the process of reading?

I can, however, quote a few short and simple lyrics, widely familiar. The first is by Robert Herrick:

> *Whenas in silks my Julia goes,*
> *Then, then, methinks, how sweetly flows*
> *That liquefaction of her clothes.*
>
> *Next, when I cast mine eyes, and see*
> *That brave vibration, each way free,*
> *O, how that glittering taketh me!*

The second is by Percy Bysshe Shelley:

> *Music, when soft voices die,*
> *Vibrates in the memory—*
> *Odors, when sweet violets sicken,*
> *Live within the sense they quicken.*

> *Rose leaves, when the rose is dead,*
> *Are heaped for the beloved's bed;*
> *And so thy thoughts, when thou art gone,*
> *Love itself shall slumber on.*

The third is by Gerard Manley Hopkins:

> *Glory be to God for dappled things—*
>   *For skies of couple-color as a brindled cow;*
>   *For rose-moles all in stipple upon trout that swim;*
> *Fresh-firecoal chestnut-falls; finches' wings;*
>   *Landscape plotted and pieced—fold, fallow, and plough;*
>   *And all trades, their gear and tackle and trim.*
>
> *All things counter, original, spare, strange;*
>   *Whatever is fickle, freckled (who knows how?)*
>   *With swift, slow; sweet, sour; adazzle, dim;*
> *He fathers-forth whose beauty is past change:*
>   *Praise him.*

Different in their objects and in the complexity of the emotions told about, these lyrics work upon us in the same way. They play upon our senses directly by the music of their words, but more than that, they evoke imaginations and memories which blend into a single whole of significant experience. Each word is counted on to do its part, not only musically in the pattern of sounds but also as a command to remember or imagine. The poet has so directed our faculties that, without being aware of how it happened, we have enjoyed an experience, not of our making but of his. We have not received something from him, as we receive knowledge from a scientific writer. Rather we have suffered ourselves to be the medium of his creation. He has used words to get into our hearts and fancies and move them to an experience that reflects his own as one dream might resemble another. In fact, by some strange manner of effluence, the poet's dream is dreamed differently by each of us.

The basic difference between expository and imaginative literature—that one instructs by communicating, whereas the other delights by recreating what cannot be communicated—leads to another difference. Because of their radically diverse aims, these two kinds of writing necessarily use language differently. The imaginative writer tries to maximize the latent ambiguities of words, thereby to gain all the richness and force that is inherent in their multiple meanings. He uses metaphors as the units of his construction just as the logical writer uses words sharpened to a single meaning. What Dante says of *The Divine Comedy,* that it must be read as having four distinct though related meanings, generally applies to poetry and fiction. The logic of expository writing aims at an ideal of unambiguous explicitness. Nothing should be left between the lines. Everything that is relevant and statable should be said as explicitly and clearly as possible. In contrast, imaginative writing relies upon what is implied rather than upon what is said. The multiplication of metaphors puts more content between the lines than in the words which compose them. The whole poem or novel says something which none of its words say or can say: it speaks the incommunicable experience it has re-created for the reader.

Taking lyric poetry and mathematics as the ideals, or perhaps I should say the two extreme forms of imaginative and expository writing, we can see another and consequent difference between the poetical and logical dimensions of

grammar. A mathematical statement is indefinitely trans-
latable into other statements expressing the same truth. The
great French scientist Poincaré once said that mathematics
was the art of saying the same thing in as many different
ways as possible. Anyone who has watched an equation
undergo the countless transformations to which it is subject
will understand this. At each stage, the actual symbols may
be different or in a different order, but the same mathematical relationship is being expressed. In contrast, a poetic
statement is absolutely untranslatable, not only from one
language to another, but within the same language from
one set of words to another. You cannot say what is said
by "Music, when soft voices die, vibrates in the memory" in
any other English words. Here is no proposition which can
be expressed in many equivalent sentences, all equally
rendering the same truth. Here is a use of words to move the
imagination, not to instruct the mind; in consequence, only
these words, and in this order, can do what the poet con-
trived them for. Any other form of words will create another experience—better or worse, but in any case different.

You may object that I have drawn the line too sharply
between the two kinds of writing. You may insist, for instance, that we can be instructed as well as delighted by imaginative literature. Of course we can, but not in the same
way as we are taught by scientific and philosophical books.
We learn from experience—the experience that we have in
the course of our daily lives. So, too, we can learn from the
vicarious, or artistically created, experiences which fiction
produces in our imagination. In this sense, poetry and
novels instruct as well as delight. The sense in which science
and philosophy teach us is different. Expository books do
not provide us with novel experiences. They comment on

such experiences as we already have or can get. That is why it seems right to say that expository books teach primarily, while imaginative books teach only incidentally, if at all, by creating experiences from which we can learn. In order to learn from such books, we have to do our own thinking about experience; in order to learn from scientists and philosophers, we must first try to understand the thinking they have done.

I have emphasized these various differences in order to state a few negative rules. They do not tell you how to read fiction. They tell you merely what not to do, because fiction is different from science. All of these "don'ts" boil down to one simple insight: don't read fiction as if it were fact; don't read a novel as if it were a scientific work, not even as if it were social science or psychology. This one insight is variously expanded by the following rules.

(1) *Don't try to find a "message" in a novel, play, or poem.* Imaginative writing is not primarily didactic. No great work of fiction is the sugar-coated propaganda that some recent critics would have us believe they all are. (If *Uncle Tom's Cabin* and *The Grapes of Wrath* are good fiction, they are so in spite of, not because of, what they preach.) I am not here making a sharp division between pure art and propaganda, for we know that fiction can move men to action, often more effectively than oratory. My point is rather that fiction has this force only when it is good as fiction—not when it is a sermon or harangue thinly wrapped in a poorly told fable. If the general precept is wise—that you should read a book for what it is—then look for the story, not the message, in books which offer themselves as narratives.

The plays of Shakespeare have been anatomized for cen-

turies to discover their hidden message—as if Shakespeare
had a secret philosophy which he cryptically concealed within his plays. The search has been fruitless. Its failure should
be a classic warning against the misreading of fiction. How
much sounder is the approach which finds each play a new
world of experience that Shakespeare opens for us. Mark
Van Doren, in his recent book on Shakespeare, wisely begins by telling us that he finds *creations*, not thoughts or doctrines, in the plays:

> The great and central virtue of Shakespeare was not
> achieved by taking thought, for thought cannot create a
> world. It can only understand one when one has been created.
> Shakespeare, starting with the world no man has made, and
> never indeed abandoning it, made many worlds within it.
> ... While we read a play of Shakespeare we are in it. We may
> be drawn in swiftly or slowly—in most cases swiftly—but once
> we are there we are enclosed. That is the secret, and it is still
> the secret of Shakespeare's power to interest us. He conditions
> us to a particular world before we are aware that it exists;
> then he absorbs us in its particulars.

The way in which Mr. Van Doren reads the plays of
Shakespeare provides a model for reading any fiction worthy
of the name.

(2) *Don't look for terms, propositions, and arguments
in imaginative literature.* Such things are logical, not poetic,
devices. They are proper to that use of language which
aims at communicating knowledge and ideas, but they are
utterly foreign when language serves as a medium for the
incommunicable—when it is employed creatively. As Mr.
Van Doren says, "In poetry and in drama statement is one
of the obscurer mediums." I think I would go further and
say that in fiction there are no statements at all, no verbal
declarations of the writer's beliefs. What a lyric poem

"states," for instance, cannot be found in any of its sentences. And the whole, comprising all its words in their reactions upon each other, says something which can never be confined within the strait jacket of propositions.

(3) *Don't criticize fiction by the standards of truth and consistency which properly apply to communications of knowledge.* The "truth" of a good story is its verisimilitude, its intrinsic probability or plausibility. It must be a likely story, but it need not describe the facts of life or society in a manner that is verifiable by experiment or research. Centuries ago, Aristotle remarked that "the standard of correctness is not the same in poetry as in politics," or in physics or psychology for that matter. Technical inaccuracies about anatomy or errors in geography and history should be criticized when the book in which they occur offers itself as a treatise on those subjects. But misstatements of fact do not mar a story if its teller succeeds in surrounding them with plausibility. When we read a biography, we want the truth about a particular man's life. When we read a novel we want a story that must be true only in the sense that it *could have happened* in the world of characters and events which the novelist has created.

(4) *Don't read all imaginative books as if they were the same.* Just as in the case of expository literature, here, too, there are differences in kind—the lyric, the novel, the play— which require appropriately different readings.

To make these "don'ts" more helpful, they must be supplemented by constructive suggestions. By developing the analogy between reading books of fact and books of fiction, I may be able to take you through another short cut to the rules for reading the latter.

- 3 -

There are, as we have seen, three groups of rules for reading expository books. The first set consists of rules for discovering the unity and part-whole structure; the second consists of rules for analyzing the whole into its component terms, propositions, and arguments; the third consists of rules for criticizing the author's doctrine so that we can reach an intelligent agreement or disagreement with him. We have called these three groups of rules *structural, interpretive,* and *critical.* If there is any analogy at all between reading expository and imaginative books, we should be able to find similar sets of rules to guide us in the latter case.

First, what are the structural rules for reading fiction? If you can remember the rules of this sort which we have already discussed (and if you cannot, you will find them summarized at the opening of Chapter Fourteen), I shall now translate them briefly into their fictional analogues:

(1) You must classify a piece of imaginative literature according to its kind. You must know whether it is a novel or a play or a lyric. A lyric tells its story primarily in terms of a single emotional experience, whereas novels and plays have much more complicated plots, involving many characters, their actions and reactions upon one another, as well as the emotions they suffer in the process. Everyone knows, furthermore, that a play differs from a novel by reason of the fact that it narrates entirely by means of actions and speeches. The author can never speak in his own person, as he can, and frequently does, in the course of a novel. All of these differences in manner of writing call for dif-

ferences in the reader's receptivity. Therefore, you should recognize at once the kind of fiction you are reading.

(2) You must grasp the unity of the whole work. Whether you have done this or not can be tested by whether you are able to express that unity in a sentence or two. The unity of an expository book resides ultimately in the main problem which it tries to solve. Hence its unity can be stated by the formulation of this question, or by the propositions which answer it. But the unity of fiction is always in its plot. I cannot stress too much the difference between *problem* and *plot* as respectively the sources of unity in expository and imaginative writing. You have not grasped the whole story until you can summarize its plot in a brief narration—not a proposition or argument. If you have an old-fashioned edition of Shakespeare at hand, you may find that each play is prefaced by a paragraph which is called "the argument." It consists of nothing more than the story in brief—a condensation of the plot. Herein lies the unity of the play.

(3) You must not only reduce the whole to its simplest unity, you must also discover how that whole is constructed out of all its parts. The parts of an expository book are concerned with parts of the whole problem, the partial solutions contributing to the solution of the whole. But the parts of fiction are the various steps which the author takes to develop his plot—the details of characterization and incident. The way in which the parts are arranged differs in the two cases. In science and philosophy, they must be ordered logically. In a story, the parts must somehow fit into a temporal scheme, a progress from a beginning through the middle to its end. To know the structure of a narrative, you must know where it begins, what it goes through, and

where it ends. You must know the various crises which lead up to the climax, where and how the climax occurs, and what happens in the aftermath.

A number of consequences follow from the points I have just made. For one thing, the parts or subwholes of an expository book are more likely to be independently readable than the parts of fiction. The first book of Euclid's thirteen—though it is a part of the whole work—can be read by itself. That is more or less the case with every well-organized expository book. Its sections or chapters, taken separately or in subgroups, make sense. But the chapters of a novel, or the acts of a play, become relatively meaningless when wrenched from the whole.

For another thing, the expository writer need not keep you in suspense. He can tell you in his preface or opening paragraphs precisely what he is going to do and how he is going to do it. Your interest is not dulled by such advance information; on the contrary, you are grateful for the guidance. But narrative, to be interesting, must sustain and heighten the suspense. Here suspense is of the essence. Even when you know the unity of the plot in advance, as that may be advertised by the "argument" which prefaces a Shakespearean play, everything that creates suspense must remain concealed. You must not be able to guess the precise steps by which the conclusion is reached. However few the number of original plots, the good writer achieves novelty and suspense by the skill with which he hides the turns his narrative takes in covering familiar ground.

Second, what are the interpretive rules for reading fiction? Our prior consideration of the difference between a poetic

and a logical use of language prepares us to make a translation of the rules which direct us to find the terms, the
propositions, and the arguments. We know we should not
do that. But what should we look for if we try to analyze
fiction?

(1) The elements of fiction are its episodes and incidents,
its characters, and their thoughts, speeches, feelings, and
actions. Each of these is an elementary part of the world
which the author creates. By manipulating these elements,
the author tells his story. They are like the terms in logical
discourse. Just as you must come to terms with an expository
writer, so here you must become acquainted with the details of incident and characterization. You have not grasped
a story until you are really familiar with its characters, until
you have lived through its events.

(2) Terms are connected in propositions. The elements
of fiction are connected by the total scene or background
against which they stand out in relief. The imaginative
writer, we have seen, creates a world in which his characters "live, move, and have their being." The fictional
analogue of the rule which directs you to find the author's
propositions can, therefore, be stated as follows: become at
home in this imaginary world; know it as if you were an
observer on the scene; become a member of its population,
willing to befriend its characters, and able to participate in
its happenings by sympathetic insight, as you would do in
the actions and sufferings of a friend. If you can do this, the
elements of fiction will cease to be so many isolated pawns
moved about mechanically on a chessboard. You will have
found the connections which vitalize them into the members
of a living society.

(3) If there is any motion in an expository book, it is the

movement of the argument, a logical transition from evidences and reasons to the conclusions they support. In the reading of such books, it is necessary to follow the argument. Hence, after you have discovered its terms and propositions, you are called upon to analyze its reasoning. There is an analogous last step in the interpretive reading of fiction. You have become acquainted with the characters. You have joined them in the imaginary world wherein they dwell, consented to the laws of their society, breathed its air, tasted its food, traveled on its highways. Now you must follow them through their adventures. The scene or background, the social setting, is (like the proposition) a kind of *static* connection of the elements of fiction. The unraveling of the plot (like the arguments or reasoning) is the dynamic connection. Aristotle said that plot is the soul of a story. It is its life. To read a story well you must have your finger on the pulse of the narrative, sensitive to its every beat.

Before leaving these fictional equivalents for the interpretive rules of reading, I must caution you not to examine the analogy too closely. An analogy of this sort is like a metaphor which will disintegrate if you press it too hard. I have used it only to give you the feel of how fiction can be read analytically. The three steps I have suggested outline the way in which one becomes progressively aware of the artistic achievement of an imaginative writer. Far from spoiling your enjoyment of a novel or play, they should enable you to enrich your pleasure by knowing intimately the sources of your delight. You will not only know what you like but also why you like it.

One other caution: the foregoing rules apply mainly to novels and plays. To the extent that lyric poems have some narrative line, they apply to lyrics also. But the heart of a lyric lies elsewhere. It really requires a special set of rules to lead you to its secret. The interpretive reading of lyric poetry is a special problem which I have neither the competence nor the space to discuss. I have already mentioned (in Chapter Seven) some books which may be helpful in this connection. To those I might add the following: Wordsworth's preface to the first edition of *Lyrical Ballads,* Matthew Arnold's *Essays in Criticism,* Edgar Allan Poe's essays on *The Poetic Principle* and *The Philosophy of Composition,* T. S. Eliot's work on *The Use of Poetry,* Herbert Read's *Form in Modern Poetry,* and Mark Van Doren's preface to *An Anthology of English and American Poetry.*

While I am recommending books, perhaps I should also mention a few that may help you develop your analytical powers in reading novels: Percy Lubbock's *The Craft of Fiction,* E. M. Forster's *Aspects of the Novel,* Edwin Muir's *The Structure of the Novel,* and Henry James's prefaces collected under the title *The Art of the Novel.* For the reading of drama, nothing has replaced Aristotle's analysis of tragedy and comedy in the *Poetics.* Where it needs to be supplemented for modern departures in the art of the theater, such books as George Meredith's essay *On Comedy* and Bernard Shaw's *The Quintessence of Ibsenism* can be consulted.

Third, and last, what are the critical rules for reading fiction? You may remember that we distinguished, in the case of expository works, between the general maxims governing criticism and a number of particular points—specific critical remarks. With respect to the general maxims, the analogy can be sufficiently drawn by one translation. Where, in the case of expository works, the advice was not to criticize a book—not to say you agree or disagree—until you can first say you understand, so here the maxim is: don't criticize imaginative writing until you fully appreciate what the author has tried to make you experience.

To explain this maxim, I must remind you of the obvious fact that we do not agree or disagree with fiction. We either like it or we do not. Our critical judgment in the case of expository books concerns their *truth,* whereas in criticizing belles-lettres, as the word itself suggests, we consider their *beauty.* The beauty of any work of art is related to the pleasure it gives us when we know it well.

Now there is an important difference here between logical and esthetic criticism. When we agree with a scientific book, a philosophy, or history, we do so because we think it speaks the truth. But when we like a poem, a novel, or play, we should hesitate, at least a moment, before attributing beauty, or artistic goodness, to the work which pleases us. We must remember that in matters of taste there is much divergence among men, and that some men, through greater cultivation, have better taste than others. While it is highly probable that what a man of really good taste likes is in itself a beautiful work, it is much less probable that the likes and dislikes of the uncultivated signify artistic perfections or failures. We must distinguish, in short, between the expression of taste which merely bespeaks liking or disliking and the ultimate critical judgment which concerns the objective merits of the work.

Let me restate the maxims, then, in the following manner. Before you express your likes and dislikes, you must first be sure that you have made an honest effort to appreciate the work. By appreciation, I mean having the experience which the author tried to produce for you by working on your emotions and imaginations. You cannot *appreciate* a novel by reading it passively, any more than you can *understand* a philosophical book that way. To achieve appreciation, as understanding, you must read actively, and that means performing all the acts of structural and analytical reading which I have briefly outlined.

After you have completed such readings, you are competent to judge. Your first judgment will naturally be one of taste. You will say not only *that* you like or dislike the book, but *why* you did or did not like it. The reasons you give will, of course, have some critical relevance to the book itself, but in their first expression they are more likely to be about you—your preferences and prejudices—than about the book. Hence, to complete the task of criticism, you must objectify your reactions by pointing to those things in the book which caused them. You must pass from saying what you like or dislike and why, to saying what is good or bad about the book and why.

There is a real difference here. No one can disagree with a man about what he likes or dislikes. The absolute authority of his own taste is every man's prerogative. But others can disagree with him about whether a book is good or bad. Taste may not be arguable, but critical appraisals can be assailed and defended. We must appeal to principles of esthetic or literary criticism if we wish to support our critical judgments.

If the principles of literary criticism were firmly established, and generally agreed on, it would be easy to enumerate briefly the main critical remarks that a reader could make about an imaginative book. Unfortunately— or fortunately—that is not the case, and you will sympathize with my discretion in hesitating to rush in. I shall, how·

ever, risk suggesting five questions which will help anyone form a critical judgment on fiction. (1) To what degree does the work have unity? (2) How great is the complexity of parts and elements which that unity embraces and organizes? (3) Is it a likely story, that is, does it have the inherent plausibility of poetic truth? (4) Does it elevate you from the ordinary semiconsciousness of daily life to the clarity of intense wakefulness, by stirring your emotions and filling your imagination? (5) Does it create a new world into which you are drawn and wherein you seem to live with the illusion that you are seeing life steadily and whole?

I shall not defend these questions beyond saying that the more they can be answered affirmatively, the more likely it is that the book in question is a great work of art. I think they will help you to discriminate between good and bad fiction, as well as to become more articulate in explaining your likes and dislikes. Although you must never forget the possible discrepancy between what is good in itself and what pleases you, you will be able to avoid the extreme inanity of the remark: "I don't know anything about art, but I know what I like."

The better you can reflectively discern the causes of your pleasure in reading fiction, the nearer you come to knowing the artistic virtues in the literary work itself. You will thus gradually develop a standard of criticism. And unless you happen to be a professional literary critic—tortured by the need to express the same few insights differently for every book, and driven by competition to avoid the obvious—you will find a large company of men of similar taste to share your critical judgments. You may even discover, what I think is true, that good taste in literature is acquired by anyone who learns to read.

- 4 -

Having gone so far toward generalizing the art of reading, by translating the expository rules into their fictional equivalents, I am impelled to take the last step and complete the job. You now have rules for reading *any book*. But how about rules for reading *anything that is fit to print?* How about reading newspapers, magazines, advertising copy, political propaganda? Can the rules be stated so generally that they apply to everything?

I think they can. Necessarily, as they become more general, the rules become fewer in number and less specific in content. In place of three sets of rules, each including three or four, the directions *for reading anything* can be summarized in four questions. To read anything well, you must be able to answer these four questions about it. In the light of all the discussion that has preceded, the questions need little explanation. You already know the steps you must take in order to answer these questions.

But, first, let me remind you of the basic distinction— between reading for information and for understanding— which underlies everything I have said about reading. For the most part, we read newspapers and magazines, and even advertising matter, for the information they contain. The amount of such material is vast, so vast that no one today has time to read more than a small fraction of the available sources of information. Necessity has been the mother of several good inventions in the field of such reading. The so-called news magazines, such as *Time* and *Newsweek,* perform an invaluable function for most of us by reading the news and reducing it to its essential elements of in-

formation. The men who write these magazines are primarily readers. They have developed the art of reading
for information to a point far beyond the average reader's
competence.

The same thing is true of *Readers Digest,* which manages
to reduce almost everything that is worth our attention in
current magazines to the compact scope of a single, small
volume. Of course, the very best articles, like the best books,
cannot be condensed without loss. If the essays of Montaigne or Lamb appeared in a current periodical, we would
scarcely be satisfied to read a digest of them. A summary
here would function well only if it impelled us to read the
original. For the average article, however, a condensation
is usually adequate, and often even better than the original,
because the average article is mainly informational. The
skill which produces *Readers Digest* each month is, first of
all, a skill in reading, and only then one of writing simply
and clearly. It does for us what few of us have the technique
—not merely the time—to do for ourselves. It cuts the core
of solid information out of pages and pages of less substantial stuff.

But, after all, we still have to read the periodicals which
accomplish these extraordinary digests of current news and
information. If we wish to be informed, we cannot avoid
the task of reading, no matter how good the digests are.
And the task of reading the digests is, in the last analysis,
the same task as that which is performed by the editors of
these magazines on the original materials they make available in more compact form. They have saved us labor, so
far as the extent of our reading is concerned, but they have
not and cannot entirely save us the trouble of reading. In
a sense, the function they perform profits us only if we can

read their digests of information as well as they have done the prior reading in order to give us the digests.

The four questions I shall now state as guides for reading *anything* apply equally to material which can inform us or enlighten us. To use these questions intelligently as a set of directions, you must know, of course, what it is you are after—whether you are reading for one purpose or the other. If you are wise, your purpose will accord properly with the nature of the thing to be read. Here are the four questions, with brief comment:

I. WHAT IN GENERAL IS BEING SAID? (To answer this question, you must perform all the steps of structural reading, according to the rules already laid down.)

II. HOW IN PARTICULAR IS IT BEING SAID? (You cannot fully discover what is being said unless you penetrate beneath the language to the thought. To do this you must observe how the language is being used, and how the thought is ordered. Here, then, you must follow all the rules of interpretative reading.)

III. IS IT TRUE? (Only after you know what is being said, and how, can you consider whether it is true or probable. This question calls for the exercise of critical judgment. You must decide to accept or reject the information being offered you. You must be especially alert to detect the distortions of propaganda in renderings of the news. In reading for enlightenment, you must decide whether you agree or disagree with what you have come to understand. The rules you must follow here are those of the third, or critical, reading.)

IV. WHAT OF IT? (Unless what you have read is true in some sense, you need go no further. But if it is, you must face this question. You cannot read for information intelligently without determining what significance is, or should be, attached to the facts presented. Facts seldom come to us without some interpretation, explicit or implied. This is especially true if you are reading digests of information which necessarily select the facts according to some evaluation of their significance, some principle of interpretation. And if you are reading for enlightenment, there is really no end to the inquiry which, at every stage of learning, is renewed by the question, *What of it?*)

These four questions summarize all the obligations of a reader. The first three indicate, moreover, why there are three ways of reading anything. The three sets of rules respond to something in the very nature of human discourse. If communications were not complex, structural analysis would be unnecessary. If language were a perfect medium instead of a relatively opaque one, there would be no need for interpretation. If error and ignorance did not circumscribe truth and knowledge, we should not have to be critical. The fourth question turns on the distinction between information and understanding. When the material you have read is itself primarily informational, you are challenged to go further and seek enlightenment. Even when you have been somewhat enlightened by what you have read, you are called upon to continue the search for significance.

Knowing these questions is, of course, not enough. You must remember to ask them as you read and, most of all, you must be able to answer them precisely and accurately. The ability to do just that is the art of reading, in a nutshell.

- 5 -

Ability to read anything well may be the goal, but the goal does not indicate the best place to begin acquiring the art. You cannot begin to acquire the right habits by reading any sort of material; perhaps I should say that some kinds of material make it easier to acquire the discipline than others. It is too easy, for instance, to get something out of newspapers, magazines, and digests, even when one reads them poorly and passively. Moreover, all our bad habits of perfunctory reading are associated with these familiar materials. That is why, throughout this book, I insisted that trying to read for understanding rather than information—because more difficult and less usual—provides you with a better occasion for developing your skill.

For the same reason, reading good books, or better, the great books, is the recipe for those who would learn to read. It is not that the rigors of difficult reading are the punishment which fits the crime of sloppy habits; rather, from the point of view of therapy, books which cannot be understood at all unless they are read actively are the ideal prescription for anyone who is still a victim of passive reading. Nor do I think that this medicine is like those drastic and strenuous remedies which are calculated either to kill or cure the patient. For in this case, the patient can determine the dosage. He can increase the amount of exercise he takes in easy stages. The remedy will begin to work as soon as he begins, and the more it works, the more he can take.

The place to begin, then, is on the great books. They are so apt for the purpose, it is almost as if they were written for the sake of teaching people how to read. They stand to the problem of learning how to read almost as water does to the business of learning how to swim. There is one important difference. Water is indispensable for swimming. But after you have learned to read by practicing on the great books, you can transfer your abilities to reading good books, to reading any books, to reading anything. The man who can keep afloat in the deeps need not concern himself about the shallows.

CHAPTER SIXTEEN

The Great Books

- I -

THERE is no end to the making of books. Nor does there seem to be any end to the making of book lists. The one is the cause of the other. There have always been more books than anyone could read. And as they have multiplied at an ever increasing rate through the centuries, more and more blue-ribbon lists have had to be made.

It is just as important to know *what* to read as *how* to read. When you have learned to read, you will still have, I hope, a long life to spend in reading. But, at best, you will be able to read only a few books of all that have been written, and the few you do read should include the best. You can rejoice in the fact that there are not too many great books to read. There seem to be fewer best books than first families, certainly less than "four hundred," as indicated by the phrase "one hundred best books," which has become a slogan. Though it should not be taken too seriously, the phrase is suggestive. The number is relatively small.

Even though that number is small, I want to repeat once more what I have already said about *quantity* of reading. Otherwise you might misinterpret the enumeration of titles which will occur in this chapter and the listing of great books in the Appendix. You might suppose that the recommendation of these books implies the desirability of reading *all* of them. In a sense, of course, it does. Ideally one should read many or even all of the great books, but the ideal is always at infinity and can only be approached. And the most important thing to know is that you approach it more genuinely by reading a few books well than many poorly. The point is to read well before you read widely. It is better by far to read a cornerstone group of the great books effectively than all of them ineffectively, for there is little or no profit in a vast amount of perfunctory reading.

If you keep this in mind I am sure you will not be frightened by the number of books that are mentioned or by titles that indicate fields with which you are unacquainted. In the course of this chapter, I shall try to group the books according to their subject matters and their leading points of interest, so that you will be able to begin reading wherever it suits your inclinations best. One book will lead to another and so, beginning with those which are at the moment nearest home, you may eventually find your way to larger and more remote circles. You *may* encompass the whole list in the end, but the most important thing about any list of books is that it should provide a good beginning.

The listing of the best books is as old as reading and writing. The teachers and librarians of ancient Alexandria did it. Their book lists were the backbone of an educational curriculum. Quintilian did it for Roman education, selecting, as he said, both *ancient* and *modern* classics. It was done again and again in the Middle Ages by Mohammedans, Jews, and Christians, and for a similar purpose. In the Renaissance, such leaders of the revival of learning as Montaigne and Erasmus made lists of the books they read. They offered themselves as models of gentlemanly literacy. Humanistic education was built on a foundation of "humane letters," as the phrase went. The reading prescribed was in the great works of Roman literature primarily, its poetry, biography, and history, and its moralistic essays.

In the nineteenth century, there were still other book lists. If you want to know the books which went into the making of a leading liberal of his day, look at John Stuart Mill's *Autobiography*. Perhaps the most famous book list made in the last century was Auguste Comte's. Comte was the French thinker who epitomized the nineteenth-century's devotion to science and to progress through science.

It is to be expected, of course, that the selection of "best books" will change with the times. Yet there is a surprising uniformity in the lists which represent the best choices of any period. In every age, both B.C. and A.D., the list makers include both ancient and modern books in their selections, and they always wonder whether the moderns are up to the great books of the past. The changes which each later age makes are mainly additions rather than substitutions. Naturally, the list of great books grows in the course of time, but its roots and outlines appear to remain the same. The tree adds new branches.

The reason for this is that the famous lists are genuinely many-sided. They try to include all that is great in the human tradition. A bad selection would be one motivated by a sectarian bias, directed by some kind of special pleading. There have been lists of this sort, which picked only the books that would prove a certain point. Such lists omit many great books. The European tradition cannot be boxed that way. It includes much that must necessarily appear false or misguided when judged from any particular point of view. Wherever one finds the truth, there will always be great errors in its company. To list the great books adequately, one must include all that have made a difference, not simply those one agrees with or approves of.

Until thirty or forty years ago, a college course was built around a set of required readings. Under the impact of the elective system and other educational changes, the requirements in this country were gradually relaxed to a point where the bachelor's degree no longer meant general literacy. The great books still appeared here and there, in this course and that, but they were seldom read in relation to one another. Frequently they were made supplementary to the textbooks which dominated the curriculum.

Things were at their worst when I entered college at the start of the twenties. As I have already reported, I also saw the upward turn begin. John Erskine had persuaded the Columbia faculty to institute an Honors course, devoted to the reading of great books. The list, which he was largely instrumental in composing, included between sixty and seventy authors, representing all fields of learning and all kinds of poetry. It differed from other current selections by having a higher standard of choice, and also by trying to include every great book, not only those of a certain period or a certain kind. It was a more comprehensive list than those used in the reading courses at Oxford, for instance, where a student specialized in "ancient greats" or "modern greats."

The Erskine list has been modified and revised many times since its inception. Mr. Hutchins and I have used it with some alterations at the University of Chicago. The four-year program of reading at St. John's College is substantially the same list, though it has been enriched by additions from the fields of mathematics and natural science. A similar list, though somewhat shorter, is being used at Columbia now in a course required for all freshmen. I think

the Erskine list, with some additions and changes, is a
fairly accurate expression of what anyone today would
name as the great works of Western culture.

I had one experience which gave me insight into this
business of listing the great books. I acted as secretary for
the faculty which taught the Honors course at Columbia
during the years when the original list was being revised.
Various members of the faculty had expressed dissatisfac-
tion. They wanted to drop some authors and include others.
To settle matters, we constructed a master list of about
three hundred books, many more than anyone would wish
included, but long enough to contain any author that anyone might name.

We then proceeded to vote, gradually excluding the
books or authors which the voting indicated as not generally
agreed on. After many ballots, we obtained a list which
satisfied everyone. It had eighty items on it, only about
fifteen more than Erskine's enumeration. It contained
almost all the titles on the original list. From those two
years of revision, I learned the extent to which there is
unanimity of judgment about the great books. It became
clear that it would be difficult to make a list much longer
than a hundred authors about whom such universal agreement could be obtained. When you got beyond that, you
would be catering to the interests of specialists in this period
or that subject matter.

I am not going to try to make up a new list of great books
for you. I think the lists now available are quite satisfactory.
As I have indicated, the revised Columbia list has been
published by the American Library Association, under the
title Classics of the Western World, and can be purchased

for less than a dollar. The slightly longer list now in use at St. John's College at Annapolis can be readily obtained from that college.

But I am going to save you the trouble of getting those lists. In the Appendix, you will find a fairly adequate enumeration. It is a selection of authors and titles from all the lists I have mentioned. I have used two criteria in making this selection: first, that the book be readily available in English; second, that it be readable by anyone without the aid of special instruction. I know, of course, that the second criterion is least applicable to the mathematical classics, and less applicable to great scientific books than to the others. Yet it holds even for them on one condition, namely, that these books be read in their historical order. An earlier work thus helps to prepare for and explain a later one.

Strictly speaking, a catalogue is not something to read. It is for reference purposes. That is why I have put the long chronological inventory of the books in the Appendix. In this chapter, I am going to try to make that list come to life by talking about the books.

I shall try here, therefore, to collect the great books into smaller groups, each group participating in a conversation about some particular problem in which you may be already interested. In some cases, the conversations will overlap, as the problems do. In other cases, conversation about one problem will lead to another. Thus, instead of lying side by side in a graveyard row, the books may appear to you as they should—the lively actors in a living tradition. I probably will not name all the books in this chapter, but I shall be able to bring enough of them into conversation

with one another, so that you can imagine the job completed. If you are induced to join in the conversation by
reading some of these books, they will take care of the rest.

- 2 -

Before I begin, however, it may be wise to say a little
more about what a great book is. I have used the phrase
again and again, hoping that what I said in Chapter Four
about great books as *original communications* would suffice for the time. In Chapter Eight, I suggested that among
poetical works there was a parallel distinction. Just as great
expository books are those which, more than others, can
increase our understanding, so the great works of imaginative literature elevate our spirit and deepen our humanity.

In the course of other chapters, I may have mentioned
other qualities which the great books possess. But now I
want to bring together in one place all the signs by which
the great books can be recognized—repeating some, adding
new ones. These are the signs which everyone uses in making lists or selections. The six I am going to mention may
not be all there are, but they are the ones some of us—
Dean Buchanan and President Barr at St. John's, and Mr.
Hutchins and I at Chicago—have found most useful in explaining the award of the library blue ribbon.

(1) I used to say jocularly that the great books were those
everybody recommends and nobody reads, or those everyone says he intends to read and never does. The joke (it is
Mark Twain's, really) may have its point for some of our
contemporaries, but the remark is false for the most part.
In fact, the great books are probably the most widely read.
They are not best sellers for a year or two. They are en-

during best sellers. *Gone with the Wind* has had relatively few readers compared to the plays of Shakespeare or *Don Quixote*. It would be reasonable to estimate, as a recent writer did, that Homer's *Iliad* has been read by at least 25,000,000 people in the last 3,000 years. When you realize the number of languages into which these books have been translated, and the number of years during which they have been read, you will not think that a number of readers running high into the millions is exaggerated.

It does not follow, of course, that every book which reaches a tremendous audience ranks as a classic by reason of that fact alone. *Three Weeks, Quo Vadis,* and *Ben-Hur,* to mention only fiction, are cases in point. Nor do I mean that a great book need be a best seller in its own day. It may take time for it to accumulate its ultimate audience. The astronomer Kepler, whose work on the planetary motions is now a classic, is reported to have said of his book that "it may wait a century for a reader, as God has waited 6,000 years for an observer."

(2) The great books are popular, not pedantic. They are not written by specialists about specialties for specialists. Whether they be philosophy or science, or history or poetry, they treat of human, not academic, problems. They are written for men, not professors. When I say they are popular, I do not mean they are popularizations in the sense of simplifying what can be found in other books. I mean they were initially written for a popular audience. They were intended for beginners. This, as I pointed out earlier, is a consequence of their being original communications. With respect to what these books have to say, most men are beginners.

To read a textbook for advanced students, you have to

read an elementary textbook first. But the great books are all elementary. They treat the elements of any subject matter. They are not related to one another as a series of textbooks graded in difficulty or in the technicality of the problems with which they deal. That is what I meant by saying that they are all for beginners, even though they do not all begin at the same place in the tradition of thought.

There is one kind of *prior* reading, however, which does help you to read a great book, and that is the other great books the author himself read. If you begin where he began, you are better prepared for the new departure he is going to make. This is the point I suggested before, when I said that even the mathematical and scientific books can be read without special instruction.

Let me illustrate this point by taking Euclid's *Elements of Geometry* and Newton's *Mathematical Principles of Natural Philosophy*. Euclid requires no prior study of mathematics. His book is genuinely an introduction to geometry, and to basic arithmetic as well. The same cannot be said for Newton, because Newton uses mathematics in the solution of physical problems. The reader must be able to follow his mathematical reasoning in order to understand how it interprets his observations. Newton had mastered Euclid. His mathematical style shows how deeply he was influenced by Euclid's treatment of ratio and proportions. His book is, therefore, not readily intelligible, even to competent scientists, unless Euclid has been read before. But with Euclid as a guide, the effort to read Newton, or Galileo, ceases to be fruitless.

I am not saying that these great scientific books can be read without effort. I am saying that if they are read in an historical order, the effort is rewarded. Just as Euclid illumi

nates Newton and Galileo, so they in turn help to make
Maxwell and Einstein intelligible. The point is not limited
to mathematical and scientific works. It applies to philosophical books as well. Their authors tell you what you
should have read before you come to them: Dewey wants
you to have read Mill and Hume; Whitehead wants you
to have read Descartes and Plato.

(3) The great books are always contemporary. In contrast, the books we call "contemporary," because they are
currently popular, last only for a year or two, or ten at the
most. They soon become antiquated. You probably cannot
recall the names of the best sellers of the twenties. If they
were recalled for you, you probably would not be interested
in reading them. Especially in the field of nonfiction books,
you want the latest "contemporary" product. But the great
books are never outmoded by the movement of thought or
the shifting winds of doctrine and opinion. On the contrary, one great book tends to intensify the significance of
others about the same subject. Thus, Marx's *Das Kapital*
and Adam Smith's *Wealth of Nations* illuminate each
other, and so do works as far apart as Claude Bernard's
Introduction to Experimental Medicine and the medical
writings of Hippocrates and Galen.

Schopenhauer said this clearly. "Looking over a huge
catalogue of new books," he said, "one might weep at thinking that, when ten years have passed, not one of them will
be heard of." His further explanation is worth following:

> There are at all times two literatures in progress, running
> side by side, but little known to each other; the one real, the
> other only apparent. The former grows into permanent litera-
> ture; it is pursued by those who live *for* science or poetry; its
> course is sober and quiet, but extremely slow; and it produces

in Europe scarcely a dozen works in a century; these, however, are permanent. The other kind is pursued by persons
who live *on* science and poetry. It goes at a gallop, with much
noise and shouting of partisans. Every twelve-month it puts
a thousand works on the market. But after a few years one
asks, Where are they? Where is the glory which came so soon
and made so much clamour? This kind may be called fleeting,
and the other, permanent literature.

"Permanent" and "fleeting" are good words to name the
persistently contemporary great books and the soon antiquated current ones.

Because they are contemporary, and should be read as
such, the word "classic" must be avoided. Mark Twain,
you will recall, defined a classic as "something that everybody wants to have read, and nobody wants to read." I am
afraid not even that is true for most people any longer.
"Classic" has come to mean an ancient and antiquated
book. People regard the classics as the great has-beens, the
great books of their times. "But our times are different,"
they say. From this point of view, the only motive for reading the classics is an historical or philological interest. It
is like poking about among the somewhat moldy monuments of a past culture. The classics, thus viewed, cannot
offer instruction to a modern man, except, of course, about
the peculiarities of his ancestors.

But the great books are *not* faded glories. They are *not*
dusty remains for scholars to investigate. They are *not* a
record of dead civilizations. *They are rather the most potent
civilizing forces in the world today.*

Of course, there is progress in some things. No one wants
to drive an old-fashioned model after the new cars are on
the market. No one suggests that we give up the electric

lights, plumbing, and vacuum cleaners of a modern apart-
ment for the spacious inconveniences of an old-fashioned
palace. There is progress in all the utilities which man can
invent to make the motions of life more efficient and easier.
There is progress in social affairs, of the sort signalized by
the advent of democracy in modern times. And there is
progress in knowledge and the clarification of problems
and ideas.

But there is not progress in everything. The fundamental
human problems remain the same in all ages. Anyone who
reads the speeches of Demosthenes and the letters of Cicero,
or if you prefer, the essays of Bacon and Montaigne, will
find how constant is the preoccupation of men with happiness and justice, with virtue and truth, and even with
stability and change itself. We may succeed in accelerating
the motions of life, but we cannot seem to change the routes
that are available to its ends.

It is not only in moral or political matters that progress
is relatively superficial. Even in theoretic knowledge, even
in science and philosophy, where knowledge increases and
understanding may be deepened, the advances made by
every epoch are laid upon a traditional foundation. Civilization grows like an onion, layer upon layer. To understand Einstein, you must, as he tells you himself, understand
Galileo and Newton. To understand Whitehead, you must,
as he also tells you, know Descartes and Plato. If any contemporary books are great because they deal with fundamental matters, then all the great books are contemporary
because they are involved in the same discussion.

(4) The great books are the most readable. I have said
this before. It means several things. If the rules of skilled
reading are somehow related to the rules of skillful writing,

then these are the best-written books. If a good reader is proficient in the liberal arts, how much more so is a great writer a master of them. These books are *masterpieces* of liberal art. In saying this, I refer primarily to expository works. The greatest works of poetry or fiction are masterpieces of fine art. In both cases, language is mastered by the writer for the sake of the reader, whether the end be instruction or delight.

To say that the great books are most readable is to say that they will not let you down if you try to read them well. You can follow the rules of reading to your utmost ability and they, unlike poorer works, will not stop paying dividends. But it is equally true to say that there is actually more in them to read. It is not merely how they are written, but what they have to say. They have more ideas per page than most books have in their entirety. That is why you can read a great book over and over again and never exhaust its contents, and probably never read skillfully enough to master it completely. The most readable books are indefinitely readable.

They are rereadable for another reason. They can be read at many different levels of understanding, as well as with a great diversity of interpretations. The most obvious examples of many levels of reading are found in such books as *Gulliver's Travels, Robinson Crusoe,* and the *Odyssey.* Children can read them with enjoyment, but fail to find therein all the beauty and significance which delight an adult mind.

(5) I have also said before that the great books are the most instructive, the most enlightening. This follows, in a sense, from the fact that they are original communications, that they contain what cannot be found in other books.

Whether you ultimately agree or disagree with their doctrines, these are the primary teachers of mankind, because they have made the basic contributions to human learning and thought. In so far as they have solved important problems, wholly or partially, the principles to be found in them are the leading principles of human knowledge. And the conclusions their authors reached are the major achievements of human thought.

It is almost unnecessary to add that the great books are the most influential books. In the tradition of learning, they have been most discussed by readers who have also been writers. These are the books *about which* there are many other books. Countless and, for the most part, forgotten are the books which have been written about them—the commentaries, digests, or popularizations.

(6) Finally, the great books deal with the persistently unsolved problems of human life. It is not enough to say of them that they have solved important problems, in whole or part. That is only one aspect of their achievement. There are genuine mysteries in the world that mark the limits of human knowing and thinking. Inquiry not only begins with wonder, but usually ends with it also.

Great minds do not, like shallower ones, despise mysteries or run away from them. They acknowledge them honestly and try to define them by the clearest statement of ultimately imponderable alternatives. Wisdom is fortified, not destroyed, by understanding its limitations. Ignorance does not make a fool as surely as self-deception.

- 3 -

You can see now how these six criteria hang together, how they follow from and support one another. You can see why, if these are the qualifications, the exclusive society of great authors has fewer than four hundred members. The shortness of the Erskine or St. John's list is inescapable when these criteria set the standard.

Perhaps you can also see why you should read the great books rather than books about them or books which try to distill them for you. "Some books," says Lord Bacon, "may be read by deputy, and extracts made of them by others. But that would be only in the less important arguments, and the meaner sort of books." With respect to the others, "distilled books are like common distilled waters, flashy things." The same reason which sends men to the concert hall and the art gallery should send them to the great books rather than to imperfect reproductions. The firsthand witness is always preferred to garbled hearsay. A good story can be spoiled by a bad raconteur.

The only excuse which men have ever given for reading books about these books does not hold here any more than it would in the case of canned music or cheap replicas of painting and sculpture. They know that it is easier, as well as better, to meet the fine artist in his own work rather than in its imitations. But they believe that the great teachers cannot be met in their own works. They think they are too difficult, too far above them, and hence they console themselves with substitutes. This, as I have tried to show, is not the case. I repeat: the great books are the most readable for anyone who knows how to read. Skill in reading is the only condition for entry into this good company.

Please do not look at the list of great books as another of those lists which men make up for the lonely island on which they are going to be shipwrecked. You do not need the idyllic solitude, which modern men can dream of only as the benefit of disaster, in order to read the great books. If you have any leisure at all, you can use it to read in. But do not make the mistake of the businessman who devotes every energy to making his pile first, and supposes that he will know how to use his spare time when he retires. Leisure and work should be components of every week, not divisions of the span of life.

The pursuit of learning and enlightenment through the great books can relieve the tedium of toil and the monotony of business as much as music and the other fine arts. But the leisure must be genuinely leisure. It must be time free from the children and from the radio, as well as unoccupied by moneygrubbing. Not only is the widely advertised fifteen minutes a day ridiculously insufficient—would anyone interested in golf or bridge think that fifteen minutes are long enough even to warm up and get started?—but the time spent in reading must not be shared with bouncing Teddy on your knee, answering Mary's questions, or listening to Jack Benny and Charlie McCarthy.

There is one point, however, in the selection of books men make for a possible shipwreck. When they are faced with having to choose a very small number, they tend to pick the best. We forget that the total amount of leisure we can rescue from our busy lives is probably no longer than a few years on a desert island. If we realized that, we might make up a list of reading for the rest of our lives as carefully as we would for a desert island. Since we do not have to pack the books in a waterproof case, we can plan on more than ten. Yet we cannot count on eternity. The bell will ring soon enough. School will be out, and unless we have laid our plans well and followed them, we are likely

to find, when reading time is over, that we might just as
well have played golf or bridge, for all the good it did our
minds.

The reading list in the Appendix is a suggestion for
those who can take the hint. It is neither too long for the
average man's leisure nor too short for those who can manage to find more time. However much of it you do, I am
sure of one thing. No time will be wasted. Whether your
economy be one of abundance or scarcity, you will find
every item on this list a profitable investment of hours and
energy.

– 4 –

I said before that I was going to make smaller groupings
of books according as their authors appeared to be talking
about the same problems, and conversing with one another. Let's begin at once. The easiest way to begin is with
the themes that dominate our daily conversation. The newspapers and radio will not let us forget about the world
crisis and our national role in it. We talk at table and in
the evening, and even during office hours, about war and
peace, about democracy against the totalitarian regimes,
about planned economies, about Fascism and Communism,
about the next national election, and hence about the Constitution, which both parties are going to use as a platform
and as a plank with which to hit the other fellow over the
head.

If we do more than look at the newspapers or listen to
the radio, we may have read such books as Walter Lippmann's *The Good Society* or James Marshall's *Swords and
Symbols*. We may even have been induced by these books,
and other considerations, to look at the Constitution itself.

If the political problems with which current books deal interest us, there is more reading for us to do in relation to them and the Constitution. These contemporary authors probably read some of the great books, and the men who wrote the Constitution certainly did. All we have to do is to follow the lead, and the trail will unwind by itself.

First, let us go to the other writings of the men who drafted the Constitution. Most obvious of all is the collection of pieces, arguing for the ratification of the Constitution, published weekly in *The Independent Journal* and elsewhere by Hamilton, Madison, and Jay. To understand *The Federalist Papers,* you should read not only the Articles of Confederation, which the Constitution was intended to supplant, but also the writings of the Federalists' major opponent on many issues, Thomas Jefferson. A selection of his political utterances has recently been made and published.

Unfortunately, it is more difficult to get the writings of another great participant in the argument, John Adams; but you will find his collected works in the library. Look especially at his *Defense of the Constitutions of Government of the United States,* written in answer to an attack by the French economist and statesman, Turgot; and also at his *Discourses on Davila.* The writings of Tom Paine are available in many editions. His *Common Sense* and his *Rights of Man* throw light on the issues of the day and the ideologies which controlled the opponents.

These writers, because they were readers as well, lead us to the books which influenced them. They are *using* ideas whose more extended and disinterested exposition is to be found elsewhere. The pages of *The Federalist Papers,* and the writings of Jefferson, Adams, and Paine, refer us to the great political thinkers of the eighteenth and late seventeenth century in Europe. We should read Montesquieu's *Spirit of the Laws,* Locke's essays *Of Civil Government,* Rousseau's *Social Contract.* To savor the rationalism of this Age of Reason, we must also read here and there in the voluminous papers of Voltaire.

You may suppose that the laissez-faire individualism of Adam Smith also belongs in our revolutionary background, but remember that *The Wealth of Nations* was first published in 1776. The founding fathers were influenced, in their ideas about property, agrarianism, and free trade, by John Locke and the French economists against whom Adam Smith subsequently wrote.

Our founding fathers were well read in ancient history. They drew upon the annals of Greece and Rome for many of their political examples. They had read Plutarch's *Lives* and Thucydides' *History of the Peloponnesian War*—the war between Sparta and Athens and their allies. They followed the fortunes of the various Greek federations for what light they might throw on the enterprise they were about to undertake. They were not only learned in history and political thought, but they went to school with the ancient orators. They reveal the influence of Cicero's orations. As a result, their political propaganda is not only magnificently turned, but amazingly effective even today. With the exception of Lincoln (who had read a few great books very well), American statesmen of a later day neither speak nor write so well.

The trail leads further. The writers of the eighteenth century had been influenced in turn by their immediate forebears in political thought. The *Leviathan* of Thomas Hobbes and the political tracts of Spinoza deal with the same problems of government—the formation of society by contract, the justifications of monarchy, oligarchy, and democracy, the right of rebellion against tyranny. Locke, Spinoza, and Hobbes are, in a sense, involved in a conversation with one another. Locke and Spinoza had read Hobbes. Spinoza, moreover, had read Machiavelli's *The Prince,* and Locke everywhere refers to and quotes "the judicious Hooker," the Richard Hooker who wrote a book about *Ecclesiastical Government* at the end of the sixteenth century, and of whom Izaak Walton, the fisherman, wrote a life.

I mention Hooker because he, more than the men of a later generation, had read the ancients well, especially the *Ethics* and *Politics* of Aristotle. He had certainly read them better than Thomas Hobbes, if we can judge by the references in the latter's work. Hooker's influence on Locke partly accounts for the difference between Locke and Hobbes on many political questions.

One other stream of influence upon our founding fathers came through a Catholic political thinker of the sixteenth century, Robert Bellarmine. Like Locke, he opposed the theory of the divine right of kings. Madison and Jefferson were acquainted with Bellarmine's arguments. I mention Bellarmine for the same reason I mentioned Hooker, because it was through him that other books entered the picture. Bellarmine reflected the great medieval works on political theory, especially the writings of St. Thomas Aquinas, who was an upholder of popular sovereignty and the natural rights of man.

The conversation about current political issues thus enlarges itself to take in the whole of European political thought. If we go back to the Constitution and the writings of '76, we are inevitably led further, as each writer reveals himself to be a reader in turn. Little has been left out. If we add Plato's *Republic* and *Laws* which Aristotle read and answered, and Cicero's *Republic* and *Laws* which were read by Roman jurists, and through them influenced the development of law throughout medieval Europe, almost all the great political books have been drawn in.

- 5 -

That is not quite true. By returning to the original conversation, and taking a fresh start, we may discover the few major omissions. Suppose there is a Nazi in our midst, and he quotes *Mein Kampf* at us. Since it is not clear that Hitler ever read the great books, the political utterances of Mussolini might be more productive of leads. Let's shift to Fascism. We may be able to detect the influence of the French philosopher, Sorel, who wrote *Reflections on Violence*. We may remember that Mussolini was once a socialist. If we pursue these lines in all their ramifications, other books inevitably find their way into the conversation.

There would be Hegel's *Philosophy of History* and *Philosophy of Right*. Here we would find the justifications of state absolutism, the deification of the state. There would also be writings of Nietzsche, especially such books as *Thus Spake Zarathustra, Beyond Good and Evil,* and *The Will to Power.* Here we would find the theory of the superman as above the canons of right and wrong, the theory of a successful use of might as its own ultimate justification. And behind Hegel, on the one hand, and Nietzsche, on the other—in the latter case through the influence of Schopenhauer—would be the greatest of German thinkers, Immanuel Kant. Anyone who reads Kant's *Philosophy of Law* will see that he cannot be held responsible for the positions of his currently more influential followers.

There might also be a Communist at our table, either Trotskyite or Stalinist. Both sorts swear by the same book. The conversation would not get very far without Karl Marx being mentioned. His great work, *Das Kapital,* would also be mentioned, even though no one had read it, not even the Communist. But if anyone had read *Das Kapital,* and other literature of revolution, he would have found a trail which led, on the one hand, to Hegel again—a starting point for both Communism and Fascism—and, on the other hand, to the great economic and social theorists of England and France: to Adam Smith's *Wealth of Nations,* to Ricardo's *Principles of Political Economy and Taxation,* and Proudhon's *Philosophy of Poverty.*

A lawyer present might turn the discussion away from economic theory by turning it to the legal aspects of business and government. He may have just read Mr. Thurman Arnold's book on *The Folklore of Capitalism,* or his earlier one on *The Symbols of Government.* That might remind someone that Mr. Jerome Frank had also written a book called *Law and the Modern Mind.* These books would bring others in their train, if they had been read with an eye on the books hidden in their backgrounds.

Becoming interested in these legal matters, we might soon leave Arnold and Frank for the company of the late Justice Holmes and that great English law reformer, Jeremy Bentham. We would go especially to Bentham's *Theory of Legislation* and his *Theory of Fictions.* Bentham would recall the whole utilitarian movement and his prize students, John Austin and John Stuart Mill. Austin's *Jurispru-*

dence and Mill's essays on *Liberty* and on *Representative Government* are being paraphrased every day, with approval or disapproval, by men who have not read them, so much have they become a part of contemporary controversy about liberalism. Bentham might also revive Blackstone, and with him the basic issues of the common law.

Blackstone, you remember, wrote the *Commentaries on the Laws of England,* which Lincoln studied so carefully. Bentham attacked him unmercifully in a book called *Comment on the Commentaries.* If this line were pursued further, we would go back to Hobbes' *Dialogue of the Common Laws* and to the great medieval and ancient writings on law and justice. Again we would find Plato and Aristotle, Cicero and Aquinas, in the background.

Our interest in Mr. Frank's book might lead in still another direction. Mr. Frank's book has a great deal to say about the neuroses of the lawmakers and judges. He had read Freud, and if we started on that, the whole history of psychology might unfold in another list of great books, including Pavlov's work on *The Conditioned Reflexes,* William James's *Principles of Psychology,* Hartmann's *Philosophy of the Unconscious,* Schopenhauer's *World as Will and Idea,* Hume's *Treatise on Human Nature,* Descartes' work on *The Passions of the Soul,* and so forth.

If we followed Mr. Arnold to his sources, we would go off on a different tangent. He is not only influenced by Bentham as a lawyer, but by Bentham's theory of language and symbols. Bentham, you will recall, is the father of the present-day semanticists, Ogden and Richards, Korzybski and Stuart Chase. If we pursued that interest, all the great works in the liberal arts would eventually have to be rediscovered, for the modern works are insufficient as an analysis of language and the arts of communication.

A list of required readings for amateur semanticists would include Locke's *Essay on Human Understanding,* especially Book III on language; Hobbes' *Leviathan,* especially the first book, and his *Rhetoric,* which closely follows Aristotle's *Rhetoric.* It should include also Plato's dialogues about language and oratory (the *Cratylus, Gorgias,* and *Phaedrus* especially), and two great medieval works on teaching and being taught, one by St. Augustine and one by St. Thomas, both called *Of the Teacher.* I dare not start on logical works, because the list might be too long, but John Stuart Mill's *System of Logic,* Boole's *Laws of Thought,* Bacon's *Novum Organum,* and Aristotle's *Organon* must be mentioned.

One other direction is possible. The consideration of political and economic issues tends to raise the basic ethical problems about pleasure and virtue, about happiness, the ends of life, and the means thereto. Someone may have read Jacques Maritain's *Freedom in the Modern World* and noticed what this living follower of Aristotle and Aquinas had to say about contemporary problems, especially the moral aspects of current political and economic issues. That would not only lead us back to the great moral treatises of the past—Aristotle's *Ethics* and the second part of Aquinas's *Summa Theologica*—but it might also get us into a many-sided dispute. To see it through, we would have to consult Mill's *Utilitarianism,* Kant's *Critique of Practical Reason,* and Spinoza's *Ethics.* We might even return to the Roman stoics and epicureans, to the *Meditations* of Marcus Aurelius, and Lucretius' *On the Nature of Things.*

- 6 -

You should have observed a number of things in this ramification of conversation or reflection about current problems. Not only does one book lead to another, but each contains implicitly a large diversity of leads. Our conversation or thought can branch out in many directions, and each time it does another group of books seems to be drawn in. Notice, furthermore, that the same authors are often represented in different connections, for they have usually written about many of these related topics, sometimes in different books, but often in the same work.

Nor is it surprising that, as one goes back to the medieval and ancient worlds, the same names are repeated many times. Aristotle and Plato, Cicero and Aquinas, for instance, stand at the fountainhead. They have been read and discussed, agreed with and disagreed with, by the writers of modern times. And when they have not been read, their doctrines have filtered down in many indirect ways, through such men as Hooker and Bellarmine.

So far we have dealt mainly with practical matters—politics, economics, morals—although you probably observed a tendency to become theoretical. We turned to psychology by way of Freud's influence on the lawyers. If the ethical controversy had been followed a bit further, we would soon have been in metaphysics. In fact, we were, with Maritain's discussion of free will and with Spinoza's *Ethics*. Kant's *Critique of Practical Reason* might have led us to his *Critique of Pure Reason,* and all the theoretic questions about the nature of knowledge and experience.

Suppose we consider briefly some theoretical questions. We have been concerned with education throughout this book. Someone who had read Mr. Hutchins' book, *The Higher Learning in America* or Cardinal Newman's *Idea of a University* might raise a question about metaphysics and its place in higher education. That usually starts a discussion about what metaphysics is. And usually someone says there is no such thing. We would probably be referred to John Dewey's *Democracy and Education* and his *Quest for Certainty* to see that all valid knowledge is scientific or experimental. If all the leads therein were followed, we might soon find ourselves back to the sources of the current antimetaphysical trend: Auguste Comte's *Positive Philosophy* and Hume's *Enquiry Concerning Human Understanding*, and perhaps even Kant's *Prolegomena to any Future Metaphysics*.

Someone, who had read such recent books by Whitehead as his *Process and Reality* and his *Science and the Modern World*, or Santayana's *Realm of Essence* and *Realm of Matter*, or Maritain's *Degrees of Knowledge*, might object to the dismissal of metaphysics. The protagonist might defend the claims of theoretic philosophy to give us knowledge about the nature of things, of a different sort and apart from science. If he had read those books well, he would have been led back to the great speculative works of modern and ancient times: to Hegel's *Phenomenology of Spirit;* to Spinoza's *Ethics,* Descartes' *Principles of Philosophy,* Leibnitz's *Discourse on Metaphysics* and his *Monadology;* to Aquinas's little work on *Being and Essence;* to Aristotle's *Metaphysics,* and to Plato's dialogues, the *Timaeus,* the *Parmenides,* and the *Sophist.*

Or let us suppose that our theoretic interests turn to the natural sciences rather than to philosophy. I have already mentioned Freud and Pavlov. The problems of human behavior and human nature open into a lot of other questions, of the sort recently treated by Alexis Carrel and J. B. S. Haldane. Not only man's nature but his place in nature would concern us. All these roads lead to Darwin's *Origin of Species* and thence, on bypaths, to Lyell's *Antiquity of Man* and Malthus's *Essay on Population.*

Recently, as you know, there have been a lot of books about the practice of medicine, and a few about the theory of it. Man's normal hypochondria makes him abnormally interested in doctors, health, and the functioning of his own body. Here there are many routes in reading, but they would all probably go through Claude Bernard's *Introduction to Experimental Medicine* and Harvey's book on *The Motion of the Heart,* all the way back to Galen's *Natural Faculties* and Hippocrates' amazing formulations of Greek medicine.

Einstein and Infeld's recent book on *The Evolution of Physics* refers us to the great milestones in the development of man's experimental knowledge. Here our reading would be deepened if we looked into Poincaré's *Foundations of Science* and Clifford's *Common Sense of the Exact Sciences.* They, in turn, would take us to such works as Faraday's *Experimental Researches into Electricity* and Boyle's *Skeptical Chymist;* perhaps even to Newton's *Opticks,* Galileo's *Two New Sciences,* and Leonardo da Vinci's *Notebooks.*

The most exact sciences are not only the most experimental but also the most mathematical ones. If we are interested in physics, we cannot avoid considering mathematics. Here, too, there have been some recent books, such as Hogben's *Mathematics for the Million,* but I think none so good as a little masterpiece by Whitehead called *An*

Introduction to Mathematics. Bertrand Russell's great work on *The Principles of Mathematics* has also just been republished.

If we read these books, we might even dare to open Hilbert's *Foundations of Geometry,* Dedekind's *Theory of Numbers,* and Peacock's *Treatise on Algebra.* Through them we could not help returning to the starting points of modern mathematics in Descartes' *Geometry* and the mathematical works of Newton and Leibnitz. The *Mathematical Lectures* of Barrow, Newton's teacher, would be extremely helpful, but I think we would also find it necessary to see the whole of modern mathematics in the light of its contrast with the Greek accomplishment, especially Euclid's *Elements of Geometry,* Nichomachus' *Introduction to Arithmetic,* and Apollonius' *Treatise on Conic Sections.*

The connection of the great books and the versatility of their authors may now appear even more plainly than before. Leibnitz and Descartes were both mathematicians and metaphysicians. Malthus's *Essay on Population* was not only a work in social science, but also influenced Darwin's notions about the struggle for existence and the survival of the fittest. Newton was not only a great experimental physicist but also a great mathematician. Leonardo's *Notebooks* contain both his theory of perspective in painting and the record of his mechanical investigations and inventions.

- 7 -

I am going to take one step further. Even though we have been primarily concerned with expository works, a recitation of the great books would be sorely deficient if the masterpieces of belles-lettres were not mentioned. Here, too, contemporary works might generate an interest in their forebears. The modern novel has a varied history which opens up when we go back from Proust and Thomas Mann, James Joyce and Hemingway, to the forms of narration they have tried to modify. Proust and, perhaps, André Gide, lead us to Flaubert, Zola, and Balzac, and to the great Russians, Dostoevski and Tolstoi. Nor will we forget our own Mark Twain, Herman Melville, and Henry James; or Hardy, Dickens, and Thackeray. Behind all these lie the great eighteenth-century novels of Defoe and Fielding. *Robinson Crusoe* and *Tom Jones* would remind us of many others, including Swift's *Gulliver.* Our travels would not be complete, of course, until we came to Cervantes' *Don Quixote* and Rabelais' *Gargantua and Pantagruel.*

The plays, both pleasant and unpleasant, by Shaw and other contemporaries follow an even longer tradition of dramatic writing. There would be not only the modern plays of Ibsen, who influenced Shaw considerably, and the earlier comedies of Sheridan and Congreve, Dryden and Molière; but behind the tragedies of Racine and Corneille, and the plays of Shakespeare and other Elizabethans, there lie the Greek comedies of Aristophanes and the great tragedies of Euripides, Sophocles, and Aeschylus.

Finally, there are the long narrative poems, the great epics: Goethe's *Faust,* Milton's *Paradise Lost,* Chaucer's *Canterbury Tales,* Dante's *Divine Comedy, The Song of Roland,* the *Nibelungenlied,* the Norse sagas, Virgil's *Aeneid,* and Homer's *Iliad* and *Odyssey.*

I have not mentioned all the great books and authors, but I have referred to a large number of them as they might group themselves in the course of conversation, or in the pursuit of interests aroused by contemporary issues or current books. There are no fixed barriers between these groups. They flow into one another at every turn.

This is not only true of such obviously related subject matters as politics and ethics, ethics and metaphysics, metaphysics and mathematics, mathematics and natural science. It appears in more remote connections. The writers of *The Federalist Papers* refer to Euclid's axioms as a model for political principles. A reader of Montaigne and Machiavelli, as well, of course, as of Plutarch, will find their sentiments and stories, even their language, in the plays of Shakespeare. *The Divine Comedy* reflects the *Summa Theologica* of St. Thomas, Aristotle's *Ethics,* and Ptolemy's astronomy. And we know how frequently Plato and Aristotle refer to Homer and the great tragic poets.

~ 8 ~

Perhaps you see now why I have said so often that the great books should be read in relation to one another and in the most various sorts of connection. Thus read, they support each other, illuminate each other, intensify each other's significance. And, of course, they make one another more readable. In reciting their names and tracing their connections, I have gone backward from contemporary books, taking each step in terms of the books an author himself read. That has shown you how the whole tradition of the great books is involved in our life today.

But if you wish to use one great book to help you read another, it would be better to read them from the past into the present, rather than the other way around. If you first read the books an author read, you will understand him better. Your mind has grown as his did, and therefore you are better able to come to terms with him, to know and understand him.

To proceed in the other direction is sometimes more exciting. It is more like doing detective work, or playing hare and hounds. Even when you get this excitement out of reading the books backwards, you will nevertheless have to understand them in the forward direction. That is the way they happened, and they can be understood no other way.

Our wanderings among the great books help me to make another point. It is difficult to say of any contemporary book that it is great. We are too near it to make a sober judgment. Sometimes we can be relatively sure, as in the case of Einstein's work or Freud's, the novels of Proust and Joyce, or the philosophy of Dewey, Whitehead, and Maritain. But, for the most part, we must refrain from such elections. The hall of fame is too august a place for us to send our living candidates, without enclosing return postage.

But current books can certainly be good, even if we cannot be sure they are great. The best sign I know that a current book is good, and that it may even be judged great some day, is the obviousness of its connection with the great books. Such books are drawn, and draw us, into the conversation which the great books have had. Necessarily their authors are well read. They belong to the tradition, whatever they think of it, or however much they seem to revolt from it. And the best way for us to read such good contemporary books is in the light of the great books. As you have noticed, conversations started by these books tend naturally to enlarge and encompass others, especially great ones. That indicates the kind of reading these good books deserve

Let me state one further conclusion. We suffer today not only from political nationalism but cultural provincialism. We have developed the cult of the present moment. We read only current books for the most part, if we read any at all. Not only shall we fail to read the *good* books of this year well, if we read only them, but our failure to read the great books isolates us from the world of man, just as much as unqualified allegiance to the swastika makes one a German first, and a man later—if ever. It is our most sacred human privilege to be men first, and citizens or nationals second. This is just as true in the cultural sphere as the political. We are not pledged to our country or our century.

It is our privilege to belong to the larger brotherhood of man which recognizes no national boundaries, nor any local or tribal fetishes. In fact, I would say it is our duty. I do not know how to escape from the strait jacket of political nationalism, but I do know how we can become citizens of the world of letters, friends of the human spirit in all its manifestations, regardless of time and place.

You can guess the answer. It is by reading the great books. Thus the human mind, wherever it is located, can be freed from current emergencies and local prejudices, through being elevated to the universal plane of communication. There it grasps the general truths, to which the whole human tradition bears witness.

Those who can read well can think critically. To this extent, they have become free minds. If they have read the great books—and I mean *really* read them—they will have the freedom to move anywhere in the human world. Only they can fully lead the life of reason who, though living in a time and place, are yet not wholly of it.

- - - - -

CHAPTER SEVENTEEN

Free Minds and Free Men

- I -

LET us not get confused about means and ends. Reading the great books is not for the sake of talking about them. Mentioning them by name may give you the appearance of literacy, but you do not have to read them to participate in parlor sports or outshine the silver at a dinner party. I hope I have made clear that there are better reasons for reading—*really* reading—the great books.

So far as conversation is concerned, it is the other way around. I have recommended discussion as an aid to reading, not reading for the sake of "brilliant" conversation. The conversation between reader and author, which is an integral part of good reading, may not take place unless the reader is accustomed to the discussion of books. If he has friends with whom he talks about books, he is more likely to talk back to the books themselves.

But there is another and more important point. Even reading the great books well is not an end in itself. It is a means toward living a decent human life, the life of a free man and a free citizen. This should be our ultimate objective. It is the ultimate theme of this book. I shall turn to it at the end of this chapter. For the present, I want to give a little more attention to the problem of discussion in relation to reading.

You can, of course, carry on a conversation with a book

alone, but that will seem to most people like talking to yourself. For lively conversation, you need more than books and the ability to read them. You need friends and the ability to talk and listen. Unfortunately, just having friends is not enough. We all have friends. But suppose our friends do not like to read books, and do not know how to read and talk about them. Suppose they are friends of the golf course or the bridge table, friends of music or of the theater, or anything except books. In that case, the kind of conversations I imagined in the last chapter will not take place.

You may have conversations which start in the same way with current topics or recent books. Someone recites the newspaper headlines or the latest news broadcast. The big news these days is full of problems. It contains the seeds for countless conversations. But do they develop? Does the talk leave the level of the newspaper and the radio? If it does not, everyone will soon find the conversation dull and, tired of repeating the same old stuff, you will decide to play cards, go to the movies, or talk about your neighbors. No special literacy is required for that.

Someone may have read a book, probably one that is now being talked about in well-informed circles. There is another chance for a conversation to begin. But it will falter and die away early unless by good luck there happen to be other readers of the same book. More likely the others will join in by mentioning *other* books they have recently read. No connections will be made. When everyone has given and taken recommendations about the next book to read, the talk will shift to the things people think they have in common. Even if several are present who have read the same book, the conversation is likely to choke because of their inability to discuss it in a way that leads somewhere.

I may be exaggerating your situation somewhat, but I speak from my own experience of too many endlessly dull social evenings. It does not seem as if there were enough people who had a common background of reading. It has become fashionable to use the phrase "frame of reference." Good conversation requires all those who engage in it to speak within the same frame of reference. Communication not only results in something common; it usually needs a common background to begin with. Our failures in communication are as much due to the lack of an initial community of ideas as to our inabilities in talking and listening.

What I am saying may sound as if it had drastic implications. Not only do I want you to learn to read, but now I am asking you to change your friends! I fear there is some truth in that. Either you yourself will not change very much, or you must change your friends. I am only saying what everyone knows, that friendship depends on a community of interests. If you read the great books, you will want friends with whom to discuss them. You do not have to find new ones if you can persuade your old ones to read along with you.

I remember what John Erskine said when he launched the group of students I belonged to on the reading of the great books. He told us that for some years past he had noticed that college students could not talk to one another intelligently. Under the elective system, they went to different classes, meeting only now and then and reading only this or that textbook in common. Members of the same college year were not intellectual friends. When he had gone to Columbia at the beginning of the century, everyone took the same courses and read the same books, many of them great ones. Good conversation had flourished and, more than that, there had been friendships with respect to ideas as well as on the playing field or in fraternities.

One of his motives in starting the Honors course was to revive college life as an intellectual community. If a group of students read the same books and met weekly for two years to discuss them, they might find a new sort of fellow-ship. The great books would not only initiate them into the world of ideas but would provide the frame of refer-ence for further communication among them. They would know how to talk intelligently and intelligibly to one an-other, not only about the books, but through the books about all the problems which engage men's thought and action.

In such a community, Erskine said, democracy would be safe, for democracy requires intelligent communication about and common participation in the solution of human problems. That was before anyone thought that democracy would ever again be threatened. As I remember, we did not pay much attention to Erskine's insight at the time. But he was right. I am sure of it now. I am sure that a liberal edu-cation is democracy's strongest bulwark.

- 2 -

I do not know what chance there is of changing the schools and colleges of this country. They are moving in the opposite direction today, away from the three R's and literacy. (Paradoxically enough, the current trends in edu-cation, which I have criticized, are also motivated by a de-votion to democracy.) But I do know that something can be done about adult education. That is not yet entirely under the control of the teachers' colleges and schools of educa-

tion. You and your friends are free to make plans for yourself. You do not have to wait for someone to come along and
offer you a program. You do not need any elaborate machinery to set up one. You do not even need any teachers. Get
together, read the great books, and discuss them. Just as you
will learn to read by reading, so you will learn to discuss
by discussing.

I have many reasons for thinking this quite feasible.
When I went to Chicago and started to teach a reading
course with President Hutchins, some people in a near-by
suburb invited me to tell them about it. The group consisted of mature men and women, all of them college graduates, some of the men engaged in professional work, some in
business, many of the women involved in local educational and political activities as well as in taking care of
their families. They decided they would like to take the
course. In college we read about sixty books in two years at
the rate of one a week. Since the suburban group would not
have as much time (what with babies and business to occupy
them), they could only read a book a month. It would take
them about eight years, therefore, to read the same list of
books. Frankly, I did not think they would stick at it.

At first they read no better than most college graduates
do. They were starting from scratch, the veneer-thin scratch
that a college education leaves. They found that their habits
of reading, adjusted to the daily paper and even the best
periodical or current book, were remarkably like no skill at
all when they came to read the *Iliad, The Divine Comedy,*
or *Crime and Punishment;* Plato's *Republic,* Spinoza's
Ethics, or Mill's *Essay on Liberty;* Newton's *Opticks* or
Darwin's *Origin of Species.* But they read them all and in
the course of doing so they learned how to read.

They kept at it because they felt their proficiency grow with each year, and enjoyed the mastery which skill provides. They can tell now what the author is trying to do, what questions he is trying to answer, what his most important concepts are, what reasons he has for his conclusions, and even what defects there are in his treatment of the subject. The intelligence of their discussion is clearly greater than it was ten years ago, and that signifies one thing surely: they have learned to read more intelligently.

This group has kept together for ten years now. So far as I can see, they plan to continue indefinitely, increasing the scope of their reading, and rereading some of the books they did poorly by in the earlier years. I may have helped them by leading their discussions, but I am sure they could now go on without my help. In fact, I am sure they would. They have discovered the difference it makes in their lives.

They were all friends before they started, but now their friendships have matured intellectually. Conversation now flourishes where before it might soon languish and give way to other things. They have experienced the pleasure of talking about serious problems intelligently. They do not exchange opinions as they would the time of day. Discussion has become responsible. A man must support what he says. Ideas have connections with one another and with the world of everyday affairs. They have learned to judge propositions and arguments by their intelligibility and relevance.

Several years before I went to Chicago, we had started a similar adult-education program in New York. Mr. Buchanan was then assistant director of the People's Institute, and he and I persuaded Mr. Everett Dean Martin to let us try reading the great books with groups of adults. We were

proposing what was then a wild experiment in adult education. It is not an experiment any longer. We should not
have thought it was one then, if we had remembered the
facts of European history. The discussion of important
problems has always been the way adults continue their
education, and it has seldom taken place except against the
common background provided by reading important books.

We started about ten groups all around the New York
area. They met in libraries, gymnasiums, church social
halls, and Y.M.C.A.'s. They consisted of all sorts of people—
some who had been to college, some who had not, rich and
poor, dull and brilliant. The leaders of these groups were
young men most of whom had not read the books themselves but were willing to try. Their chief function was to
conduct the discussion, to start it off by asking some leading
questions, to keep it going when it bogged down, to clarify
disputes when they threatened to becloud the real issues.

It was a great success. It stopped only because it needed
financial support it did not get to pay for staff and main-
tenance. But it can be revived anywhere and any time by
any group of people who decide they will read and talk
about the great books together. All you need are some
friends to begin with, and you will be better friends before
you are through.

You may say that I have forgotten one thing. In both the
New York and Chicago groups I have described, there were
leaders responsible for conducting the discussion, leaders
who may have had a little more experience than the rest
of the group in reading the books. Trained leaders would
help you get started, I admit. But they are a luxury, not a
necessity.

You can proceed in the most democratic fashion by electing a leader for each meeting. Let different people take turns at it. On each occasion the leader will probably learn more about reading and discussing the book than all the others. If every member of the group gets this experience in turn, the whole group will learn more quickly than if they imported a leader from the outside. There is this compensation in the plan I am suggesting, though it may be more difficult at the start.

I do not have to tell you how a book should be discussed. All the rules for reading tell you that. They are a set of directions for discussing a book as well as reading it. Just as they should regulate the conversation you have with the author, so they govern the conversation you can have with your friends about the book. And, as I have said before, the two conversations mutually support each other.

A discussion is led by the asking of questions. The rules for reading indicate the major questions which can be asked about any book, in itself or in relation to other books. The discussion is sustained by the answering of questions. Those who participate must, of course, understand the questions and be relevant in the remarks they make. But if you have acquired the discipline of coming to terms with an author, you and your friends should have no difficulty in coming to terms with each other. In fact, it is easier, because you can help one another reach an understanding. I am supposing, of course, that you will have good intellectual manners, that you will not judge until you understand what the other fellow is saying, and that when you do judge, you will give reasons.

Every good conversation is a unique thing. It has never happened that way before and will never happen again. The order of the questions will be different in every case

The opinions expressed, the way they are opposed and clarified, will vary from book to book and from group to group discussing the same book. Yet every good discussion is the same in some respects. It moves freely. The argument is followed wherever it leads. Understanding and agreement are the constant goals, to be reached by infinitely various routes. A good conversation is neither aimless nor empty. When something worth discussing has been well discussed, discussion is not the stale and unprofitable thing most people think it is.

Good discussion of important problems in the light of great books is almost a complete exercise in the arts of thinking and communicating. Only writing is left out. Bacon said: "Reading maketh a full man, conference a ready man, and writing an exact man." Perhaps even exactitude can be attained through the precision which well-regulated discussion demands. In any case, the mind can be sufficiently disciplined by reading, listening, and talking.

- 3 -

The mind which is trained to read well has its analytical and critical powers developed. The mind which is trained to discuss well has them further sharpened. One acquires a tolerance for arguments through dealing with them patiently and sympathetically. The animal impulse to impose our opinions upon others is thus checked. We learn that the only authority is reason itself—the only arbiters in any dispute are the reasons and evidences. We do not try to gain ascendancy by a show of force or by counting the noses of those who agree with us. Genuine issues cannot be decided by the mere weight of opinion. We must appeal to reason, not depend on pressure groups.

We all want to learn to think straight. A great book may help us by the examples it affords of penetrating insight and cogent analysis. A good discussion may give further support by catching us when we are thinking crooked. If our friends do not let us get away with it, we may soon learn that sloppy thinking, like murder, will always out. Embarrassment may reduce us to making an effort we had never supposed was within our power. Unless reading and discussion enforce these demands for straight and clear thinking, most of us go through life with an amazingly false confidence in our perceptions and judgments. We think badly most of the time and, what is worse, we do not know it because we are seldom found out.

Those who can read well, listen and talk well, have disciplined minds. Discipline is indispensable for a free use of our powers. The man who has not the knack of doing something gets tied up in knots when he tries to perform. The discipline which comes from skill is necessary for facility. How far can you go in discussing a book with someone who does not know how to read or talk about it? How far can you get in your own reading without a trained ability?

Discipline, as I have said before, is a source of freedom. Only a trained intelligence can think freely. And where there is no freedom in thinking, there can be no freedom of thought. Without free minds, we cannot long remain free men.

Perhaps you are now prepared to admit that learning to read may be significantly related to other things—in fact, to all the rest of a reader's life. Its social and political implications are not remote. Before I consider them, however, let me remind you of one immediate justification for bothering to learn to read.

Reading—and with it thinking and learning—is enjoyable for those who do it well. Just as we enjoy being able to use our bodies skillfully, so we can derive pleasure from a competent employment of our other faculties. The better we can use our minds, the more we appreciate how good it is to be able to think and learn. The art of reading can be praised, therefore, as intrinsically good. We have mental powers to use and leisure in which to employ them disinterestedly. Reading is certainly one way of fulfilling them.

If such praise were all, I should not be satisfied. However good reading may be as an immediate source of pleasure, it is not completely an end in itself. We must do more than think and learn in order to lead a human life. We must act. If we wish to preserve our leisure for disinterested activities, we cannot shirk our practical responsibilities. It is in relation to our practical life that reading has its ultimate justification.

Reading the great books has been for nought unless we are concerned with bringing about a good society. Everyone wants to live in it, but few seem willing to work for it. Let me say briefly what I mean by a good society. It is simply the enlargement of the community in which we live with our friends. We live together with our friends in peaceful and intelligent association. We form a community to the extent that we communicate, share common ideas and purposes. The good society, in the large, must be an association of men made friends by intelligent communication.

- 4 -

Where men lack the arts of communication, intelligent discussion must languish. Where there is no mastery of the medium for exchanging ideas, ideas cease to play a part in human life. When that happens, men are little better than the brutes they dominate by force or cunning, and they will soon try to dominate each other in the same way.

The loss of freedom follows. When men cannot live together as friends, when a whole society is not built on a real community of understanding, freedom cannot flourish. We can live freely only with our friends. With all others, we are constantly oppressed by every sort of dread, and checked in every movement by suspicion.

Preserving freedom, for ourselves and our posterity, is one of our major concerns today. A proper respect for liberty is the heart of sound liberalism. But I cannot help wondering whether our liberalism is sound. We do not seem to know the origins of liberty or its ends. We cry out for all sorts of liberty—freedom of speech, of the press, of assembly—but we do not seem to realize that freedom of thought is the basis for all these others. Without it, freedom of speech is an empty privilege, and a free conscience nothing but a private prejudice. Without it, our civil liberties can be exercised only in a *pro forma* way, and we are unlikely to retain them long if we do not know how to use them well.

As President Barr, of St. John's College, has pointed out, American liberalism today asks for too little, not too much. We have not demanded, as our ancestors did, a mind freed from ignorance, an awakened imagination, and a disciplined reason, without which we cannot effectively use our other freedoms or even preserve them. We have paid attention to the external uses of liberty rather than its essence. The reigning educational system suggests, moreover, that we no longer know how free minds are made and, through them, free men.

It is not just a play on words to connect *liberalism* and *liberal* education, or to say that training in the *liberal* arts *liberalizes*—makes us free. The arts of reading and writing, listening and speaking, are the arts which make it possible for us to think freely, because they discipline the mind. *They are the liberating arts.* The discipline they accomplish frees us from the vagaries of unfounded opinion and the strictures of local prejudice. They free our minds from every domination except the authority of reason itself. A free man recognizes no other authority. Those who ask to be free from all authority—from reason itself—are false liberals. As Milton said, "license they mean, when they cry liberty."

I was invited last year by the American Council on Education to address its annual meeting in Washington. I chose to speak about the political implications of the three R's, under the title "Liberalism and Liberal Education." I tried to show how false liberalism is the enemy of liberal education, and why a truly liberal education is needed in this country to correct the confusions of this widely prevalent false liberalism. By false liberalism, I mean the sort which confuses authority with tyranny and discipline with regimentation. It exists wherever men think everything is just a matter of opinion. That is a suicidal doctrine. It ultimately reduces itself to the position that only might makes right. The liberal who frees himself *from* reason, rather than *through* it, surrenders to the only other arbiter in human affairs—force, or what Mr. Chamberlain has called "the awful arbitrament of war."

The political implications of the three R's, or the liberal arts, are not far to seek. If democracy is a society of free men, it must sustain and extend liberal education or perish. Democratic citizens must be able to think for themselves. To do this, they must first be able to think, and have a body of ideas to think with. They must be able to communicate clearly with one another and receive communications of all sorts critically. It is for such ends that skill in reading and reading the great books are obviously only means.

In Shakespeare's *Henry VI*, the following speech occurs:

> Thou hast most traitorously corrupted the youth of the realm in erecting a grammar-school; and whereas before, our forefathers had no other books but the score and the tally, thou hast caused printing to be used, and, contrary to the king, his crown and dignity, thou hast built a paper-mill.

Reading and writing looked like high treason to the tyrant. He saw in them the forces which might shake him from his throne. And for a while they did, in the gradual democratization of the Western world through the spread of learning and the growth of literacy. But we see today a different turn in human affairs. The means of communication which once were used by liberators to free men are now used by dictators to subdue them.

Today the pen is as potent as the sword in the making of a despot. Tyrants used to be great generals. Now they are strategists in communication, beguiling orators or propagandists. Their weapons are the radio and the press as much as secret police and concentration camps. And when men are pushed about by propaganda, they are as servile as when they are coerced by brute force. They are political puppets, not free men democratically ruled.

Hobbes was suspicious of democracy because he feared its tendency to degenerate into an oligarchy of orators. Though our aims be different from his, we must admit that recent history supports his point. We have seen abroad how the leading orator in the land can become its tyrant. We must save democracy from these inherent weaknesses by closing such roads to despotism. If we are being oppressed by organizations of force, we fight to disarm them. So we must disarm the orators, and we must do so in advance of the day when their spell begins to bind. There is only one way of doing that in a land where free speech is everybody's privilege. The citizens must become critical of what they read and what they hear. They must be liberally educated. If the schools fail to give them such education, they must get it for themselves by learning to read and by reading. But, for their children's sake, they may ultimately realize that something will have to be done about the schools.

The fact that liberally disciplined minds make it harder for those who try to misuse the means of communication is a negative point. There are positive advantages as well. A democracy needs both competent leaders and responsible followers. Neither is possible unless men can exercise free judgment and are in possession of principles which direct action to the right ends. A democratic citizen is an independent subject, because he is ultimately subject to his own free choices. A democratic leader rules only by guiding, not imposing upon, that freedom.

Just as a good teacher tries to elicit active learning on the part of his students, so the art of ruling in a democracy is one of inviting active participation on the part of citizens.

But just as good teaching cannot succeed unless the students have the art of being taught—the skills involved in learning actively from a teacher—so democratic ruling fails unless the citizens possess the reciprocal art of being ruled. Without the art of being taught, students must receive instruction passively. They can learn only through being *indoctrinated,* in the vicious sense of that word. As we have seen, we are properly teachable, or docile, only to the extent that we have the mental discipline to learn by the active and free use of our powers. Similarly, without the art of being ruled, we can be governed only by force or imposition.

A democracy, in short, depends on men who can rule themselves because they have the art of being ruled. Whether they occupy the offices of government or merely the rank of citizens, such men can rule or be ruled without losing their integrity or freedom. Brute force and insidious propaganda are evils with which they are prepared to cope. To maintain the reciprocity between ruling and being ruled is to guarantee political and civil liberty. They do not suffer because all men are not in the government or because just laws must be enforced.

The art of being ruled and the reciprocal art of ruling, like the arts of being taught and of teaching, are arts of the mind. They are liberal arts. The democratic ruler must move us by rational persuasion. If we are good democratic citizens, we must be capable of being moved that way—*and only in that way.* The appeal to fact and reason distinguishes rational persuasion from vicious propaganda. Men who are moved by such persuasion remain free because they have moved themselves. They have been persuaded *knowingly.*

To know how to be ruled is thus the primary qualification for democratic citizenship. A liberal education is needed to qualify men for their political duties as well as for their intellectual life. The art of reading is related to the art of being ruled as well as to the art of being taught. In both cases, men must be able to engage in communication actively, intelligently, critically. Democratic government, more than any other, depends upon successful communication; for, as Walter Lippmann has pointed out, "in a democracy, the opposition is not only tolerated as constitutional, but must be maintained because it is indispensable." The consent of the governed is fully realized only when, through intelligent debate of issues, all colors of political opinion share in the formation of decisions. Debate which is not founded on the communication of all parties is specious. The democratic process is a sham when men fail to understand each other. We must be able to meet other minds in the processes of government and social life as well as in the processes of learning; and, in both cases, we must be able to make up our own minds and act accordingly.

We must act, however. That is the final word in every phase of human life. I have not hesitated to praise the reading and discussion of great books as things intrinsically good, but I repeat: *they are not the ultimate ends of life.* We want happiness and a good society. In this larger view, reading is only a means to an end.

If, after you have learned to read and have read the great books, you act foolishly in personal or political affairs, you might just as well have saved yourself the trouble. It may have been fun at the time, but the fun will not last long. Unless those who are well read can act well also, we shall soon find ourselves deprived of the pleasures we get from these accomplishments. Knowledge may be a good in itself, but knowledge without right action will bring us to a world in which the pursuit of knowledge itself is impossible—a world in which books are burned, libraries closed, the search for truth is repressed, and disinterested leisure lost.

I hope it is not too naïve to expect the contrary from genuinely liberal education, in school and out. I have some reason to believe that those who have *really* read the great books will probably think well and soundly on the issues we face today. The man who thinks clearly about practical problems certainly knows that they are well solved only by right action. Whether he will respect the obligation to act accordingly is, of course, beyond the province of the liberal arts. Nevertheless, they prepare for freedom. They make free minds and form a community of friends who share a common world of ideas. Beyond that the responsibility for acting like free men is ours to accept or shirk.

A List of the Great Books

--

THE following list is not intended as a complete bibliog-raphy of worthwhile reading, nor even as a complete inventory of the greatest books of Western culture. I have limited myself to naming only those great books which are readily available in current English translations. I have also limited myself to books which do not require, for the most part, any special background or preparation.

These two limitations naturally tend to exclude some of the classics of mathematics and experimental science. In these two fields, the work of translation into English is far from being completed, and in many cases where an English translation has been made it is not available in an inexpensive edition. It may be questioned, furthermore, whether some of the great mathematical and scientific works I have included can be profitably examined by the untutored in these fields. I have already answered this question affirmatively and suggested that these books are intelligible if taken in their historical order. Even if I am wrong about this point, as I may be, I think everyone will agree that a list of great books would be sadly deficient if all mathematical and scientific books were omitted. And certainly there are many people who already do have sufficient background, provided by textbook courses in mathematics and science, to warrant their looking into the original communications which textbooks can never replace.

Most of the authors and most of the titles are, I am sure,

generally familiar names, even when the books themselves have not been seen. (In most cases, you can probably guess from the title the kind of book it is and the field to which it belongs.) Names which are strange to some may be familiar to others. I hope that the strangeness of some of these authors and titles will not dismay or deter you. There is nothing here so recondite that it is esoteric, nothing that a little courage will not conquer.

It is wise, of course, to begin with those books that interest you most, for whatever reason. As I have said many times before, the primary aim is to read well, not widely. A list of books should not be regarded as a *challenge* which you can meet only by finishing every item on it. It should be regarded as an *invitation* which you can accept graciously by beginning wherever you feel most at home.

The authors are listed chronologically, according to the known or conjectured date of their birth. The several works by a particular author are also arranged chronologically, where this is possible. I have tried to give the date when a book was *first* published in the *original* language of its author. This is fairly easy to do for modern books, but relatively difficult for most of the ancient ones. In the latter case, I have used the dates which reliable scholarship has assigned, though even here in many instances the scholars disagree. Minor inaccuracies in the dating of works need not concern us. Wherever a date of publication is not assigned, it is simply because the knowledge is lacking or because there is too much scholarly disagreement about the matter.

I have not listed all the works of every author. I have cited only the more important titles, selecting them, in the

case of expository books, to show the diversity of an
author's contribution to different fields of learning. In
some instances, I have found it necessary to speak of the
author's *Works,* and to specify in brackets underneath the
titles which are especially important.

In making a list of this kind, the greatest difficulty always
arises with respect to the relatively contemporary items.
The nearer one comes to one's own day, the more difficult
it is to exercise a detached judgment. Here one's judgment
must be tentative, and there is much room for reasonable
differences of opinion. For this reason, I have separated the
contemporaries from the main list. The *great* authors are
numbered consecutively. The *good* contemporary authors
are marked by the letters of the alphabet. The separation
here is not between the living and the dead, because some
authors who have died recently are as contemporary as
those still living.

Disagreement about inclusions or exclusions will probably focus on the contemporary list. I offer it only as a suggestion. Everyone must decide for himself whether these
authors are truly great and should be added to the main
list. The verdict of history will determine whether your
judgment is right. As to the main list, there may also be
some minor disagreements. I can think at once of names
and titles that will be suggested: the *Enneads* of Plotinus,
the *Little Flowers* of St. Francis, the works of Schopenhauer, the novels of Thomas Hardy, the apologetical and
historical writings of John Henry Newman—to mention a
few of the more obvious omissions. In some cases, such
omissions are due to lack of an adequate English rendering; in others, to the judgment, which I had to make, that

a particular work was not of the same magnitude as those listed; and in still others, to the judgment that an author's importance was more attributable to his life and actions than to his writings. One could not hope to construct a list of this sort without encountering differences of opinion, precisely because such judgments have to be made, one way or the other. I can only hope that the number of additions or subtractions which anyone might wish to make would constitute a small percentage of the total list. If that turns out to be the case, I shall feel satisfied that the list is fairly representative—that it encompasses what is generally recognized to be the European tradition.

Ultimately everyone should make his own list of great books. I think it would be wise, however, to read a few of the books which have been unanimously acclaimed before you start. The more you read, of course, the better. This list is a starter.

For the convenience of the reader in acquiring copies of the great books, either at a bookstore or at a library, I have indicated the good, inexpensive editions, wherever they exist. The key to the abbreviations, used to signify these editions, is given on the opposite page. Most of the books available in popular editions are also available in other editions which are not listed here. These other editions are frequently worth consulting for they are often better translations or more authoritative renderings of the text; and in some cases, they present the complete work which the popular and inexpensive editions give in an abbreviated form. In the case of books which are not available in popular editions, the most readily procurable edition is listed, though again this may not be the only published version of the work. As all prices are somewhat subject to change, they are not listed here.

KEY

ANC:	Anchor	LC:	Loeb Classical Library
BM:	Bobbs-Merrill	ML:	Modern Library
COL:	Collier	NAL:	New American Library
DOV:	Dover	OCL:	Open Court Library
EL:	Everyman's Library	PEN:	Penguin
HAF:	Hafner	PS:	Peter Smith

WC: World's Classics (Oxford)

(pa): paperbound   (op): out of print

1. HOMER (c. 850 B.C.)
   Iliad . . . . EL, LC, ML, PEN (pa), WC
   Odyssey . . . . EL, LC, ML, PEN (pa)
2. *The Old Testament*
3. AESCHYLUS (c. 525-456 B.C.)
   Tragedies
   (esp. *House of Atreus, Prometheus Bound*)
   EL, LC, PEN (pa)
4. SOPHOCLES (c. 497-406 B.C.)
   Tragedies
   (esp. *Oedipus the King, Antigone, Electra*)
   EL, LC, Oxford (pa), WC
5. EURIPIDES (c. 485-406 B.C.)
   Tragedies
   (esp. *Medea, Electra, Hippolytus, Bacchae*)
   EL, LC, University of Chicago (pa)
6. HERODOTUS (c. 484-425 B.C.)
   History (of the Persian Wars) (c. 444-425 B.C.)
   LC, ML, PEN (pa)
7. THUCYDIDES (c. 470-400 B.C.)
   History of the Peloponnesian War (c. 404-401 B.C.)
   EL, LC, ML, PEN (pa)
8. HIPPOCRATES (c. 460-357? B.C.)
   Collection of Medical Writings (c. 320-300 B.C.) . . . LC

9. ARISTOPHANES (*c.* 444-380 B.C.)
   Comedies
   (esp. *Lysistrata, Clouds, Birds, Frogs*)
                          Bantam (pa), EL, LC, WC

10. PLATO (*c.* 427-347 B.C.)
    Dialogues (*c.* 404-347 B.C.)
    (esp. *Republic, Symposium, Phaedo, Meno, Apology,
    Lysis, Phaedrus, Protagoras, Gorgias, Cratylus, Sophist,
    Philebus, Thaetetus, Parmenides*)   EL, LC, ML, NAL (pa)

11. ARISTOTLE (384-322 B.C.)
    Works (*c.* 335-323 B.C.)
    (esp. *Organon, Physics, Metaphysics, De Anima, Ethics,
    Politics Rhetoric, Poetics*) . . . . . EL, LC, PEN (pa)

12. EUCLID (*c.* 323-283 B.C.)
    Elements of Geometry . . . . . . DOV (pa), EL

13. CICERO (106-43 B.C.)
    Orations (*c.* 66-57 B.C.) LC
    Republic (54 B.C.) LC
    Laws (52 B.C.) LC
    Tusculan Disputations (45 B.C.) LC
    Offices (44 B.C.) . . . . EL, LC

14. LUCRETIUS (*c.* 95-52 B.C.)
    Of the Nature of Things (*c.* 55 B.C.) . . . EL, EL (pa), LC

15. VIRGIL (70-19 B.C.)
    Aeneid (*c.* 27-20 B.C.) . . . . . . EL, LC, ML, PEN (pa)

16. HORACE (65-8 B.C.)
    Odes and Epodes (22-13 B.C.)
                    EL, LC, ML, University of Chicago (pa)
    The Art of Poetry (13 B.C.) . . . . EL, ML

17. LIVY (59 B.C.-A.D. 17)
    History of Rome (*c.* 27-25 B.C.) . . . . . . EL, LC

18. OVID (43 B.C.-A.D. 17)
    Metamorphoses (*c.* 9-17) . . . . . . EL, LC, PEN (pa)

19. QUINTILIAN (*c.* 40-118)
    Institutes of Oratory (94-95) LC

20. PLUTARCH (*c.* 45-120)
    Lives . . . . EL, LC, ML

59. RACINE (1639-1699)
      Tragedies (1667-77)
      (esp. *Andromache, Phaedra, Athaliah*) . .   ML, PEN (pa)
60. NEWTON (1642-1727)
      Mathematical Principles of Natural Philosophy (1687)
                                University of California Press
      Opticks (1704) . . . . DOV (pa)
61. LEIBNITZ (1646-1716)
      Discourse on Metaphysics (1686) . . . . OCL
      New Essays Concerning Human Understanding (1704)
                                                      OCL
      Monadology (1714) . . . . Oxford University Press
62. DEFOE (1661-1731)
      Robinson Crusoe (1719) . . . . EL, ML, NAL (pa)
      Moll Flanders (1722) . . . . EL, ML, ML (pa)
63. SWIFT (1667-1745)
      Battle of the Books (1704) . . . . EL, ML
      Tale of a Tub (1704) . . . . EL, ML
      Journal to Stella (1712) . . . . EL
      Gulliver's Travels (1727) . . . . EL, ML, ML (pa), WC
64. MONTESQUIEU (1689-1755)
      Persian Letters (1721) . . . . BM (pa)
      Spirit of Laws (1748) . . . . HAF (pa)
65. VOLTAIRE (1694-1778)
      Candide (1758) . . . . EL, ML, NAL (pa)
      Philosophical Dictionary (c. 1764-73) . . Basic Books
      Toleration . . . . G. P. Putnam (op)
66. BERKELEY (1684-1753)
      A New Theory of Vision (1709) . . . . .BM (pa), EL
      The Principles of Human Knowledge (1710)
                                            OCL, OCL (pa)
67. FIELDING (1707-1754)
      Joseph Andrews (1742) . . . . . . EL, ML, ML (pa)
      Tom Jones (1749) . . . . EL, ML, ML (pa)
68. HUME (1711-1776)
      A Treatise of Human Nature (1739-40)
                                      Dolphin (pa), EL

78. GOETHE (1749-1832)
     Faust (1774) . . . . EL, ML, ML (pa), WC
     Poetry and Truth (1775) . . . . G. Bell (op)
79. RICARDO (1772-1823)
     The Principles of Political Economy and Taxation
     (1817) . . . . EL
80. MALTHUS (1766-1834)
     Essay on the Principles of Population (1798)
                                             EL, NAL (pa)
81. DALTON (1766-1844)
     A New System of Chemical Philosophy (1808)
82. HEGEL (1770-1831)
     Phenomenology of Spirit (1807) . . . . . Macmillan
     Science of Logic (1812-16) . . . . Macmillan
     Philosophy of Right (1820) . . Oxford University Press
     Philosophy of History (1837) . . . . PS
83. GUIZOT (1787-1874)
     History of Civilization in France (1845)
                                 D. Appleton-Century (op)
84. FARADAY (1791-1867)
     Experimental Researches in Electricity (1839-1855) . EL
85. LOBACHEVSKI (1793-1856)
     Geometrical Researches on the Theory of Parallels
     (1840) . . . . DOV (pa), OCL
86. COMTE (1798-1857)
     Positive Philosophy (1830-42) . . . . . P. Eckler (op)
87. BALZAC (1799-1850)
     Works (1829-42)
     (esp. *Le Père Goriot, Cousin Pons, Eugénie Grandet,
     Cousin Betty, César Birotteau*)
                       EL, ML, ML (pa), Modern Student's Library
88. LYELL (1797-1875)
     The Antiquity of Man (1863) . . . . EL (op)
89. J. S. MILL (1806-1873)
     System of Logic (1843) . . . . Longmans, Green (op)
     Principles of Political Economy (1848)
                                       Augustus M. Kelley

On Liberty (1859) . . . . BM (pa), WC
Of Representative Government (1861) . . BM (pa), WC
Utilitarianism (1863) . . . . .BM (pa), EL
Autobiography (1873) . . . . . . BM (pa), WC
90. DARWIN (1809-1882)
    The Origin of Species (1859) . . . . EL, ML, NAL (pa)
91. THACKERAY (1811-1863)
    Works (1846-62)
    (esp. *Vanity Fair, Henry Esmond, The Virginians,
    Pendennis*) . . . . EL, ML, ML (pa)
92. DICKENS (1812-1870)
    Works (1834-70)
    (esp. *Pickwick Papers, Our Mutual Friend, David Cop-
    perfield, Dombey and Son, Oliver Twist, A Tale of Two
    Cities*) . . . . Dolphin (pa), EL, ML
93. CLAUDE BERNARD (1813-1878)
    Introduction to Experimental Medicine (1876)
                     Abelard-Schumann, DOV (pa)
94. BOOLE (1815-1864)
    Laws of Thought (1854) . . . . . . DOV (pa), PS
95. MARX (1818-1883)
    Capital (1867)
    (along with *The Communist Manifesto*)
                     EL, Gateway (pa), ML
96. MELVILLE (1819-1891)
    Typee (1846) . . . . COL (pa), EL, WC
    Moby Dick (1846) . . . . . . .COL (pa), EL, ML, WC
97. DOSTOEVSKI (1821-1881)
    Crime and Punishment (1866) . . . Dell (pa), EL, ML
    The Idiot (1869) . . . . Dell (pa), EL, ML
    The Brothers Karamazov (1881) . . . Dell (pa), EL, ML
98. BUCKLE (1822-1862)
    A History of Civilization in England (1857)
                     D. Appleton-Century (op)
99. FLAUBERT (1821-1880)
    Madame Bovary (1857)
              EL, ML, ML (pa), Modern Student's Library

100. GALTON (1822-1911)
Inquiries into Human Faculty and Its Development
(1883) . . . . EL (op)
101. RIEMANN (1826-1866)
The Hypotheses of Geometry (1867) . . . . DOV (pa)
102. IBSEN (1828-1906)
Plays (1850-1900)
(esp. *Peer Gynt, Brand, Hedda Gabler, Emperor and
Galilean, A Doll's House, The Wild Duck, The Master
Builder)* . . . . EL, ML, ML (pa)
103. TOLSTOI (1828-1910)
War and Peace (1861-68) . . . . .EL, ML, PEN (pa), WC
Anna Karenina (1875-78) . . . . . EL, ML, ML (pa), WC
What is Art? (1898) . . . . BM (pa), WC
104. DEDEKIND (1831-1916)
Theory of Numbers (1872) . . . . .OCL
105. WUNDT (1832-1920)
Physiological Psychology (1880) . . Allen and Unwin
Outline of Psychology (1896) . . . A. Kröner, Leipzig
106. MARK TWAIN (1835-1910)
Innocents Abroad (1869) . . . . . . Harper's
Adventures of Huckleberry Finn (1884)
Harper's, PEN (pa)
A Connecticut Yankee in King Arthur's Court (1889)
Harper's, ML, Washington Square Press
107. HENRY ADAMS (1838-1918)
History of the United States (1889-91) Scribner's (op)
Mont-Saint-Michel and Chartres (privately published,
1904; pub., 1913) . . . . Houghton Mifflin, NAL (pa)
The Education of Henry Adams (privately published,
1906; pub., 1918) . . . . ML
Degradation of the Democratic Dogma (1919) . . . PS
108. CHARLES PEIRCE (1839-1914)
Chance, Love, and Logic (Collected, 1923)
Harcourt, Brace (op)
Collected Papers (Edited, 1931-34)
Harvard University Press

109. WILLIAM SUMNER (1840-1910)
    Folkways (1907) . . . . Ginn, NAL (pa)
110. OLIVER WENDELL HOLMES (1841-1935)
    The Common Law (1881) . . . . . . Little, Brown
    Collected Legal Papers (1921) . . . . PS
111. WILLIAM JAMES (1842-1910)
    Principles of Psychology (1890) . . . . PS
    The Varieties of Religious Experience (1902)
                    ML, NAL (pa)
    Pragmatism (1907) . . . . .Meridian (pa)
    A Pluralistic Universe (1909). . . . . . . McKay
    Essays in Radical Empiricism (1912) . . . . McKay
112. NIETZSCHE (1844-1900)
    Thus Spake Zarathustra (1883-92) . . EL, ML, PEN (pa)
    Beyond Good and Evil (1886) . . . Henry Regnery
    The Genealogy of Morals (1887) . . . . .ANC (pa)
    The Will to Power (1895) . . . . . Macmillan (op)
113. GEORG CANTOR (1845-1918)
    Transfinite Numbers (1895-97) . . . . DOV (pa), OCL

A. PAVLOV (1849-1936)
    Conditioned Reflexes (1926) . . . . . DOV (pa), PS
B. POINCARÉ (1854-1912)
    The Foundations of Science (1902-09)
                        Science Press (op)
C. FREUD (1856-1939)
    Three Contributions to a Theory of Sex (1905) EL (pa)
    Introductory Lectures on Psychonanalyis (1917)
                        W. W. Norton
    Beyond the Pleasure Principle (1920)
                  Bantam (pa), Liveright
    Group Psychology and the Analysis of the Ego (1920)
                  Bantam (pa), Liveright
    The Ego and the Id (1923) . . . . Hogarth Press (op)
    Civilization and Its Discontents (1930) W. W. Norton
D. THORSTEIN VEBLEN (1857-1929)
    The Theory of the Leisure Class (1899) . ML, NAL (pa)

The Higher Learning in America (1918)
                                    Hill & Wang (pa), PS
The Place of Science in Modern Civilization (1919)
                                    Russell & Russell
Vested Interests and the State of Industrial Arts (1919)
                                    Viking Press (op)
*Absentee Ownership and Business Enterprise in Recent
Times* (1923) . . . . Viking Press (op)

E. LENIN (1870-1924)
    Imperialism (1917) . . . . International Publishers

F. PROUST (1871-1922)
    Remembrance of Things Past (1913-1926)
                                    Random House

G. SHAW (1856-1950)
    Plays Pleasant and Unpleasant (1898)
                                    Dodd, Mead, PEN (pa)
    Man and Superman (1903) . . Dodd, Mead, NAL (pa)
    Androcles and the Lion (1903) . Dodd, Mead, PEN (pa)

H. BOAS (1858-1938)
    The Mind of Primitive Man (1911)
                                    COL (pa), Macmillan
    Anthropology and Modern Life (1928)   W. W. Norton

I. DEWEY (1859-1952)
    How We Think (1910) . . . . D. C. Heath
    Democracy and Education (1916) . . . Macmillan
    Experience and Nature (1925) . . . . DOV (pa), OCL
    The Quest for Certainty (1929) . . . Capricorn (pa)
    Logic (1938) . . . . Henry Holt

J. BERGSON (1859-1941)
    Time and Free Will (1889) . Harper Torchbooks (pa)
    Matter and Memory (1896) . . . . . . ANC (pa)
    Creative Evolution (1907) . . . . .ML
    Two Sources of Morality and Religion (1932) ANC (pa)

K. WHITEHEAD (1861-1947)
    A Treatise on Universal Algebra (1898) . . HAF (pa)
    An Introduction to Mathematics (1911)
                                    Oxford University Press (pa)

Science and the Modern World (1925)

Macmillan, NAL (pa)

Process and Reality (1929)

Harper Torchbooks (pa), Macmillan

Adventures of Ideas (1933) . . Macmillan, NAL (pa)

L. SANTAYANA (1863-1952)

  Skepticism and Animal Faith (1923) . . . . . DOV (pa)

  Realm of Essence (1927) . . . . . Scribner's (op)

  Realm of Matter (1930) . . . . . Scribner's (op)

  Realm of Truth (1938) . . . . . . Scribner's (op)

M. RUSSELL (1872-   )

  Principles of Mathematics (1903) . . W. W. Norton

N. THOMAS MANN (1875-1955)

  The Magic Mountain (1925) . . . . Alfred A. Knopf

  Joseph in Egypt (1938) . . . . . . Alfred A. Knopf

O. EINSTEIN (1879-1955)

  The Theory of Relativity (1916) . Crown, Crown (pa)

  Sidelights on Relativity (1920-21) . . . Methuen (op)

  The Evolution of Physics (with Infeld) (1938)

Simon & Schuster, Simon & Schuster (pa)

P. TROTSKY (1879-1940)

  The History of the Russian Revolution (1932)

Simon & Schuster (op)

Q. JOYCE (1882-1941)

  Ulysses (1922) . . . . ML

R. MARITAIN (1882-   )

  Art and Scholasticism (1920) . . . . . . Scribner's

  Degrees of Knowledge (1932) . . . . . . Scribner's

  Freedom in the Modern World (1933) . Scribner's (op)

  A Preface to Metaphysics (1940) NAL (pa), Sheed & Ward

Publisher's Note

SINCE the original publication of *How to Read a Book*, there has been a vast proliferation of editions in English of many of the great books, especially in cheap editions. The preceding bibliography lists only unabridged editions and those which are most readily available as of 1963, with the exception of a few titles which are now out of print but which may still be found in many libraries or secured through secondhand bookstores.

A preponderance of the entire list is available as a set entitled *Great Books of the Western World,* published by the Encyclopaedia Britannica under the general editorship of Dr. Adler.

About the Author

DR. MORTIMER ADLER, a native New Yorker, earned the degree of Doctor of Philosophy at Columbia University in 1928. Subsequent to six years of teaching at Columbia, he became professor of the philosophy of law at the University of Chicago, and he has been director of the Institute for Philosophical Research in San Francisco since 1952. Among the many books he has publised are *Dialectic*, 1927; *Art and Prudence*, 1937; *What Man Has Made of Man*, 1938; *A Dialectic of Morals*, 1941; *How to Think About War and Peace*, 1944; *The Idea of Freedom*, 1958; *The Capitalist Manifesto* (with Louis Kelso), 1958; and *The New Capitalists*, 1961.